PRIVATE CLIENT
Wills, Trusts and Estate Planning

PRIVATE CLIENT
Wills, Trusts and Estate Planning

Robin Riddett, Solicitor

JORDANS

1998

Published by
Jordan Publishing Limited
21 St Thomas Street
Bristol BS1 6JS

British Library Cataloguing-in-Publication Data
A catalogue record for this book is available from the British Library.

ISSN 1353–3649
ISBN 0 85308 462 9

Photoset by Pentacor PLC, High Wycombe, Buckinghamshire
Printed in Great Britain by Hobbs The Printers Ltd of Southampton

PREFACE

The aim of this book is to provide a comprehensive introduction to the legal and taxation implications arising from estate planning work for clients within the private client department of a solicitor's practice. At the beginning of Chapter 1, there is reference to the problem of definition of private client. In view of this it has been necessary, but difficult, to define the scope of the text, although the subtitle to this book has helped to a considerable extent.

I have had the benefit of helpful, and often long, discussions with many practitioners from whose suggestions I hope to have arrived at a consensus. However, I remain aware that the private client department of a London firm is often very different from a provincial practice. I should like to express my appreciation to the many busy private client partners who have so willingly provided their advice and suggestions, and their time, in relation to the content of this book.

This book is written primarily to complement The College of Law's Legal Practice elective Private Client but it is hoped it will provide a useful introduction to others interested in this type of work. Students studying for this elective will have already completed the compulsory part of the Legal Practice Course; there are, therefore, some references to that course, in particular to the LPC Resource Book *Wills, Probate and Administration* (Jordans, 1997).

The permission to reproduce a number of precedent forms and clauses from the following publications is acknowledged with thanks: *Practical Trust Precedents* (FTLT), *Practical Will Precedents* (FTLT) (permission obtained from Withers); and P White *Post-Death Rearrangements: Practice and Precedents* 2nd edn (FTLT, 1992).

For brevity, I have used the masculine pronoun throughout to include the feminine.

The law is stated as at 31 October 1997.

Throughout, I have endeavoured to provide the principal statutory references to enable further research to be made into a topic where this is required. In a subject as broad-based as Private Client (even as interpreted within this book), there are many relevant textbooks and precedent books to which a student or practitioner may wish to refer; these include:

FINANCIAL SERVICES
Camp *Solicitors and Financial Services: A Compliance Handbook* 2nd edn (The Law Society, 1996)

ENDURING POWERS OF ATTORNEY
Aldridge *Powers of Attorney* 8th edn (FTLT, 1991)

TRUST LAW
Parker and Mellows *The Modern Law of Trusts* 5th edn (Sweet & Maxwell, 1983)
Hanbury and Martin *Modern Equity* 14th edn (Sweet & Maxwell, 1993)

PRECEDENTS
Practical Will Precedents (FTLT)
Practical Trust Precedents (FTLT)
Potter and Monroe's Tax Planning With Precedents (Sweet & Maxwell)
Forms and Encyclopaedia of Precedents (Butterworths), Trusts and Settlements
Practical Tax Planning and Precedents (FTLT)

ESTATE AND TAX PLANNING
Estate Planning (Tolley)
Tax Planning (Tolley)
Taxation of UK Trusts (Tolley)
McKie *Capital Gains Taxation of Non-Resident Settlements: The New Rules* (Sweet & Maxwell)
White *Post-Death Rearrangements: Practice and Precedents* 4th edn (FTLT, 1992)

REVENUE LAW
Whitehouse et al *Revenue Law: Principles and Practice* 14th edn (Butterworths, 1996)
British Tax Library *Capital Taxes* (Sweet & Maxwell)

ROBIN RIDDETT
Guildford

CONTENTS

TABLE OF CASES

References in the right-hand column are to paragraph numbers.

TABLE OF STATUTES

References in the right-hand column are to paragraph numbers.

TABLE OF STATUTORY INSTRUMENTS

References in the right-hand column are to paragraph numbers.

ABBREVIATIONS

The following abbreviations are used throughout this book.

AEA 1925	Administration of Estates Act 1925
AEA 1971	Administration of Estates Act 1971
EPAA 1985	Enduring Powers of Attorney Act 1985
FA	Finance Act
F (No 2) A 1997	Finance (No 2) Act 1997
FSA 1986	Financial Services Act 1986
ICTA 1988	Income and Corporation Taxes Act 1988
IHTA 1984	Inheritance Tax Act 1984
PAA 1964	Perpetuities and Accumulation Act 1964
SLA 1925	Settled Land Act 1925
TA 1925	Trustee Act 1925
TCGA 1992	Taxation of Chargeable Gains Act 1992
TIA 1961	Trustee Investments Act 1961
TLA 1996	Trusts of Land and Appointment of Trustees Act 1996
VTA 1958	Variation of Trusts Act 1958

Chapter 1

PRIVATE CLIENT

1.1 WHAT IS PRIVATE CLIENT WORK?

Lord Denning in *Griffiths v JP Harrison (Watford) Ltd* [1962] 1 All ER 909, HL said, 'We can recognise a "trade" when we see it. ... But we are hard pressed to define it.' In that case, he was considering whether an activity was a trading activity. He might have said much the same thing had he been considering 'private client work'.

At its broadest, private client work may be said to include all work except commercial work, although even commercial work has a private client dimension. At its narrowest, it will generally be taken to exclude such topics as conveyancing, family law, litigation and employment law, so that it may be seen as covering a residual category of personal taxation, wills, probate and trust work.

Some firms, generally the larger firms, have separate departments with partners and assistant solicitors who concentrate exclusively on serving the needs of their private clients. Smaller firms often have a number of partners and assistant solicitors who do private client work but not necessarily within a separate department. These firms will not usually define this work as private client work as such. If asked, they would probably see it as covering most of the firm's clients except the purely commercial clients. In recent years, some large practices have developed a policy of concentrating on commercial work and referring any private client work to other firms specialising in that area.

The subtitle to this Resource Book, 'Wills, Trusts and Estate Planning', is descriptive of, and places a limit on, the scope of the book. Therefore, it covers private client work in the narrow sense. Other aspects of private client work as more broadly defined are the subject of other books in this series.

Extensive discussion with City of London firms, provincial city firms and many other firms with private client departments has confirmed that the main emphasis of their work within the private client department is 'estate planning'. This emphasis has led to an equivalent main theme for this LPC Resource Book.

1.2 PRIVATE CLIENT AND THE COMPULSORY SUBJECTS OF THE LEGAL PRACTICE COURSE

1.2.1 Wills, probate and administration

The study of private client work follows naturally on from a study of wills, probate and administration. Many of the topics introduced in the LPC Resource Book *Wills, Probate and Administration* (Jordans, 1997), for example lifetime gifts and the use of annual tax exemptions, are developed further. Many new topics and ideas for estate planning are also introduced. In some cases, reference is made to particular aspects of the LPC Resource Book *Wills, Probate and Administration*. It will, therefore, be necessary to read some of the material contained in that book.

1.2.2   Revenue law

The three principal taxes applicable to private individuals are relevant to this area of work. The principles of these taxes are set out in the LPC Resource Books *Pervasive Topics*; *Wills, Probate and Administration*; and *Business Law and Practice* (Jordans, 1997).

1.2.3   Financial services

Estate planning for clients will inevitably involve a consideration of financial planning, particularly in relation to investments. For example, it may be necessary to advise clients in relation to their existing shares, or clients may need advice as to what investments they should make in the immediate future.

In some cases, a solicitor may become involved in other investment activity for a client. After giving advice, the solicitor may follow this up by making arrangements for the client to acquire (or sell) investments. In some cases, the solicitor may even be prepared to manage a client's investment portfolio.

Not all solicitors' firms will wish to carry out investment business for clients, even though they undertake a substantial amount of private client work. Many practitioners prefer to 'hive off' the financial aspects of a client's business to specialist financial services advisers leaving the solicitor to concentrate on the purely legal aspects of the work. However, some of the larger firms, as well as many medium-sized or smaller firms, take the opposite approach. They see financial services work as potentially lucrative for the practice. Thus, using their existing client database as their prime source of investment business, firms which decide to become involved in financial services work may often set up a separate financial services department. This may be 'headed up' by a solicitor with the necessary expertise or by an individual brought into the firm for the purpose. Such a person would normally have qualifications and experience gained from working in the financial services industry. Departments of this type will work closely with the private client department but will also provide a support role for other areas of the practice.

No solicitor, or sole practitioner, may give investment advice, or be involved in other aspects of investment activity, unless he is authorised to do so (FSA 1986, s 3). It is usual for a solicitor's firm to receive authorisation to conduct investment business from The Law Society. It will issue either a category 1 Investment Business Certificate (to firms not carrying out discrete investment business (DIB)) or a category 2 Investment Business Certificate to DIB firms only. A firm may not carry out DIB 'unless it is conducted by or under the direct supervision of a principal who is a Qualified Person' (Solicitors' Investment Business Rules 1995, r 20). Solicitors wishing to carry out DIB can obtain Qualified Person status by either passing The Law Society approved investment business examination or gaining exemption from it. Solicitors who have passed the Professional Skills Course are permitted to carry out non-DIB work only.

This book presupposes that the solicitor's firm has obtained an investment business certificate and that the investment activity will be carried out within the requirements of the Financial Services Act 1986 and the Solicitors' Investment Business Rules 1995. On occasion, it may be necessary to reconsider the relevant parts of the LPC Resource Book *Pervasive Topics* (Jordans, 1997). Using the preliminary study as a basis, emphasis will be given to the nature of the various investment products available on the market, their similarities and differences and their suitability or otherwise for any particular client. Such a client, within the context of this book, may either be an individual or a trustee.

1.3 OWNERSHIP AND DISPOSITION OF ASSETS

Private client work for any client will involve the solicitor in two separate, though closely related, matters.

1.3.1 Ownership of assets

The decision to acquire assets, for example the family home or investments, is for the client to make, although the solicitor may be asked to offer advice. Even where clients do not require advice as to the selection of particular assets, it is unlikely that they will consider how family assets should be owned. The solicitor is frequently concerned to advise on the advantages and disadvantages of sole ownership or joint ownership (as joint tenants or as tenants in common) or whether to hold assets through a trust. Hence, this book deals with (inter alia):

(1) financial planning; and
(2) estate planning.

1.3.2 Disposition of assets

Once substantial assets have been acquired, it becomes necessary for the client to consider their devolution among the family, particularly as part of IHT planning. There are various ways in which this can be achieved. Broadly, the methods involved include lifetime gifts, whether as absolute gifts or gifts into trust, and gifts by will in trust for the benefit of the testator's family. Chapters dealing with these matters include:

(1) outright inter vivos gifts;
(2) identifying, drafting and using inter vivos settlements; and
(3) wills, particularly wills creating will trusts.

Chapter 2

FINANCIAL PLANNING

2.1 PLANNING THE CLIENT'S FINANCIAL AFFAIRS

The purpose of this chapter is to introduce some of the concepts which lie behind financial and investment planning advice for individual clients as part of their estate planning.

Financial planning is a continuing process. It requires the development of a strategy based on short, and long-term forward planning. Ideally, a plan, an investment strategy, should be developed for the client. Any immediate needs identified by the plan can be implemented at once. Longer-term planning can be given effect as the opportunities develop.

The range of financial planning and investment opportunities available to private clients is very wide. In view of this, the key to successful advice to clients lies in:

(1) knowing all the circumstances of the particular client; and
(2) devising a financial and investment plan which is appropriate to meet those circumstances.

2.1.1 Financial planning

Financial planning covers savings, for example, in a bank or building society, investments, life assurance and pension arrangements, mortgages, school fee schemes (see Appendix 2) and tax planning generally (see Chapter 4).

2.1.2 Investment planning

Investment planning is one aspect of financial planning. In everyday use the phrase is understood as covering a wide range of investments from unit trusts, investment trusts and other stocks and shares (see Appendix 2) to specialist items such as works of art, stamp collections and investment in woodlands. It is not confined to 'investments' as defined in the Financial Services Act 1986 (see **2.2**).

2.2 THE FINANCIAL SERVICES ACT 1986

The Financial Services Act 1986 (FSA 1986), and the Solicitors' Investment Business Rules 1995 (the Rules) are discussed in the LPC Resource Book *Pervasive Topics* (Jordans, 1997). Any solicitor who is involved in developing and implementing an investment strategy for a client must comply with the relevant provisions of the Act and the Rules.

2.2.1 Authorisation to conduct investment business

The everyday meaning of 'investments' is wider than the definition of investments adopted for the purposes of the FSA 1986. Thus, if the solicitor is to give advice, or to carry out any other activity in relation to investments which falls outside the meaning of the Act, his firm will not require authorisation to conduct investment business from The Law Society. For example, advice in relation to savings in a building society or a bank, and in relation to mortgages, does not require authorisation. By contrast, specific advice in relation to a shareholding will require authorisation. However, if the firm is authorised to conduct investment business for clients generally, it will not particularly matter whether an investment is within the Act or not since any investment business requiring authorisation will be covered automatically.

2.2.2 Discrete investment business

Any solicitor providing investment advice, or conducting other investment activity for clients, will be carrying out investment business for those clients. Without a category 2 Investment Business Certificate, the firm may not carry out DIB for its clients and it will not be affected by the extra compliance requirements of the Rules where DIB is conducted. The principal method of avoiding DIB is to instruct a permitted third party (PTP), usually a stockbroker, to act in the investment transaction for the solicitor's clients leaving the solicitor to do only the legal work involved.

Generally, a solicitor's firm will have a well-defined policy in relation to DIB. Only the firms which have established financial services departments will feel able to offer DIB services to their clients as part of their financial planning advice. Non-DIB firms will use a PTP and so avoid carrying out DIB.

2.2.3 Fees and commissions

It is, of course, usual for a solicitor to charge a client a fee for work done for the client.

Investment business gives rise to payment of commission by the provider of the investment product. If a solicitor arranges an endowment policy for a client he will receive a commission from the life company. If, instead, the transaction is carried out through a PTP, it will usually be agreed that the PTP shares the commission he receives with the solicitor.

Receipt of fees and commissions gives rise to the need to consider the Solicitors' Practice Rules 1990 and Codes of Practice and the general principle that there must be no conflict of interest between the solicitor and the client.

Practice Rule 1
The solicitor must remain independent and act in the best interests of his client. This does not prevent receipt of commission. However, placing a client's business with the company which pays the biggest commission may be in the solicitor's best interest, not the client's. A breach of Rule 1 would occur.

Practice Rule 10
The solicitor must account to the client for any commission received of more than £20 unless the client, in full knowledge of the amount or basis of calculation of the commission, agrees that the solicitor should retain the commission. Commissions for investment business will frequently exceed £20.

Solicitors' Introduction and Referral Code 1990
By this Code a solicitor is entitled to receive commissions for placing business for clients, provided the Practice Rules are complied with.

Fees or commission?

A solicitor has a choice:

(1) To charge a fee for the work and account to the client for the entire commission received.

(2) To charge a fee for the work but to offset this (with the client's agreement) with the commission received.

(3) To retain the commission with the client's agreement in lieu of charging a fee.

There are advantages and disadvantages to each method. One particular point to note is that the amount charged, whether as fees or by way of commission, can always be challenged if not 'fair and reasonable' for the amount of work done (Solicitors' (Non-Contentious Business) Remuneration Order 1994).

2.3 DEVELOPING THE INVESTMENT STRATEGY FOR CLIENTS

2.3.1 'Know your client'

Where a solicitor is carrying on DIB for a client, one of the specific obligations imposed on him by the Rules is the requirement to 'know your client' (Rule 22). This is a term which is well known in the financial services industry where it is called the client 'fact find'.

Even where a solicitor is not intending to conduct DIB for the client, so that Rule 22 will have no application, it is none the less useful to have its content in mind as providing broad guidelines when taking instructions in relation to any financial planning for clients. The principal features of Rule 22, ie the client's personal details, his financial details and the suitability of investments for the client, are developed in the context of financial planning, in the following paragraphs.

The obligation imposed on solicitors by Rule 22 has two main aspects;

(1) an investigation of facts, ie the obligation is to ascertain from the client all relevant personal and financial details before performing any investment service for the client (see **2.3.2**); and

(2) a suitability of investments provision. By this requirement, inter alia, 'only investments suitable to the particular client may be recommended' (see **2.3.4**).

2.3.2 The client's personal details

The information which should be obtained will include the following four major categories:

(1) Personal details:

    (a) name, address and occupation;

    (b) dates of birth and retirement;

    (c) whether single, married, divorced, or widow(ed);

    (d) whether employed, or self-employed.

(2) Family details:

    (a) spouse (name and age);

    (b) children, grandchildren (names and ages).

(3) Gifts previously made (including the amounts and whether outright or in trust).
(4) Provision by any will (including the date of will).

2.3.3 The client's financial details

The financial details which will be obtained from the client, and consequently any financial planning advice which can be given, will generally concentrate on two broad areas:

(1) the client's current assets and liabilities; and
(2) the client's current income and expenditure.

Generally, there will be some 'signpost' or 'indicator' in the client's existing financial affairs which leads to the opportunity to provide financial planning advice. Some of these indicators are as follows.

Savings predominantly on deposit in a bank or building society account
Savings in the bank or building society are 'safe' and convenient in that the money can be withdrawn quickly (although some accounts do require up to 90 days' notice to be given unless interest is to be lost, see further Appendix 2). Interest payable is subject to income tax. The main danger in holding a lot of money in such an account is the loss of purchasing power because of inflation. Inflation is the investor's number one enemy. At 5 per cent inflation, £100 today will be worth £95 next year. Although it is prudent to hold some money in savings accounts as a ready source of money in case of emergency, consideration could be given to withdrawing the majority of it for investment elsewhere.

Investments all yielding high income returns
High income yields will be superficially attractive to the client but there are features of such a return which indicate a review of the investment strategy, for example, because:

(1) high yields may be earned at the expense of high risk, ie there may be a higher risk of losing the invested capital because of the nature of the investment. If so, it may be prudent to diversify the investment portfolio to an appropriate extent; and
(2) high income indicates the probability of income tax rates of 40 per cent. This may be alleviated by the transfer of some investments into the name of the client's spouse if he or she pays income tax at a lower rate or by rearranging the investment portfolio into assets where the concentration is on capital growth rather than income yield.

No payment of life policy premiums
For a consideration of the available types of life policy, see Appendix 2. Although premiums do not generally attract income tax relief, it is always prudent to use life policies as a method of saving to produce substantial sums of money on the occurrence of anticipated future events. Traditionally, these are the repayment of a mortgage, the retirement of the client and the death of a client.

No contributions to an occupational pension scheme or a personal pension
Ideally, anyone who is in work should be able to look forward to retirement in the knowledge that he will then benefit from a pension which provides an acceptable level of income. Payment of national insurance contributions during working life will ensure receipt of the state retirement pension. This is payable at state pension age which is currently 60 for women and 65 for men. In some cases a 'top up' pension

will be payable as well, ie the state earnings related pension. However, further 'top up' through an occupational pension scheme or a private pension is also desirable.

OCCUPATIONAL PENSION SCHEMES

The absence of contributions by an employee to an occupational pension scheme should not necessarily be taken as meaning that the employee will not benefit from an occupational pension on retirement. These schemes are often offered by employers on a 'non-contributory' basis, ie only the employer pays contributions. If approved by the Inland Revenue, occupational pension schemes attract considerable tax advantages for employer and employee contributions and for the pension fund itself.

PERSONAL PENSION SCHEMES

Personal pension schemes are available to the self-employed and to those employed in 'non-pensionable' employment, ie to employees who are not offered an occupational pension scheme by their employers. They are also available to employees who prefer not to join the pension scheme provided by their employer. If approved by the Inland Revenue, these schemes also attract considerable tax advantages for contributions to the scheme as well as for the fund itself.

See Appendix 2 for a more detailed discussion of pensions.

Assets held in the name of one spouse alone

The home, investments and other assets may, with advantage, be transferred into the joint ownership of spouses through the use of a joint tenancy or a tenancy in common. The various estate planning opportunities available to spouses are discussed in detail in Chapter 4.

2.3.4 Suitability of investments for a particular client

The last of the features of Rule 22 relates to the 'suitability' of investments. The investment strategy for the client will reflect the information obtained during the client 'fact find'. Two particular factors will be the age of the client, and his existing investments and earnings.

The client's age

(1) Younger clients, especially if married with children, may have little spare money beyond what is needed for everyday life, including mortgage payments. Because of the possibility of moving house and other changing circumstances, ideally such clients should place any spare money in savings accounts whereby the income is reasonably high but the capital is free from risk and can easily be recovered if needed. For example, high interest building society and bank deposit accounts provide safe, high returns. Should further money be available, a more complex strategy will be needed.

(2) Middle-aged clients, with growing families, should begin planning for retirement and old age by improving their income and capital position as far as possible. Maximum affordable pension contributions should be made. Spare earnings and investment income should be invested to produce maximum capital growth.

(3) Retirement-age clients, who no longer have mortgage and school fee commitments, may need to change the emphasis of their investment strategy from capital growth to income yield. Loss of earnings will need to be balanced as far

as possible by investment yields and pension income. If a tax-free capital lump sum is withdrawn from the pension fund at retirement, this should be invested to improve the income position.

(4) Elderly clients, often with low incomes, need to ensure that maximum advantage is taken of the increased levels of personal tax allowances – the age related allowances (see Appendix 1) – by holding high income yielding investments where possible. By s 480A of the ICTA 1988, interest payable to depositors in banks and building societies is paid net of lower rate tax (20%) from 6 April 1996. Non-tax payers can recover this tax if they submit an appropriate claim to the Inland Revenue. However, if the client is not a tax payer, there is considerable advantage to be gained from holding money in a bank or building society because interest can be paid without deduction of lower rate tax at source. The elderly client will need to certify to the bank or building society that he is not a tax payer so that he can receive gross interest payments.

Planning the financial and other affairs of elderly clients will become difficult where they are unable to take part in decision-making through loss of mental capacity. In order to overcome problems caused by loss of mental capacity, it is appropriate for the solicitor to recommend to an elderly client that he makes an enduring power of attorney (EPA). The client may choose to appoint a member of the family or perhaps the solicitor to be his attorney under the EPA. Timing the recommendation of an EPA requires considerable care and tact but it is often convenient to raise the matter at the same time as the elderly client is making a new will or codicil. EPA's are considered in detail in Chapter 3.

The client's existing investments and earnings

For most young and elderly clients, an investment strategy should be followed which, consistent with a policy of spreading risk, develops maximum income potential. A similar policy may be prudent for middle-aged clients but for them earnings may be sufficiently high to permit a policy favouring capital growth instead. The actual selection of investments will be influenced by the particular interests and prejudices of the client as well as by the taxation position.

2.4 PORTFOLIO PLANNING

Every client is different, and each client will have different requirements. Excluding house purchase, a general plan for investments will probably be:

(1) 'ready cash' saved in a bank or building society;
(2) protection through life assurance for the client and dependants;
(3) pension; and
(4) longer term investments purchased with any spare cash.

2.4.1 High risk/low risk

Investments can be categorised as low, medium or high risk. Often the higher the return, the higher the risk. Each category might include the following:

Low risk
(a) Savings accounts in the bank or building society.
(b) Government stock ('gilts').
(c) National Savings, for example National Savings Certificates, income bonds or premium bonds.

Medium risk

(a) Unit trusts.

(b) Investment trusts.

(c) Shares in public companies, ie in blue chip 'equities'.

High risk

(a) Shares in small public companies and in private companies.

(b) 'Collectibles' such as works of art and stamp collections.

(c) Woodlands.

2.4.2 Longer term/short term

Short term

'Savings' ie short term cash investments for the purchase of a particular item such as a new car. Probably the bank or building society offers the best opportunity but interest rates may be low (and no capital growth).

Longer term

Longer term 'investment' depends on the client's available resources, personal likes and dislikes etc and may include many of the investments in Appendix 2.

2.4.3 Capital growth/income yield

If the client has adequate income, he may prefer to invest for capital growth rather than for dividends or interest. Company shares are the probable type of investment if capital growth is required, although companies showing good capital growth usually pay good dividends as well.

If income yield is required, savings in higher rate bank and building society accounts may be sensible. So too may be investment in certain companies where the dividend record is good or even government stocks ('gilts').

2.4.4 Income tax and capital gains tax

'Savings' producing an income and 'investments' producing both an income and capital growth will mean that both income tax and capital gains tax will be relevant for the client. Some savings and investments are tax free and should always feature in the portfolio planning for clients who are, or who become because of the investment, tax payers. Examples include TESSAs and PEPs (see further Appendix 2).

2.5 INTRODUCTION TO TYPES OF INVESTMENT PRODUCTS

There are very many different types of investment product on the market. The term 'investment product' covers savings, ie money deposited in a bank or building society, as well as stocks, shares, unit and investment trusts, PEPs, life policies etc. All these products have different characteristics, uses and tax positions associated with them. They must be selected with care to suit the particular type of client. Details of some of the more usual investment products appear in Appendix 2.

2.6 INCOME TAX

The structure of the system for charging income tax has built into it many opportunities for reducing the amount of tax otherwise payable. Sound financial and investment planning for clients involves ensuring that so far as possible the client takes full advantage of these opportunities including:

(1) receipt of tax-free income (and capital gains);
(2) deductions from earnings giving tax relief;
(3) relief for 'charges on income';
(4) full use of personal reliefs; and
(5) full use of the lower and basic rate income tax bands, particularly under independent taxation for husband and wife clients.

2.6.1 Tax-free income

The main categories of savings and investments producing tax-free income are detailed in Appendix 2. Where possible a gross income should be obtained if the client is not a tax payer so as to avoid the need to obtain a refund of tax deducted at source from the Inland Revenue. Some of these investments are free of capital gains tax as well as income tax.

2.6.2 Deductions from income giving tax relief

The various Schedules and Cases in ICTA 1988 permit certain deductions when calculating the statutory income from the particular source. For example, when computing profits for Schedule A a landlord may deduct expenditure incurred 'wholly and exclusively' in connection with the receipt of the rent such as expenditure on maintenance, repairs, insurance and management; expenses incurred 'wholly and exclusively' for the purposes of his business can be deducted by a sole trader under Schedule D Case 1.

In addition, statutory provision often allows other deductions. Where this is so, there is often a sound investment opportunity as well. Pension contributions provide a particularly good example of this.

The employed and the self-employed client should be advised of the benefits which can be obtained through pension provision. Apart from the 'employee relations' factor, there are also tax benefits for an employer whose contributions to an exempt approved occupational pension scheme are deductible under Schedule D Case 1. The investment and tax saving opportunities for individual clients through occupational pension schemes and personal pensions are discussed in Appendix 2.

2.6.3 Charges on income

Technically, charges on income are 'amounts which fall to be deducted in computing total income', ie they are deducted from a taxpayer's statutory income. They are not defined but include payments which the taxpayer is obliged to make (even if the commitment is entered into voluntarily, for example payments under a deed of covenant). Interest payments and annual payments are the most common deductions made as charges on income.

Interest payments
The general rule is that payments of interest, such as bank overdraft interest, give

no tax relief to the person making the payment. To this principle, there are important exceptions:

(1) Interest paid on loans of money borrowed for trade purposes is deductible as a business expense under Schedule D Case 1 if made wholly and exclusively for the purposes of the trade. Here, tax relief is available but not in the form of a change on income.

(2) Interest paid on loans to purchase a main residence can also attract tax relief. If the various conditions are satisfied, relief is generally available under the MIRAS scheme (see later) and, again, not as a charge on income.

Interest paid on 'qualifying loans' does, however, attract income tax relief as a charge on income. In most cases interest is paid in full to the lender but in a few cases tax at basic rate should be deducted by the borrower before making the payment. In particular this applies where yearly interest is paid by a person to another person whose 'usual abode' is outside the UK. The borrower pays the basic rate tax which he has deducted from the interest payment to the Inland Revenue authorities in the UK.

Qualifying loans include:

(1) A loan to buy a share in a partnership or contribute capital or make a loan to a partnership.

(2) A loan to invest in a close trading company.

(3) A loan to PRs to pay IHT.

MIRAS AND LOANS TO PURCHASE A MAIN RESIDENCE

Interest on loans of up to £30,000 attracted tax relief at 20 per cent (1994/95). Since then, relief has been given at 15 per cent and will continue at that rate for 1997/98. For 1998/99 it will reduce to 10 per cent. The interest must be paid on a loan taken out by the owner of an interest in land in the UK to purchase or develop the land for use as his only or main residence. He must therefore both pay the interest and occupy the property. Where the loan is made by one of the major lending institutions (including the lending banks, building societies and local authorities) the relief is usually given by allowing the interest to be paid net of tax, even if the borrower is not a taxpayer. Because most taxpayers obtain their relief under the MIRAS system (mortgage interest relief at source) the interest can be ignored when making an income tax calculation, ie it is not deducted as a charge on income. If for any reason the MIRAS scheme does not apply, relief is given by way of a reduction of tax at the end of the income tax calculation. The loss to the lender in receiving only a net payment from the borrower is made up by an equivalent payment from the Inland Revenue.

Example

Sonia has bought her house with the assistance of a mortgage loan from the Abbeyfax Building Society. Monthly interest is £400. The MIRAS scheme applies.

	£
monthly interest	400
less: £400 at 15%	60
payment to building society	340

The Abbeyfax Building Society recovers the additional £60 from the Inland Revenue and so receives the full £400 per month.

As MIRAS applies, any income tax liability Sonia may have is calculated without reference to her mortgage interest payments. If MIRAS had not applied, Sonia would obtain her tax relief by a reduction of her tax bill for the tax year by an amount equal to tax at 15% on the gross annual interest paid to the building society.

ELDERLY TAXPAYER – LOAN TO BUY A LIFE ANNUITY (ICTA 1988, s 365)

This section gives relief at basic rate (23%) to elderly taxpayers for interest paid in connection with 'home income plans' (see Appendix 2, para (19)). In these cases, the rate of relief has not been reduced to 15 per cent, as in the case of other loans to purchase land. Interest payments on loans of up to £30,000 taken out by individuals or couples aged 65 or over to purchase an annuity attract the relief if certain conditions are satisfied:

(1)   at least 90 per cent of the loan is used to buy an annual income (an annuity) for the elderly person;
(2)   the loan is secured on land in the UK used as the borrower's only or main residence when the interest is paid.

Annual payments

Over many years 'annual payments' have been used by taxpayers as charges on income to save income tax. When tax rates were high, the tax saving involved was considerable. Traditionally, an annual payment was an 'allocation' or an alienation of income to another, whose income it then became for tax purposes. The payer thereby avoided tax on the income alienated at basic rate and higher rate. The recipient became liable at rates appropriate to his income level. If the recipient was not a taxpayer, for example a child of the payer or a charity, or paid tax at rates lower than the payer, there was an obvious overall saving on tax on the income allocated to the payee. Anti-avoidance legislation has cut back the tax saving which can be made through annual payments. In particular, a payment of income by a parent to an infant unmarried child ceased to attract tax relief (ICTA 1988, s 663 and see further **4.6.4**) although covenanted payments to charity remain unaffected.

To be within the meaning of 'annual payment' the following conditions need to be satisfied (*IRC v Whitworth Park Coal Co Ltd* [1958] 2 All ER 91):

(1)   There must be a binding obligation under which the payment is made, for example a court order. Even if entered into voluntarily there may be a binding obligation, such as a deed of covenant.
(2)   There must be an element of recurrence attached to the obligation, ie it must be 'annual'.
(3)   A payment must be 'pure income' of the recipient, ie there is no expense involved for the recipient of the payment.

The covenanted charitable donation is the principal category of payment which remains within the meaning of annual payment and which is not outlawed by statute (ICTA 1988, s 347A). There are, however, further conditions which must be satisfied. The covenant must be drafted so as to be capable of exceeding 3 years (hence the common fixed 4-year charitable covenant – although a covenant for any period capable of exceeding 3 years suffices; for example, the life of the donor); further, the covenant must not be capable of revocation within that period.

Sections 348 to 350 of the ICTA 1988 provide the machinery whereby the recipient's tax at basic rate on the covenanted payment is to be collected at source from the payer; the charity (exempt income tax) being in receipt of a net sum can recover the tax deducted at source from the Inland Revenue.

Example

Donald, who has an investment income of £20,000 covenants to pay his favourite charity, the RNLI, £1,000 per annum for 5 years.

(1) Donald may deduct basic rate tax (£230) from the payment. He pays the RNLI £770 and gives it a tax deduction certificate R 185. He pays the Inland Revenue £230 (see (3) below). Donald's obligation to pay the charity is then satisfied.

(2) Donald's statutory income is reduced to £19,000 (he deducts the annual payment – £1,000 – as a charge on his income).

(3) Donald's tax position

	Covenant	No covenant
	£	£
statutory income	20,000	20,000
less: charge on income	1,000	—
	19,000	20,000
personal allowance (1997/98)	4,045	4,045
	14,955	15,955
tax: £4,100 @ 20%	820	820
balance @ 23%	2,496.65	2,726.65
	3,316.65	3,546.65
£1,000 @ 23%	230	—
(see para (1) above)	3,546.65	3,546.65

Note (i): the cost to Donald of providing the charity with £1,000 is only £770 because although his total outlay is £770 paid to the charity and £230 to the Inland Revenue, his *own* tax bill is reduced by £230 (£3,546.65 – 230 = £3,316.65).

Note (ii): if Donald had been a 40% tax payer the cost to him of giving the charity £1,000 would have been less (he would have saved tax at his highest marginal rate).

(4) The RNLI

	£
It receives from Donald	770
It receives from the Inland Revenue	230
gross receipt	1,000

Only if the taxpayer has sufficient income to 'support' his covenanted payment will the benefit of tax relief be available. In husband and wife cases it is possible to 'transfer' an existing covenant to the other spouse where this is appropriate to obtain relief. Instead, the couple might prefer to take full advantage of independent taxation and transfer income-producing investments between them.

Drafting the covenant calls for care in choice of the appropriate 'formula of words' if the intention is to give the charity a fixed sum each year. It is not possible for the payer and the payee to agree that the payment is to be made without deduction of tax (ICTA 1988, s 106). Compare the following:

(1) Donald covenants to pay the RNLI £1,000.
    If basic rate is 23%, he pays the charity £770.
    If basic rate is 30%, he pays the charity £700.

(2) Donald covenants to pay the RNLI 'such sum as after deduction of tax at the basic rate currently in force leaves £770', ie the covenant is phrased in net terms.

    If basic rate is 23%   £1,000 – (1,000 × 23%) = £770.
    If basic rate is 30%   £1,100 – (1,100 × 30%) = £770.
    The variation here is in the gross amount, not the net sum received by the RNLI.

(3) Donald covenants to pay '£770 free of tax'. Here, the question is whether 'tax free' means free of all taxes the recipient might pay. If the recipient were other than an exempt individual this might be of concern; for example, a higher rate taxpayer might claim to be free of all income tax on the covenanted amount, ie free of any excess liability 40% – 23% = 17%. This problem still exists but only for 'old' covenants, ie those started before covenanted payments to individuals ceased to be possible.

2.6.4   Personal reliefs (Appendix 1)

The relief to which an individual is entitled depends upon his personal circumstances. Under independent taxation husbands and wives are separate people for this purpose. It is important that married couples ensure that each has sufficient income to support not only their own personal reliefs but also their individual charitable covenants. Transfer of income-producing investments between spouses will make this possible. In addition, each spouse should, where possible, be in receipt of sufficient income to attract the lower and basic rate bands. Again, this can be achieved by transfer of income-producing assets from the spouse paying tax at the higher rate.

Elderly taxpayers
In the case of elderly taxpayers, the personal relief and the married couple's allowance are 'age related', ie they are increased for taxpayers aged 65 to 74 years and then again for those aged 75 or over. If the elderly taxpayer has income exceeding £15,600 (1997/98), the age-related allowances are reduced by 50 per cent of income over the limit until such time as the level of the ordinary personal allowance (£4,045) or the married couple's allowance (£1,830) is reached. Thus, the lower level of allowance is available even though the extra age-related part has been lost because of the excess income.

   Example: 1997/98 – reduction of age-related personal allowance
   (1) Widow aged 80 with income of £16,000 (50% excess = £200)
        personal allowance reduced to £5,200

(2) Widow aged 80 with income of £19,000 (50% excess = £1,700)
no age allowance but entitled to personal allowance of £4,045

For a married couple, the husband's income only is relevant to reduction of the married couple's allowance. His age related personal allowance is reduced first (to the basic £4,045) and then the age related married couple's allowance is reduced (to the basic £1,830). In neither case is the allowance reduced below the basic figure.

Example: 1997/98 – reduction in age-related personal and married couple's allowance

(1) Winifred is aged 78 with an income of £5,000. She has no tax liability: her age-related personal allowance of £5,400 exceeds her income by £400. The unused excess cannot be transferred to her husband Henry nor can it be carried forward to 1998/99.
(2) Henry (aged 80) has an income of £18,600. 50% of his excess income over the limit (£18,600 – £15,600 = £3,000 × 50% = £1,500) will reduce his age-related allowances as follows:

	Personal allowance	*MCA*
	£	£
Age related	5,400	3,225
Reduction	1,355*	145*
	4,045	3,080

* £1,500 excess first reduces the personal allowance. Henry will receive only the basic personal allowance but will not lose the whole of his age-related MCA.

Until 1 July 1998, elderly taxpayers are also entitled to tax relief at 23 per cent for premiums paid on certain private medical insurance contracts. Either the individual or one of a married couple must be aged 60 or over. If the premium is paid by another for the elderly person, the payer obtains the relief, provided the insurance contract is eligible. Relief is obtained by deducting an amount equivalent to 23 per cent of the premium as a reduction in the individual's tax liability. This relief is withdrawn on premiums paid on policies taken out on or after 2 July 1998 under Finance (No 2) Act 1997 (F (No 2) A 1997).

2.6.5 Rates of tax

Subject to personal and other allowances, income tax is an annual tax charged in bands: in 1997/98, 20 per cent on the first £4,100 of taxable income, 23 per cent on the next £22,000 and 40 per cent on the balance.

Chapter 3

ENDURING POWERS OF ATTORNEY

3.1 WHAT IS AN EPA?

An ordinary power of attorney, whether granted under the Trustee Act 1925 (TA 1925) or as a short form power under the Powers of Attorney Act 1971, ceases to have effect when the donor of the power loses his mental capacity. This means that the attorney appointed by the power is no longer able to act at just the moment when the power is most needed.

The EPA was introduced by the Enduring Powers of Attorney Act 1985 (EPAA 1985) as a means of allowing the authority of the attorney to continue notwithstanding the intervening lack of mental capacity of the donor. An EPA has a number of features including the following:

(1) It must be granted by an adult donor with the appropriate mental capacity to make the EPA. He will have such capacity if he understands the nature and effect of the power, ie that the attorney may assume authority over his affairs and that the power may continue if he becomes mentally incapable.

(2) An EPA can appoint one or more attorneys. Where two or more are appointed they may be joint attorneys or joint and several attorneys. If joint attorneys are appointed, they must act together and the power will cease if either should die or lose mental capacity. If the appointment is as joint and several attorneys then each can act independently of the other or others. This may be convenient but could lead to lack of protection for the donor's property.

(3) The EPA may continue despite the loss of mental capacity of the donor but special duties then arise for the attorney (see **3.3**).

(4) The EPA may give the attorney general or specific authority to act on the donor's behalf. If general authority is given, this confers authority 'to do on behalf of the donor anything which the donor can lawfully do'. If specific authority is given, the authority is limited to the particular activity, for example, to contract to sell and execute a transfer of the donor's freehold property.

(5) Any authority given by the EPA is limited to acts relating to the donor's property and financial affairs. Thus, it can cover such transactions as buying and selling shares or a house on behalf of the donor. But even an EPA giving general authority is significantly limited. It does not cover such matters as where the donor should live, whether or not medical treatment should be given or withheld or the execution of a will for the donor. This limitation on the authority of the attorney will not necessarily matter until such time as the donor of the power loses mental capacity. Decisions relating to matters not covered by the EPA must be taken by individuals other than the attorney acting under the power. If the donor of the EPA does not have sufficient mental capacity to make a will, the Court of Protection may be asked to make a 'statutory will' on behalf of the donor.

(6) The attorney has authority to use the donor's property to provide for the needs of any persons in the way the donor might be expected to have done. He may also make gifts out of the donor's property provided they are of a reasonable

amount and are made on limited occasions to people related to or connected with the donor, or to charity. In either case the attorney may benefit himself, for example, wedding gifts to the donor's daughter can be made even if the daughter is the attorney.

3.2   CREATION OF AN EPA

3.2.1   The Enduring Power of Attorney (Prescribed Form) Regulations 1990

An EPA can be validly created only if the instrument complies with the following requirements:

(1)   The EPA is in the form prescribed in the 1990 Regulations (see Appendix 3). The Act provides that 'immaterial differences in form' can be ignored thus making it possible for firms of solicitors to have their own forms of EPA on word processor. It may, however, be considered safer to use printed versions of the form purchased from law stationers.

(2)   The EPA form incorporates the prescribed explanatory information together with all the relevant marginal notes. Part A of the form entitled 'About using this form' must be included together with Parts B and C. The entire form must be explained to the donor of the power before it is signed.

(3)   The EPA must be executed in the prescribed manner by both the donor and the attorney, in each case in the presence of an independent witness. If the donor (or the attorney) is physically disabled, then the EPA can be executed on his behalf but in this case the signature must be made in the presence of two independent witnesses.

3.2.2   Postponing the attorney's authority to act

Once the EPA has been correctly executed, the attorney may act under its authority immediately, and without further formality. The execution of the EPA does not deprive the donor of the ability to take decisions on his own behalf should he so wish; indeed, he can revoke the power at any time. However, he will need to retain sufficient mental capacity if he is to act on his own behalf or to revoke the power.

Some donors prefer the attorney's authority to act only to arise at a future date and not immediately the power is executed. Even though there is no duty placed on the attorney to act under the EPA, there is a natural reluctance on the part of the donor to allow the attorney to act while he still retains capacity to do so. If the attorney's authority is to be delayed, the EPA should be drafted to include an appropriate restriction on the attorney's authority. For example, the authority may be delayed until such time as the attorney believes that 'the donor either is, or is becoming, mentally incapable', ie the authority will arise at the same time as the EPAA 1985 places a duty on the attorney to register the EPA with the Court of Protection (see **3.3**). Great care must must be exercised when drafting this type of restriction.

3.2.3   Restricting the automatic delegation of the donor's position as trustee

Section 3 of the EPAA 1985 provides that an attorney acting under an EPA may 'execute all trusts, powers and discretions vested in the donor as trustee'. Thus, automatically, the attorney may act in place of the donor as trustee under existing will trusts and inter vivos settlements. Section 3 is confined to the position as trustee and so does not cover cases where the donor is a personal representative of a deceased person's estate.

The effect of s 3 should be drawn to the donor's attention when he is considering making an EPA. He may prefer (as may his co-trustees) to restrict the attorney's authority by a suitable provision in the EPA whereby the position as trustee is not automatically delegated in this way. Once again, considerable care will be needed when drafting such a restriction.

3.3 REGISTRATION OF THE EPA WITH THE COURT OF PROTECTION

3.3.1 Donor's mental incapacity

Unlike an ordinary power of attorney, an EPA is not revoked by the donor's subsequent loss of mental capacity. However, once the donor has become incapacitated the attorney is unable to act under the authority of the EPA until it has been registered with the Court of Protection. The EPAA 1985 imposes special duties on the attorney which arise once the attorney 'has reason to believe that the donor is or is becoming mentally incapable'.

3.3.2 Special duties

The attorney is required to notify the donor of the EPA and certain specified relatives of his intention to apply to the Court of Protection for registration of the EPA.

The specified relatives who must receive notification of intention to apply for registration of the EPA include:

(1) the donor's husband or wife;
(2) the donor's children (including illegitimate children);
(3) the donor's parents;
(4) the donor's brothers and sisters, whether of the whole or half blood;
(5) the widow or widower of a child of the donor;
(6) the donor's grandchildren.

The list continues with further remoter categories of relatives.

The EPAA 1985 requires that three individuals be ascertained by working from the top of the list. All members of a particular category must be notified once any member of the category is counted to establish the minimum number of three. However, there is no requirement for the attorney to notify (inter alia) a person who has not attained 18, or himself, even if he is a specified relative but he should be included when counting the number of relatives to notify.

> *Example*
> Adam is married with five adult children and a number of other surviving relatives. He has appointed his solicitor, Brian, to be his attorney. When Adam becomes incapable of managing his affairs Brian must notify Adam's wife and all five children (plus Adam himself unless the court dispenses with this).

The Court of Protection has a general power of dispensation from the duty of notification. It can order dispensation if satisfied that it would be undesirable or impractical for the attorney to give notice, or if no useful purpose is likely to be achieved by it. However, clear medical evidence of detriment to health would be required before the court dispenses with notification to the donor.

The application to the Court of Protection for registration of the EPA should be made within 10 days of giving notice to the donor and the specified relatives.

3.3.3   Effect of registration

The registration of the EPA with the Court of Protection effectively revalidates the EPA and restores to the attorney the powers granted by the EPA. Once registered, the donor can no longer revoke, extend or restrict the extent of the EPA.

3.4   WHEN SHOULD AN EPA BE GRANTED?

As in the case of an ordinary power of attorney, there is no precise occasion when an EPA should be granted. However, it may be appropriate to do so:

(1)   when the donor is intending to be absent abroad for a given period of time. If the EPA is not restricted, the attorney would be able to act during the donor's absence;

(2)   at the same time as the donor is making a will. Most clients will raise the question of a will with their solicitor but, apart from unusual circumstances, it is not likely that a client will consider making an EPA. It is, therefore, generally necessary for the solicitor to find an appropriate occasion when the subject of an EPA can be introduced. Often this will be when instructions are taken for the will. It is good practice to consider giving advice about a will and an EPA at the same time, particularly if the client is elderly. Although a younger testator is unlikely to be keen on the idea of an EPA, it should be remembered that either accident or illness can result in loss of mental capacity. Without an EPA the person's affairs would be managed by a receiver appointed by the Court of Protection.

Chapter 4

ESTATE PLANNING

4.1 INTRODUCTION

For the person who declines advice during his lifetime and wishes to die intestate, estate planning is of little relevance. Anyone else is a candidate for estate planning.

Estate planning can range from advising on a will leaving everything to a spouse to complex 'off-shore' tax avoidance schemes. The majority of practitioners find that their cases fall somewhere between these extremes. The client offering the greatest scope for estate planning is wealthy, married with children (and possibly grandchildren).

4.1.1 Estate planning

Estate planning is a combination of: financial planning (see Chapter 2); lifetime giving, outright and/or into trusts (see Chapter 5); and will drafting (see Chapter 11). For clients with relatively limited means, it may only be possible to plan through a will, for example, by leaving a legacy to the children to take advantage of the nil rate band with the residue passing to the surviving spouse. Wealthy clients, however, should be encouraged to use a combination of lifetime transfers and gifts by will. Where lifetime estate planning is contemplated, it is essential that consideration should also be given to a complementary will. If a client dies intestate or leaves a will that does not take lifetime planning into account, unexpected claims can arise: from the Inland Revenue for additional tax, and negligence suits against the solicitor by a surviving spouse or children who receive less than was intended.

4.1.2 Aims

The aims of a client are nearly always twofold:

(1) the provision of financial security for himself and his family; and
(2) the avoidance of tax.

It is not always possible to achieve both objectives and many practitioners believe that tax savings should not be achieved at the expense of financial security.

Estate planning often involves a person giving away assets during his lifetime, perhaps to a spouse or children. Once the gift is made, it cannot be claimed back, for example, if the parties subsequently divorce or the donor parent falls on hard times. If planning through a will, the will of the deceased spouse should not prejudice the standard of living of the survivor by leaving too much property away from that surviving spouse.

Whereas with basic tax planning through wills the intention is to limit the amount of inheritance tax (IHT) payable on a death, the tax planning element of inter vivos estate planning is often as much concerned with avoiding capital gains tax (CGT) or minimising an income tax bill as it is with IHT. Because of the interaction of the taxes, clients may have to accept a small CGT bill as part of the cost of avoiding a large IHT bill, or a potential IHT charge for a considerable saving of CGT.

Example

James has been told that to give away assets which are likely to increase in value is sound IHT planning. Accordingly, he plans to give his daughter his 10,000 shares in Widgets plc which have considerable growth potential. He hopes to reduce the IHT payable at death on his already large estate. Stockbrokers have advised that he will realise a gain of £10,000 if he gives the shares away now. There are no relevant reliefs which James can claim.

Compare the following:

Lifetime gift

(1) CGT: chargeable gain of £3,500 (10,000 – 6,500 annual exemption) taxed at 40% = £1,400.
(2) IHT, PET: even if death occurs within 7 years, IHT will be calculated on the value of the shares at the date of the gift. The increase in value will occur in James's daughter's estate, not in his estate.

No lifetime gift: tax on death

(1) CGT: none (tax-free uplift to value of shares at the date of death).
(2) IHT: on value of the shares at death as part of James's estate attracting tax of up to 40%.

Where a client is contemplating estate planning, the solicitor must balance the cost of the legal work involved against the tax saving to ensure that the costs of the scheme do not outweigh the advantages. Making property transfers inter vivos may give rise to an immediate tax bill which may make it difficult to persuade clients that the proposal will save tax in the long run. Clients may also have to accept that the payment of some tax is inevitable (whether during their lifetime or on death) in order to ensure the best practical financial arrangements for the family.

In this chapter, consideration is given to estate planning by lifetime transfers. Estate planning through wills is dealt with in Chapter 11.

4.1.3   Some ground rules

Advice to clients should be against a background of well-established criteria including the following.

How much to give away?

Apart from the obvious – not too much – other factors to be taken into consideration are: ill health, separation or divorce, retirement, death of one of the parties to the marriage and the effects of inflation on the purchasing power of income and on the value of retained capital. Any of these may suggest retaining more rather than less.

What to give away?

Where possible, assets likely to appreciate in value should be considered for lifetime giving. Shares in a private company following flotation on The Stock Exchange will often rise substantially in value. So too may the value of a painting following the death of the artist. Gifts before the increase in value ensures the growth occurs in the estate of the donee and 'freezes the value' of the gift (PET) at the value at the time of the gift, which will be relevant should death occur within 7 years. A 'disposal' for CGT will occur but the disposal consideration will be the market value at the date of the gift.

How to give away?

Outright gifts are straightforward but are inflexible; if circumstances change the gift once made cannot be recovered. If the proposed donee is a minor, such a gift (if substantial) would not be sensible. An outright gift may become inappropriate; for example, the donee may become addicted to drugs and so be better able to fund the addiction, or may become mentally or physically handicapped, when the money might be better spent for him rather than given to him.

Gifts into trust provide flexibility

Because unexpected events do occur, flexibility is an important part of planning. However, trusts require proper administration. Dealing with income and investment of trust funds, preparing trust accounts and making tax returns for the trust all cost time and money. This must be weighed against the advantages of flexibility. So too must possible adverse change in tax law affecting trusts. Over recent years, this has made discretionary trusts less attractive to estate planners and their clients.

Don't let the tax tail wag the dog!

The objective is to plan affairs so that the client's property is enjoyed by his beneficiaries (often the family) to the best advantage. In achieving this, tax avoidance is only one aspect.

4.2 TAX AND ESTATE PLANNING

The following paragraphs contain some reminders of the basic rules relating to the taxation of individuals, many of which rules also apply to the taxation of trustees. Some of these points will have been encountered already (see the LPC Resource Books *Pervasive Topics*, *Wills, Probate and Administration* and *Business Law and Practice* (Jordans, 1997). The aim is to group together those points which are relevant when considering the various estate planning ideas put forward in this chapter. Where new tax law is required, both for estate planning and elsewhere, it will be explained in detail either here or in context.

4.3 INHERITANCE TAX

IHTA 1984, s 7 provides that tax is charged in accordance with the table of rates in Sch 1 to the Act.

4.3.1 Rates of IHT chargeable on death

0% on the first £215,000 (nil rate band) from 6 April 1997.
40% on the balance.

4.3.2 Rates of IHT for lifetime chargeable transfers

0% on the first £215,000 (nil rate band).
20% on the balance.

The majority of lifetime transfers are PETs (potentially exempt transfers) but the creation of a no interest in possession trust, for example a discretionary settlement, is immediately chargeable. IHT must be re-assessed at death rates if the settlor (the person creating the settlement) dies within the following 7 years. Credit is given in the re-calculation for any tax already paid, ie when the settlement was created.

Example

Helen gives property with a value of £261,000 to the trustees of her discretionary trust (ignore exemptions and reliefs). The trustees agree to pay the IHT.

			£
IHT at lifetime rates	£215,000 @ 0%	=	nil
	£ 46,000 @ 20%	=	9,200

Helen dies 14 months later – the IHT is reassessed.

			£
IHT at death rates	£215,000 @ 0%	=	nil
	£ 46,000 @ 40%	=	18,400
			18,400
Less : IHT already paid at lifetime rates			9,200
Additional IHT as result of Helen's death			9,200

If Helen, not the trustees, had agreed to pay the IHT when she created the settlement, the loss to her estate then would have included the IHT payable, ie grossing up would have applied to calculate the value transferred. This is considered further in Chapter 5.

4.3.3   Potentially exempt transfers (IHTA 1984, s 3A)

Potentially exempt transfers (PETs) are transfers made by an individual on or after 18 March 1986 which, apart from the section, are chargeable transfers. The following are PETs:

(i)   Gifts to other individuals provided the donee's estate is increased or the property transferred becomes comprised in his estate.

(ii)   Transfers to the trustees of an interest in possession settlement because the estate of the beneficiary with the life interest includes the property in which that interest subsists, ie the settled property (IHTA 1984, ss 5 and 49).

(iii)   Transfers to the trustees of an accumulation and maintenance trust and trusts for the disabled (IHTA 1984, ss 71 and 89).

Transfers to trustees of interest in possession settlements and accumulation and maintenance trusts are considered further in Chapter 5.

No charge arises at the time the PET is made and it is treated as fully exempt unless the transferor dies within the following 7 years. There is no obligation on the transferor to notify the Inland Revenue of the PET. Should the transferor die within the 7 years following the PET, it becomes chargeable and must be reported to the Inland Revenue.

4.3.4   Exemptions applying to lifetime transfers (IHTA 1984, ss 18–23)

(1)   Any property passing to a spouse (there is a limit of £55,000 on the exempt amount if the recipient spouse is non-UK domiciled – IHTA 1984, s 18(2) (see further **14.3**)).

(2)   Gifts to charity. Various ways of giving to charity are considered in **4.9**.

(3)   Small gifts. Gifts not exceeding £250 to any one person in any one year are exempt. Because of this limitation, it is not possible to combine the small gift

exemption with another exemption, for example the annual exemption. The gift must be outright, not in trust.

(4) Transfers of £3,000 per annum (any unused annual exemption can be carried forward one year).

Example

In Year 1 a donor makes his first ever gift of £1,000. In Year 2 he may give away £5,000. If the £2,000 carried forward from Year 1 is not used in the following year, it is lost and may not be carried further forward.

Used by a husband and wife with adequate resources, over a 25-year period they could give their children a total of £156,000. By the simple use of an exemption considerable estate planning for the parents could be achieved.

(5) Gifts in consideration of marriage: up to £5,000 per parent of the couple (lesser amounts for other donors). The gift may be outright or into trust if the beneficiaries are the couple, their issue (or spouses). It must be 'in contemplation' of a particular marriage and should be so evidenced in writing.

(6) Normal expenditure out of income: if claimed (it is not given automatically) this exemption applies to a gift of cash that:

(a) is part of the normal expenditure of the donor;

(b) taking one with another, is made out of income; and

(c) after other such gifts, leaves the donor with sufficient income to maintain his usual standard of living.

It is a question of fact whether a gift qualifies. What is 'normal expenditure' for one person is not necessarily so for another. If not one of a series of regular payments, a gift may nonetheless be 'normal' if of a type which by its nature is likely recur (see further *Bennett v IRC* [1995] STC 54).

The exemption is most commonly used to fund the payment of premiums on policies of assurance written in trust, for example:

(a) an endowment policy written in trust by a parent in favour of a child on which the parent pays the annual premiums;

(b) premiums on a policy written in trust to be used to fund a potential IHT liability should the donor die within 7 years of a PET.

4.3.5 Valuation

Market value

The IHT legislation contains provisions relating to the valuation of property given away by a donor. The normal rule is that property is valued at 'the price [it] might reasonably be expected to fetch if sold on the open market at the time; but that price shall not be reduced on the grounds that the whole property is to be placed on the market at one and the same time'. Thus, it is not possible to argue for a reduced valuation because 'the market is flooded' where a lot of a similar type of property is available at once (IHTA 1984, s 160).

The 'open market rule' applies on a death although changes in value of an estate caused by the death can be taken into account (IHTA 1984, s 171). For example, life policies which mature on death are valued at the maturity value (not the surrender value) and personal goodwill in a business is valued at a figure (usually lower) after allowing for the loss of the proprietor of the business.

Joint ownership of assets

Co-owners of land can discount the value of their respective shares to take into account the fact that it may be difficult to sell a share in co-owned property on the market; the purchaser will occupy the property with the other co-owner. A discount of 10–15 per cent is normal.

> *Example*
> Two brothers own a house equally. If the open market value of the house is £200,000, the value of a one-half share may be agreed by the Inland Revenue to be £90,000.

Valuation of other jointly owned assets does not attract such a discount. In these cases, the open market value is divided proportionately between the joint owners.

The related property rules (see later) deny this discount to a husband and wife who co-own property.

Quoted shares

As for CGT, the price is taken to be the price 'one quarter up' from the lower to the higher price for dealings on the day in question on the stock market. Thus, if a share is shown as 100p–104p for the day of dealing, the valuation would be 101p per share held by the donor.

Shares in unquoted companies

Shares in private/family companies are notoriously difficult to value; such a valuation is not an exact science. The principal reason for the difficulty is the lack of any real market. Final agreement of value will take many years of negotiation between the donor's valuers and the Unlisted Securities Division of the Inland Revenue. Many factors will be relevant:

(1)   The success or otherwise of the company.
(2)   Other recent dealings in the shares (if any).
(3)   The number of shares as a percentage of the entire issued capital of the company:

- a 75% holding   can pass special resolutions
- a 51% holding   can pass ordinary resolutions
- 50% or less   a minority holding, with less voting influence (especially if small holding).

(4)   The existence of typical pre-emption rights in the company's articles of association requiring shares first to be offered to other shareholders. Here the lack of a market is the real problem. Nevertheless, the courts have over a long period held that shares must be valued on the assumption that there is a market but that the purchaser will then himself become subject to the restrictions contained in the articles of association.

To reach agreement the Inland Revenue will need from the company or its advisers much information including:

(a)   A full description of the business carried on by the company.
(b)   The last 3 years' accounts of the company published before the date of valuation.
(c)   If minority holdings are to be valued, details of any restrictions on the transfer of shares.

(d) If there are different classes of shares, a statement of the rights of each class, in particular those concerning voting, dividends and distributions on a liquidation of the company.

Related property (IHTA 1984, s 161)

Assets as a pair or set are worth more than the aggregate value of each item valued separately; for example, one valuable earring is not worth a lot on its own. The related property rules are designed to avoid loss of IHT by splitting asset ownership. Section 161(1) provides 'where the value of any property comprised in a person's estate would be less than the appropriate proportion of the value of the aggregate of that and any related property, it shall be the appropriate proportion of the value of that aggregate'.

Example

Harriet and her husband, Tiny, each owned 30% of the shares in H and T Ltd, their personal company. Taken separately, each holding is valued at £25,000, but together the controlling holding of 60% is valued at £75,000. Harriet considers giving her shareholding to their child, Rowland. Under the related property rule, her shareholding would be valued as the appropriate proportion of the value of their total holding, ie £75,000 ÷ 2 = £37,500.

If Harriet makes her gift, she will make a PET. If she dies within 7 years the PET will have become a chargeable transfer. Business property relief at 100% will be available if Rowland owns the shares when his mother dies.

4.3.6 Reliefs

Agricultural property relief (IHTA 1984, ss 115–124)

Agricultural property relief is given automatically for transfers of value of 'agricultural property'. 'Agricultural property' is defined as including agricultural land and pasture; and cottages, farm buildings and farmhouses together with the land occupied with them as are of a character appropriate to the property.

The relief is given against the 'agricultural value' of the agricultural property. 'Agricultural value' is defined as the value which would be the value of the property if the property were subject to a perpetual covenant prohibiting its use otherwise than as agricultural property. Thus, any value attributable to possible development or to mineral deposits under the land would not be eligible.

Agricultural property relief applies to property which was either:

(1) occupied by the transferor for agriculture throughout the 2 years immediately before the transfer; or
(2) owned by the transferor throughout the 7 years immediately before the transfer (provided it was occupied by someone (the transferor or another) for agriculture throughout the 7-year period).

For these purposes, periods of occupation and ownership of a deceased spouse can be included.

100 per cent relief

Available where the transferor had the right to vacant possession immediately before the transfer or the right to obtain it within 12 months, although by concession (ESC F17) this period is extended to 24 months from the date of the transfer. To encourage agricultural tenancies, this relief is now available where property is let on a tenancy starting on or after 1 September 1995 (FA 1995, s 155).

50 per cent relief
Available on any other qualifying agricultural property.

> *Examples*
>
> (1) Giles, who farmed Greenacre for 28 months has just died. Agricultural property relief is available at 100% against the vacant possession value due to the owner occupation.
> (2) Jim ceased farming Blackacre 10 years ago. He let the farm to his son, who has continued to farm it, and he retained the freehold reversion himself. Jim has just died. His PRs will be able to claim agricultural property relief at 50% against the tenanted value of the agricultural property.

AGRICULTURAL PROPERTY IN SETTLEMENTS
Subject to the time-limits, the relief can apply to agricultural property held by trustees whether or not there is an interest in possession in the settled property. If there is an interest in possession, the life tenant (whose 'estate' under general principle is deemed to include the settled property, ie the agricultural property) is the 'transferor' and 'owner' of the agricultural property for the purposes of the relief. The life tenant must therefore satisfy the conditions of 2 years' occupation of the property or 7 years' ownership of it. If there are discretionary trusts, the trustees will instead be the 'transferors' and 'owners' of the agricultural property. The occasions of charge to IHT on discretionary trusts are discussed at **10.2**.

Agricultural property relief is given in priority to business property relief.

Business property relief (IHTA 1984, ss 103–114)
Business property relief operates to reduce the value transferred by a transfer of value of relevant business property by a certain percentage.

A reduction of 100 per cent of the value transferred is allowed for transfers of certain assets. They are:

(1) A business or interest in a business (eg a partnership share).
(2) Shares which are not quoted on the Stock Exchange (companies on the Unlisted Securities Market and the Alternative Investment Market count as unquoted for this purpose).

A reduction of 50 per cent of the value transferred is allowed for transfers of any other assets which qualify for business property relief. They are:

(1) Shares which are quoted on the Stock Exchange and where the transferor had control; control exists broadly where the transferor's entire holding yields over 50 per cent of the votes on all resolutions.
(2) Land, buildings, machinery or plant owned by the transferor personally but used by a partnership of which he is a member or by a company of which he has control.

The relevant business property must have been owned by the transferor for at least 2 years immediately prior to the transfer. An exception to this rule applies where a spouse inherits business property under the will or intestacy of the deceased spouse. In that circumstance only, the surviving spouse is deemed to have owned the property from the time it was originally acquired by the deceased spouse.

Example 1

In 1989 James acquired 75% of the shares in X Ltd, a private company. James died in 1993 leaving those shares to his wife Kim. In 1994 Kim died leaving all her estate, including the shares, to her son. The 100% relief will be available on Kim's death.

The exception does not apply where the relevant business property is transferred to the spouse inter vivos.

Example 2

In Year 1 Judy sets up her own business, Y Ltd, and holds 100% of the shares.
In Year 5 she transfers 20% of those shares to her husband, Keith.
In Year 6 Keith dies leaving the 20% shareholding to his son.
No relief is available against the value of the 20% holding as Keith has only owned the shares for one year.

These inter-spouse transfer rules also apply to agricultural property relief.

INTER VIVOS TRANSFERS – AVAILABILITY OF RELIEF

Where the charge to IHT arises as a result of a PET or chargeable lifetime transfer (a transfer to discretionary trustees) which is followed by the death of the transferor within 7 years, any IHT (or additional IHT) may be calculated with the benefit of business property relief provided:

(i)   the transferees still own the assets (or replacement assets which qualify as business property) at the death of the transferor (or if earlier, the transferee's own death); and

(ii) the asset qualified as business property immediately before the transferor's death but (for this purpose) ignoring the 2-year ownership requirement.

BUSINESS PROPERTY IN SETTLEMENTS

As with agricultural property relief, relief can be available where business property is held by trustees.

In an interest in possession settlement, the availability of this relief is gauged by reference to the position of the life tenant; as with agricultural property relief the life tenant's 'estate' includes the settled property. If the life tenant satisfies the 2-year ownership test, 100 per cent relief is available where the assets in the trust are either a business or are unquoted shares. 50 per cent relief is available for controlling holdings in quoted companies and for land, buildings, machinery or plant in the trust used in the life tenant's own business or a company which he controls.

If property is held on discretionary trusts, relief will be available if the trustees satisfy the conditions. The occasions of charge to IHT on a discretionary trust are discussed at **10.2**.

4.4   CAPITAL GAINS TAX

4.4.1   Rates

CGT is charged on gains on disposals by treating them as the top slice of the tax payer's income, ie at 20 per cent, 23 per cent and/or 40 per cent. For trustees the rates are 23 per cent or 34 per cent (see Chapter 13).

4.4.2   Calculation

The gain is calculated as the difference between the disposal consideration and the acquisition cost, less indexation allowance and other permitted deductions.

Capital losses are set against chargeable gains for the same tax year and to the extent that losses exceed any gain for that year they can be carried forward to set against future chargeable gains.

4.4.3   Exemptions

(1)   The first £6,500 (£3,250 for trustees) of chargeable gains each year.
(2)   A husband and wife are each entitled to the annual exemption.
(3)   Any gain arising on the disposal by gift or sale of the taxpayer's main or only residence. Where a taxpayer owns more than one residence he may elect for one to be treated as his main residence. A husband and wife living together have only one principal private residence exemption.
(4)   Any gain on the disposal of a property owned by trustees where the property is the residence of a beneficiary entitled to occupation under the terms of the trust or at the discretion of the trustees.

For a further discussion of the points mentioned in paragraphs (3) and (4) above and other matters relating to the main residence, see **4.8.4**.

4.4.4   Death (TCGA 1992, s 62)

Death provides an automatic CGT-free revaluation of assets. The probate value becomes the acquisition cost for subsequent disposals by PRs, beneficiaries and trustees if a trust arises under the will or intestacy. This is because there is no disposal on death but there is an acquisition by the PRs etc. One consequence is that gains accruing during the lifetime are not charged to CGT. This point needs careful consideration as part of general estate planning. Disposal of the same asset inter vivos could well result in immediate liability to tax if the gain exceeds the annual exemption and where neither hold-over relief nor retirement relief is available.

No liability arises when assets are vested in legatees by the PRs; the PRs' acquisition (on death) is taken to be the legatees' acquisition for their future CGT purposes. A 'legatee' includes any person inheriting under a will or intestacy whether beneficially or as a trustee if a trust arises following the death.

> *Example*
> Shares worth £50,000 at death were acquired by the testator 10 years earlier for £5,000. Ignoring the indexation allowance, the gain of £45,000 over the period of ownership does not attract CGT. Gains on all subsequent disposals will be based on an acquisition cost of £50,000. If instead the shares were given away inter vivos the gain on the disposal would attract CGT unless relief was available.

A similar CGT-free revaluation of trust assets occurs when the life tenant under an interest in possession settlement dies. This is in line with the general approach that CGT is not payable as a result of a death.

> *Example*
> Under a testator's will the trustees are holding £100,000 of quoted shares 'for Susan for life, George in remainder'. Susan has just died and the shares are worth £250,000. Ignoring the indexation allowance:

(1)   the gain of £150,000 during the trust period is exempt CGT.

(2)   the investments transferred to George are 'deemed' acquired by him for his future CGT purposes at their market value at Susan's death. Not all the investment will be transferred to George because some will have been sold by the trustees to pay IHT due as a result of Susan's death.

The position of the trustees where a 'deemed disposal' occurs is considered further in **10.1.4**.

4.4.5   Reliefs

(1) Inter-spouse transfers

Inter-spouse transfers are deemed to occur at no gain no loss. Effectively, tax on any gain since the acquisition by the donor spouse is deferred until there is a disposal by the donee spouse (TCGA 1992, s 58).

Example

In 1987, Archie bought a painting for £10,000. He gave his painting to his wife Belinda in 1992 when its value had increased to £18,000. Indexation for the period was £500. Belinda's acquisition cost for future disposals is £10,500.

	£
Archie's deemed disposal consideration	10,500
less: acquisition cost	10,000
	500
indexation allowance	500
	nil

Belinda's acquisition cost is Archie's disposal consideration, ie £10,500.

(2) Hold-over relief

Before 14 March 1989, hold-over relief was generally available for gifts by individuals and trustees to individuals or trustees resident in the UK. Relief is now provided in relatively limited circumstances by TCGA 1992, ss 165 and 260. These provisions operate in the same way, by permitting gains which accrue to the donor to be held over. Tax is effectively deferred by permitting the donee to acquire the gifted property at the donor's acquisition cost after allowing for indexation. Tax remains deferred until the donee disposes of the property when he either cannot or chooses not to make a further hold-over election.

To obtain hold-over relief, an election is required by both the transferor and the transferee although where the transferee is a trustee only the election of the transferor is required. Once made, the result of the election is:

'(a)   the amount of any chargeable gain which, apart from this section, would accrue to the transferor on the disposal, and

(b)   the amount of the consideration for which, apart from this section, the transferee would be regarded with the purposes of CGT as having acquired the asset or, as the case may be, the shares or securities, shall be reduced by an amount equal to the held-over gain on the disposal' (s 165).

A similar result is achieved under s 260.

Example

John gives his shares in his personal company to his daughter Julia. Their market value is £100,000.

A joint election for hold-over relief is made.

		£
(1)	disposal consideration (market value)	100,000
	less: cost price (say)	10,000
		90,000
	indexation allowance (say)	20,000
	held-over gain	70,000

1.   John's gain on disposal is reduced to nil
2.   Julia's acquisition cost is reduced to £30,000 (£100,000 – £70,000)

(2)   Julia sells her shares for £150,000. Her gain is calculated as follows:

	£
disposal consideration (sale proceeds)	150,000
less: cost price (see above)	30,000
	120,000
indexation allowance (say)	30,000
gain	90,000

Julia's chargeable gain is made up of the gain during her period of ownership of £20,000 (150,000 – (100,000 + 30,000)) and £70,000 (the gain held over).

DISPOSAL OF BUSINESS ASSETS WITHIN s 165

Section 165 applies to gifts by individuals and deemed disposals by trustees on the ending of a trust of:

(1)   An asset, or an interest in an asset, used for the purposes of a trade, profession or vocation carried on by:

    (a)   the donor; or
    (b)   his personal company; or
    (c)   a company which is a member of a trading group of companies of which the holding company is the donor's personal company.

(2)   Shares or securities of a trading company or of the holding company of a trading group where:

    (a)   the shares or securities are neither quoted on a recognised stock exchange nor dealt in on the Unlisted Securities Market or the Alternative Investment Market; or
    (b)   the trading company or holding company is the transferor's personal company.

(3)   Agricultural property, or an interest in agricultural property, which is not used for the purposes of a trade carried on as mentioned in paragraph (1) above.

A 'personal' company is a company as defined for retirement relief.

Business assets in settlements

Section 165 relief in a modified form is extended to business assets owned by trustees by TCGA 1992, Sch 7. The asset must be used in a business carried on by the trustees, ie the trustees of a discretionary settlement, or by a beneficiary of a settlement with an interest in possession in the settled property, ie the life tenant. Disposals of shares by trustees in unquoted trading companies and shares with 25 per cent of the voting rights exercisable by the trustees also attract the relief.

DISPOSALS WITHIN s 260

Disposals by individuals or deemed disposals by trustees within s 260 include:

(1) chargeable transfers within the meaning of the Inheritance Tax Act 1984 (and transfers which would be chargeable transfers but for IHTA 1984, s 19 (the annual exemption)) and which are not potentially exempt transfers;
(2) exempt transfers within IHTA 1984, s 24 (transfers to political parties), s 26 (transfers for public benefit), s 27 (transfers to maintenance funds for historic buildings) and s 30 (transfers of designated property);
(3) termination of an accumulation and maintenance settlement where a beneficiary becomes absolutely entitled to the settled property.

Not being immediately chargeable, PETs do not attract this relief. If the donor dies within 7 years so that the PET becomes chargeable relief is not available since, again, it was not immediately chargeable when made. The main type of gift which is not a PET but is a chargeable transfer occurs on the creation and termination of trusts with no interest in possession. Clearly, discretionary trusts are included (even if the value transferred falls within the nil rate band because the IHT charge is at nil per cent) but so too is the termination of accumulation and maintenance trusts (see further Chapter 10). As the creation of an accumulation and maintenance trust is a PET, relief under s 260 is not available.

Example
Kathy transfers assets valued at £215,000 to the trustees of her newly created discretionary trust. She has made no other transfers. Even though no IHT is actually payable there is an occasion of immediate charge (at 0%). Hold-over relief is available at Kathy's election. The trustees do not need to join in the election.

The effect of this relief is that a gift which attracts IHT (or which does not but which reduces the donor's nil rate band) is not also charged to CGT. A double charge to tax is thus avoided. PETs do not attract IHT (at least immediately) and so CGT will normally arise on the disposal (unless s 165 relief applies).

HOLD-OVER RELIEF AND THE FOREIGN ELEMENT

Neither s 165 nor s 260 applies where the transferee is neither resident nor ordinarily resident in the UK. Thus, disposals of chargeable assets to non-resident individuals or settlements are, for this reason, not particularly attractive.

A clawback of CGT can arise where the donee emigrates within 6 years following a hold-over election. If the donee ceases to be resident and ordinarily resident in the UK, CGT liability on the held-over gains is immediately triggered. The CGT is primarily payable by the donee (now overseas). If he fails to pay the tax within 12 months it can be recovered from the donor who has a (probably worthless) right of recovery from the donee.

Because of the risk of a clawback charge, the donor should be advised to consider insurance cover, retention of part of the gifted property for 6 years and indemnities from the donee.

GIFTS ATTRACTING IHT AND CGT

A disposal may lead eventually to charges to both taxes. IHT may arise immediately if the gift is to discretionary trustees (at 20 per cent) and/or subsequently should the donor die within 7 years of a PET or an immediately chargeable transfer. CGT may arise on a future disposal of the gifted property by the donee. If such a charge to IHT does occur, the donee may deduct the IHT paid when calculating his gain on the future disposal. However, in making his deduction it cannot be used to create a loss on the disposal. Only if a hold-over election has been made under either s 165 or s 260 can the IHT be deducted in this way.

> *Example*
>
> Jason transferred assets worth £200,000 to the trustees of his recently established discretionary settlement. They elected to hold-over the gain of £80,000. Assume £10,000 IHT was paid. The trustees now sell the assets for £250,000 and re-invest the proceeds. The calculation of the trustees' CGT liability is:

	£	£
Disposal consideration		250,000
less: acquisition cost	120,000	
IHT paid	10,000	130,000
		120,000
indexation allowance (say)		30,000
chargeable gain		90,000

Note: the principle illustrated in the example also applies if a PET becomes chargeable. Provided a CGT hold-over election was made by the donor and donee the IHT payable can be deducted as in the example.

SOME PLANNING CONSIDERATIONS

Because hold-over relief is not generally available on gifts, for example on gifts of quoted shares to the donor's children, estate planning gifts should be given careful thought.

(1) A gift which attracts CGT at 40 per cent made purely to save IHT at 40 per cent may not be particularly attractive in cash flow terms. The same gift made by will would avoid CGT and give to the donee the benefit of an uplift in his acquisition price (to market value at the date of death) for future CGT purposes.

(2) CGT is charged on gains (after allowing for indexation) whereas IHT is charged on full values (subject to reliefs).

(3) Gifts of assets expected to appreciate in value may attract an immediate CGT charge on the gain but IHT will be limited to the value of the asset at the time of the gift, ie 'asset freezing' applies should the PET become chargeable.

(4) Section 165 of the IHTA 1984 provides that CGT paid by the donee reduces the value transferred by the chargeable transfer for IHT. Normally CGT is payable by the donor but, in circumstances where hold-over relief is not available, consideration should be given to the donee paying the tax to take advantage of s 165. For this to happen, agreement must be reached between the donor and donee.

A disposal (PET) giving rise to a chargeable gain which cannot be held-over, followed by the death of the donor within 7 years, could cause IHT to become payable by the donee. If the donee pays the CGT, the value transferred is reduced, and therefore the IHT bill for the donee would also be reduced.

Example

A gift (PET) of quoted shares worth £500,000 results in a CGT liability of £50,000.

(1) If the donor pays the CGT, the value transferred for IHT is £500,000. It is not £550,000, ie the loss to the estate of the donor is not increased by the CGT paid.

(2) If the donee pays the CGT, the value transferred for IHT is £450,000, ie it is reduced by the CGT paid.

Obviously the donee will need to be in a position to fund both tax liabilities. Insurance against the potential IHT may be possible but not the CGT because this is an immediately quantifiable amount.

Retirement relief (TCGA 1992, ss 163–164)

Retirement relief is available to reduce or eliminate gains made on disposals by sale or gift of a business interest (see below) provided the individual (or, in certain cases, trustees – see below) making the disposal is either then at least 50 years of age or is forced to retire before that age because of ill health. As the requirement is that disposal is at a certain age (or due to ill health) it is not essential that the individual actually retires; he must dispose of the business interest at retirement age. For example, an individual may decide to continue working, perhaps as an employee on a reduced salary instead of as sole proprietor, after giving his business to his daughter.

Assuming the conditions are satisfied, in order to obtain full relief the individual must have owned the business asset for 10 years prior to the disposal (the relief is scaled down for periods of ownership of between one and 10 years). No relief is available if ownership is for less than one year. To determine the length of ownership it is possible to aggregate previous periods of ownership of business interests. Similarly, periods of ownership by spouses may be aggregated following an inter vivos transfer between spouses living together (Sch 6, paras 15 and 16).

Retirement relief exempts gains on disposals of business interests of up to £250,000 and relieves 50 per cent of gains between £250,000 and £1m. The interest must be either a business (or part) or shares in a personal company (see below).

A BUSINESS OR PART OF A BUSINESS

This includes the disposal of a sole trader's business or part of it on the introduction of a partner. It also includes the disposal by a partner of his interest in the partnership assets.

The relief is not available on the disposal of a mere business asset; it is necessary for there to be a disposal of an interest in the business. For example, the sale by a farmer of one field (for development) from a farm of 100 acres would not attract retirement relief (*McGregor v Adcock* [1977] 3 All ER 65). Furthermore, the relief only applies to gains on the disposal of the business interest which relate to chargeable business assets. Business assets include the goodwill and premises but not investments such as stocks and shares held as reserves.

SHARES IN A PERSONAL COMPANY

Relief is available to the shareholder on gains on disposal of his shares. If the company owns chargeable business assets and investments, only a proportion of the shareholder's gains will attract relief. That proportion is the same proportion as reflects the proportion of the company's chargeable assets which are chargeable business assets (and not investments).

To qualify for relief the shareholder must be a full-time working officer or employee of the company devoting substantially the whole of his time to it (accepted by the Inland Revenue as 30 hours per week). Semi-retirement is possible, providing the individual continues to work 10 hours per week, but in such a case the period of ownership is based on the number of years of full-time service.

In addition, the company must be the individual's 'personal' company, ie a trading company in which he exercises at least 5 per cent of the voting rights.

ASSOCIATED DISPOSALS

An 'associated disposal' by an individual of a business asset which has been used in a partnership (of which he was a partner) or his personal company also attract retirement relief. It is necessary for the disposal of the asset to be associated 'with the retirement' from the business but it need not necessarily coincide, for example a delay in selling a freehold site used by the individual's former partnership if throughout he had an intention to dispose of both interests.

BUSINESS INTERESTS OWNED BY TRUSTEES

Disposals by trustees can also attract retirement relief where shares in a personal company or assets used in a business were held by the trustees as settled property. Only settlements with an interest in possession qualify; discretionary trusts are therefore excluded. Following the sale by the trustees, the beneficiary must cease to be a full-time working officer or employee of the company or cease to carry on the business (as the case may be). The retirement relief on the disposal by the trustees is calculated by treating the disposal as if made by the beneficiary.

4.5   TRANSFERS BETWEEN HUSBAND AND WIFE

4.5.1   Financial and estate planning

It is advisable for the wealth of a married couple to be split between them. Whilst the division need not be equal it is inadvisable for one spouse to own the majority of the assets. 'Equalisation' will provide greater financial security for the 'poorer' spouse, and the greatest scope for tax planning.

Life insurance

INSURANCE ON THE TAXPAYER'S OWN LIFE

Most clients who are married or with young children should consider the need for personal life insurance (see Appendix 2). If nothing further is done when the life cover is purchased, the insured sum will be paid to the PRs on the death of the insured and will form part of his estate.

A grant of representation will be required before the proceeds are available, and the amount will be taxable if left to a beneficiary other than the deceased's spouse (or charity). Both problems can be avoided if the life insurance policy is written in trust.

Where a new policy is being purchased as part of financial advice, it can be written in trust from the outset. Life insurance companies have standard trust documents which the insured can complete with the names of the trustees and the chosen beneficiary or beneficiaries.

Existing policies can also be written in trust but whenever possible it is better to create the trust at the time of purchase. Because existing policies may have a surrender value if the insured cancels the policy before his death he will receive a lump sum based on the amount of premiums he has paid. By writing the policy in trust, the insured is giving up this surrender value to his beneficiary and this is a transfer of value for IHT purposes. Usually the policy will be valued at the higher of the market value or cost of providing the policy, ie the premiums already paid (IHTA 1984, s 167). In practice this is rarely a problem as the surrender value is relatively small compared with the maturity value and is likely to be covered by the insured's £3,000 annual IHT exemption. To the extent this is exceeded the transfer of the surrender value will be a potentially exempt transfer (PET). It does mean, however, that in the year the policy is put into trust, the annual IHT exemption may not be available to set against other non-exempt gifts.

Once a policy has been written in trust the annual premiums paid by the insured to the insurance company are paid by the insured for the benefit of the beneficiary. These premiums are transfers of value for IHT but, unless disproportionately large when compared with the annual income of the insured, they should be exempt as normal expenditure out of income, or if not then covered by the £3,000 annual exemption. They are not PETs (IHTA 1984, s 3(A)).

INSURANCE ON THE LIFE OF ANOTHER

Where a couple have young children it is quite possible that one parent, usually the mother, does not have paid employment. Thought should be given to the costs of employing a housekeeper and nanny or purchasing child care in the event of the mother's death. Where the father's income is unlikely to be sufficient in such circumstances he might consider insuring the mother's life, ie he pays the premiums and receives the lump sum if the mother dies. As the insurance cover is likely to be required only whilst the children are of school age, term assurance (see Appendix 2) could be considered.

Example

Adam and Betty have 2 children aged 6 and 4 respectively. Betty does not work and Adam's income is £12,000 per annum. He calculates the family's expenditure to be £9,000 per annum and believes home help and child care would cost an extra £5,000 per annum if Betty died. This could not be supported by his income. If he insured Betty's life he would receive a lump sum on her death from which to pay the £5,000 per annum.

The matrimonial home

This is often the major asset owned by an individual or married couple. Whilst care should be taken in using it purely as an object of tax planning, certain steps might be considered by most married couples.

SOLE OWNERSHIP v JOINT OWNERSHIP

Unless there are personal reasons for not doing so, consideration should be given to the property being owned jointly by a husband and wife. This might be done in order to reflect the contribution each has made to the purchase price or to provide a non-contributing spouse with the security of legal ownership. The property can be purchased in joint names or purchased in a sole name and subsequently transferred into joint names. Most lenders insist that a property which is to be used as a matrimonial home is jointly owned.

JOINT TENANCY

Holding a property as joint tenants means that on the death of one spouse his or her interest in the property immediately and automatically passes to the surviving spouse, ie accrues by survivorship. This cannot be prevented by anything said about the property in the will. All that the surviving joint owner needs to prove absolute ownership of the property is the death certificate of his or her spouse. Joint tenancy therefore avoids the costs and delays involved in obtaining a grant of representation on the death of the first joint tenant to die and, because the survivor is the spouse, the interest in the property is IHT exempt on that first death.

> *Example*
>
> Carla and David own a house worth £245,000 as joint tenants. David dies and the house vests in Carla absolutely. There is no IHT payable. Carla dies 6 weeks later leaving her estate (the house) to Emma. IHT of £12,000 is payable.

Where, however, the combined value of a husband and wife's assets (including the house) exceed the IHT nil rate band consideration should be given to them owning the matrimonial home as tenants in common. Coupled with appropriate wills this can provide a limited opportunity for tax avoidance whilst ensuring security for a surviving spouse.

TENANCY IN COMMON

Property held under a tenancy in common passes by will or intestacy, not automatically to the surviving co-owner. A tenancy in common does allow the first spouse to die to leave his share away from the survivor. The effect would be shared ownership between the surviving spouse and children or other relative(s) or friend(s) of the deceased. The danger is that the child etc may want the house sold to realise his inheritance. This risk should only be contemplated where the value of the property is such that the surviving spouse's share is sufficient to purchase suitable alternative accommodation and the survivor is happy at the possibility of having to move.

An alternative solution is for a husband and wife to make wills leaving their respective interests in the property to each other subject to a survivorship period. In the normal course of events, one spouse will survive the other by a considerable period of time, in which case the property passes to the survivor, whose right to the home is thus guaranteed. Where, however, both die within a short period of time their respective interests in the property pass to, for example their children, and both nil rate bands are utilised.

> *Example*
>
> Carla and David own a house as tenants in common. They make wills leaving their respective shares of the house to each other conditional on surviving at least 3 months and if not, to Emma. David and Carla die within 6 weeks of each other.
>
> David's $\frac{1}{2}$ share (£107,500) is held by his PRs for Carla if she survives by 3 months. As she dies within this period it passes to Emma. There will be no IHT because it falls within his nil rate band.

Carla's ½ share (£107,500) passes to Emma. There is no IHT because it falls within her nil rate band.

Where a house is held on a joint tenancy either co-owner may sever the joint tenancy converting it into a tenancy in common. The consent of the other co-owner is not required to the severance which is effected by giving notice to the co-owner in signed writing that the joint tenancy is terminated and that the parties now hold as tenants in common.

MORTGAGE

Where the matrimonial home, however owned, is subject to a mortgage, that mortgage debt should be covered by suitable insurance (see Appendix 2). This will enable the mortgage to be paid off in full on the death of the borrower without the need for the house or other assets to be sold to meet the debt. Where two people are jointly responsible for the mortgage they can choose whether the insurance should pay out on the first or second death.

4.5.2 Transferring assets (other than the matrimonial home) on to a joint tenancy

Practical reasons

The reasons for making such a transfer are likely to be practical. The transfer allows each spouse access to particular assets and means that on the death of the first spouse to die the survivor automatically becomes sole owner of those assets. There is no need to obtain a grant of representation (so the administration is quicker and cheaper) and the survivor has immediate access to finances.

Effect for IHT

Joint tenancy offers no IHT saving. Although on the first death the transfer is spouse exempt, the combined estates are taxed on the second death.

Effect for income tax

The basic rule is that any income arising from a jointly held asset will be treated as belonging equally to the husband and wife (ICTA 1988, s 282A). This is so irrespective of how they contributed to the account or purchase of the asset or account (eg with a bank or building society).

> *Example*
> Harry has a building society account into which he periodically pays additional savings. He transfers this account into the joint names of himself and his wife Isobel. Isobel makes no contributions to the account. For income tax purposes she is nevertheless treated as owning one half of the annual income.

Spouses can override this general 50:50 rule by making a declaration to the Inland Revenue of how they in fact beneficially enjoy the income. The declaration relates to the income and to the underlying property. The income cannot be shared in proportions different from the property which produces it. The declaration has effect from its date; notice must be given to the Inspector of Taxes within 60 days of a declaration which must be made on Form 17.

Where one spouse has insufficient income from his or her own resources to be paying income tax, or is paying income tax at the lower (20 per cent) or basic (23 per cent) rate whilst the other spouse is a higher (40 per cent) rate income tax payer, it may be sensible to transfer some part of the beneficial ownership in the jointly owned property to the spouse with the lower tax rate, followed by a declaration that that spouse is entitled to an equivalent proportion of the income. The transfer of the beneficial ownership will generally be by declaration of trust made by the spouses.

Example

John and Kate are the joint holders of a building society account. The annual interest is £100 gross. John pays income tax at 40%. Kate pays income tax at 20%.

(1) Without a declaration

John will pay 40% tax on his one half £50 × 40%	=	£20
Kate will pay 20% tax on her one half £50 × 20%	=	£10
Total income tax		£30

(2) Transfer of beneficial ownership and declaration that Kate is entitled to 90% of the interest

John will pay 40% tax on his 10% share £10 × 40%	=	£ 4
Kate will pay 20% tax on her 90% share £90 × 20%	=	£18
Total income tax		£22

Care should be taken where a declaration of trust is contemplated in respect of income from an asset which is a chargeable asset for CGT (see below).

Effect for CGT

The transfer of an asset from a sole name into the joint names of the husband and wife is at 'no gain no loss' (see **4.4.5**).

On a subsequent disposal, whether a sale or by gift, each spouse will be regarded as owning a half share of the asset and charged to CGT accordingly. Where a husband and wife, who pay income tax at different rates, contemplate the disposal of an asset with an inbuilt capital gain, the effect is that up to one half of the gain will be taxed, if at all, at the lower of their rates.

Example

Len transfers a shareholding which he bought for £2,000 into the joint names of himself and his wife Mary.

Len pays income tax at 40% and Mary at 23%. The shares are sold for £17,000 (assume indexation nil).

	Len will pay £	Mary will pay £
Disposal consideration	8,500	8,500
less Acquisition cost	1,000	1,000
	7,500	7,500
less Annual exemption	6,500	6,500
	1,000	1,000
Chargeable gain:	£1,000 @ 40%	£1,000 @ 23%
	= £400	= £230

Where a declaration as to the beneficial enjoyment of the income from a jointly owned asset has been made, it will have a corresponding effect for CGT purposes.

Example

Neville and Olive declare that the income from a shareholding is enjoyed 25:75. They will have a corresponding beneficial ownership of the shareholding. The shares were bought for £400 and have just been sold for £10,000. Assume indexation nil.

	Neville's chargeable gain		Olive's chargeable gain	
	£	£	£	£
Disposal		2,500		7,500
less Acquisition cost	100		300	
Annual exemption	6,500		6,500	
		6,600		6,800
Chargeable gain:		nil		700

Conclusion

Transferring assets into joint names may provide beneficial effects. It allows both spouses access to the assets. It is a means of making provision for the recipient spouse without the donor spouse losing control of the property. However, holding property jointly may cause IHT to be payable when the couple die. If all assets are in joint names, the IHT nil rate band of the first spouse to die will not be utilised and their estates will be aggregated on the second death. Clients whose combined assets do not exceed the nil rate band will find that the practical and income tax advantages of owning property jointly exceed the theoretical IHT disadvantages. For wealthier clients, particularly those with combined estates of £430,000 or more, there may be practical reasons for holding some assets in joint names but the IHT disadvantage of losing one IHT nil rate band means that the majority of assets should be held in individual names.

4.5.3 Absolute transfers

The motive for such a gift may be altruistic but inter-spouse transfers play an important part in the process of 'equalisation' and maximise the scope for tax saving both during the joint lives of the couple and on death.

Care should be taken when selecting the assets to be transferred in order that any available tax reliefs are not lost or reduced by the gift, for example business property relief or retirement relief.

Example

Peter and Rose wish to minimise the amount of IHT that their daughter Susan will pay on their deaths. Peter transfers his 40% shareholding in their private company Z Ltd worth £200,000 to Rose as part of the 'equalisation' process. He has owned the shares for 4 years. Rose dies 6 months later leaving everything to Susan. The shareholding is taxable on its full value as Rose has not owned the shares for 2 years (see **4.3.6**). Had Peter retained the shares and given them inter vivos or by will to Susan, 100% business property relief would have been available.

Now that agricultural property relief and business property relief are at 100 per cent, provided the basic conditions are satisfied, there is effectively exemption from IHT. Gifts by will to chargeable beneficiaries (the children) are therefore sensible planning considerations. Inter vivos transfers to the children are PETs but there is always the possibility of IHT if the donor should die within the following 7 years at a time when the donee fails to qualify for the reliefs. A change of government could see a change in the availability of these reliefs so that a gift by will on death might again seem less attractive compared to the PET.

Income tax reasons

Wherever possible, a husband and wife should ensure that they each utilise their own personal allowances and lower rate band before either of them start paying income tax at the basic rate. Where only one spouse is a higher rate tax payer, as much investment income as possible should be attributed to the other spouse.

As seen in **4.5.2** above, this can be achieved by a transfer of assets into joint names with a declaration as to the beneficial ownership of the income. The couple must remember to make the declaration if the income is to be apportioned other than 50:50. The maximum split is 1:99 and the division will have to be declared by the couple on their income tax returns. Many couples may prefer assets to be transferred outright as all the income then belongs to the transferee spouse from the date of the transfer.

CGT reasons

Where a large capital gain is anticipated on the disposal of an asset held by one spouse who will pay CGT at 40 per cent, consideration should be given to transferring (without liability to CGT) that asset to the 'poorer' spouse who will then pay tax on the whole or a substantial part of the subsequently realised gain at 20 or 23 per cent.

A husband and wife are both entitled to an annual exemption of £6,500 but any unused annual exemption cannot be transferred to the other spouse nor can it be carried forward for use in future years. All clients (whether married or not) should be advised to use the exemption each year if possible.

BED AND BREAKFASTING

Some clients 'play the stock market' regularly by buying and selling shares. Successful 'players' will make annual gains on their dealings against which they will set their annual exemption.

Where a client has an active financial planning strategy but is not changing shareholdings regularly it is advisable to limit the build-up of unrealised gains within his investments. With a share portfolio this can be achieved by doing what is colloquially known as 'bed and breakfasting'. The idea is that each year sufficient shares are sold to realise a gain which does not exceed the available annual exemption of the shareholder. The day following the sale the shares are bought back with the new higher cost price as the acquisition cost for future disposals. Commission will be payable to the stockbroker who carries out the transactions.

> *Example*
>
> Three years ago Tina bought shares in A plc for £500. They are now worth £7,000. Stockbrokers advise that A plc is a good investment and the value is likely to increase further. Tina does not plan to make any other capital gains this year (ignore indexation).
>
> Day 1: Tina sells her A plc shares.
>
> Gain of £6,200 covered by her annual exemption.

Day 2: Tina buys £7,000 worth of A plc shares.

The following year Tina needs to buy a car so she sells her A plc shares for £9,000. The gain of £2,000 (£9,000 less acquisition cost of £7,000) is covered by her annual exemption.

If Tina had not 'bed and breakfasted' her shareholding the gain on the sale this year would have been chargeable.

	£
Disposal consideration	9,000
less Acquisition cost	500
	8,500
less Annual exemption	6,500
Chargeable gain	2,000

IHT reasons

IHT savings are often perceived as the main purpose in making inter-spouse transfers. Whilst no tax saving is achieved from the transfer itself, because such transfers are IHT exempt, having assets in the individual ownership of each spouse does allow maximum use of exemptions, reliefs and the nil rate band for passing on family wealth. The inter-spouse transfer should be made to permit both spouses to make gifts by will and lifetime gifts to children and other relatives.

USING THE NIL RATE BAND

Example 1

Ursula and Victor are married with two children. Ursula has assets worth £500,000 and Victor assets of £100,000. They have undertaken no estate planning and have made no previous transfers. Neither owns property attracting any relief for IHT. Their estates pass by will to each other, and their children inherit the entire estate on the second death.

IHT on the first death will be nil (spouse exemption).

IHT on the second death calculated on the combined estates of £600,000 will be £154,000.

Note: the tax bill would be identical if the estates were equalised but the wills remained unaltered.

Example 2

Facts as before, but Ursula and Victor do some limited planning through their wills. As a result the children will inherit some property on the death of the first parent.

Ursula's will leaves £215,000 to the children and the residue to Victor or to the children if he has predeceased her.

Victor's will leaves all his estate to the children.

(1) Assume Victor dies first

IHT on Victor's death:	£100,000 @ 0% = nil
IHT on Ursula's death:	£215,000 @ 0% = nil
	£285,000 @ 40% = £114,000

(2) Assume Ursula dies first

IHT on Ursula's death: £215,000 @ 0% = nil

                            £285,000 exempt = nil

IHT on Victor's death: £215,000 @ 0% = nil

                            £170,000 @ 40% = £68,000

Example 3

Ursula and Victor have undertaken estate planning by lifetime equalisation of the value of their estates, and made wills utilising their respective nil rate bands.

(1) Ursula transfers £215,000 to Victor
     IHT exempt

(2) Ursula's will :   £215,000 to children
                                residue to Victor

     Victor's will :   £215,000 to children
                                residue to Ursula

     IHT on first death :   £215,000 @ 0% = nil
                                residue exempt = nil

     IHT on second death :   £215,000 @ 0% = nil
                                £170,000 @ 40% = £68,000

Note: although the tax bill in Example 3 is the same as in Example 2(2), that depended upon Ursula dying before Victor. In Example 3 it does not matter which parent dies first as the tax bill will be the same.

USING LIFETIME EXEMPTIONS

There is scope for the tax bill to be reduced further by each parent making lifetime gifts to or for the benefit of their children. For example, each parent can give £5,000 to a child on the occasion of the child's marriage; each parent can make annual gifts of £3,000. Before these exemptions can be claimed, each parent must have sufficient assets to make the gifts. Unused exemptions cannot be transferred from one spouse to the other.

ANTI-AVOIDANCE RULES

The anti-avoidance legislation and cases (see **4.10** below) should not be a problem in the context of straightforward family estate planning provided that at the time of the inter-spouse transfer the recipient spouse is not under a binding obligation to use the property as directed by the donor spouse.

4.6   TRANSFERS FROM PARENTS TO CHILDREN AND REMOTER ISSUE

Most parents wish to provide for their children and those who can actually afford to do so wish to ensure that such provision is made in the most tax-effective way.

It is not always possible to achieve the client's intentions and avoid a tax bill. The skill is to put forward ideas that will satisfy the practical objectives at the minimum tax cost.

In addition to balancing practical objectives and the overall tax cost the solicitor must be aware of the interaction of the capital taxes; for example, is the CGT cost of a course of action less than the IHT bill which will arise if the action is not taken?

The choice for parents is a lifetime gift either outright or through the creation of a trust (see **4.6.4**), or by will which is either an outright gift or gift into trust. The use of will trusts is discussed in Chapter 11 and will not be discussed in detail here.

4.6.1   Outright gifts

A gift is an immediate outright transfer of property from one person to another. There can be no conditions attached.

When making gifts of small sums of money or family possessions, or wishing to benefit an adult child, an outright gift may be the most sensible and appropriate course of action. However, where the intended recipient is a minor or is irresponsible with money, the donor may feel that it is inappropriate to hand over valuable assets or large amounts of cash. In such circumstances it might be advisable to provide the intended benefit via a trust (but see **4.6.4** 'Parental settlements for minor children'). A minor is unable to hold the legal estate in land so it is impossible to make an outright gift of land to a person under 18 years of age. Where such a gift is attempted, statute imposes a trust (SLA 1925, s 27(1) and see TLA 1996, s 2(6), Sch 1(1)).

4.6.2   The taxation of outright gifts

Inheritance tax
The current IHT legislation encourages lifetime giving whether by a parent, grandparent or others and wherever possible clients should take full advantage of the exceptions and reliefs offered.

THE ANNUAL EXEMPTION (IHTA 1984, s 19)
Every taxpayer can make gifts of £3,000 per annum and as the unused exemption can only be carried forward for one tax year, it should be used every year if the client can afford to do so. A husband and wife each have their own annual exemption.

PETS (IHTA 1984, s 3A) – 'ASSET FREEZING'
All gifts between individuals are PETs when they are made, as indeed are gifts into accumulation and maintenance trusts and trusts for the disabled. Gifts on to discretionary trusts are immediately chargeable transfers (charged at half the death rate). The effect of the PET is that no IHT is payable at the time of the transfer. The transfer becomes exempt from IHT if the transferor lives for 7 years. Should the transferor die within the 7-year period, the PET becomes chargeable. The value which is taxed is the value of the property at the date of the transfer, unless the value has fallen when it is the lower value which is taxed – see below. It is therefore sensible for clients to consider giving away assets which are likely to increase in value. Rates at the date of the death are used unless they have increased since the gift. If so, the rates at the date of the gift are used instead.

> *Example*
> Keith owns a painting by an elderly living artist. He paid £20,000 for it and believes that its value will quadruple after the artist's death. Keith utilises his annual exemptions on other transfers.

Year 1: Keith gives the painting (value £20,000) to Laura (PET).

Year 4: Keith dies and the painting is valued at £115,000. IHT rates have not increased subsequently. The gift of the painting becomes a chargeable transfer and tax is charged on £20,000, which, assuming Keith had made no previous transfers, will be covered by his nil rate band.

Where a PET is of an amount which exceeds the transferor's nil rate band, IHT will be payable by the donee if the transferor dies within 7 years. Whilst this tax cannot be avoided, the transferee or transferor can mitigate its effect by insuring the transferor's life for 7 years (for an explanation of such term assurance, see Appendix 2(16)) for a sum equal to the potential tax bill. If the transferor insures his own life the insurance policy should be written in trust for the transferee.

Example
Mike, who has made no gifts other than of £3,000 per annum, gives his daughter Nina £250,000 to buy a house.

If Mike dies within 7 years, Nina could face a tax bill of up to £14,000.

Unless she insures her father's life (which she may not be able to afford to do) Nina therefore has the choice of only spending £236,000 and putting the rest aside to meet the anticipated tax bill or having to sell or mortgage the house on Mike's death to raise the tax.

Alternatively, Mike could insure his life for £14,000 for 7 years and give the benefit of the insurance to Nina. The annual premiums should be covered by his normal expenditure out of income exemption. If Mike dies within 7 years Nina receives cash of £14,000 with which to pay the tax and so can safely spend the full £250,000 on buying her house.

If property other than cash is given away and the value of that property falls between the date of the PET and the death, relief is provided by IHTA 1984, s 131. IHT is calculated on the reduced value instead of the original value (the relief applies similarly following a lifetime chargeable transfer). This relief reduces the value which is taxed; it does not affect the value of the original PET. This means that the original value remains in the transferor's cumulative total when calculating any IHT on later lifetime transfers and on the estate on the death. Any taper relief is based on the IHT actually payable, ie the IHT payable on the reduced value.

IHT is charged at the rate at death unless this has increased when the rates in force at the date of the PET are used.

Example
In January 1993, Harold gave his grandson his shares in Z plc. Harold died in April 1997 when the shares were worth £250,000; in 1993 they had been worth £300,000. Apart from using his annual exemptions, Harold has made no other transfers.

(1) On Harold's death within 7 years, the PET becomes chargeable on the reduced value of £250,000.

(2) IHT, at rates in force when Harold died:

		£
nil rate band	£215,000	nil
balance	£35,000 @ 40%	14,000
		14,000

(3) Taper relief – Harold died 4 years later.

£14,000 @ 60% = £8,400 (payable by Harold's grandson).

(4) The original value of £300,000 remains in Harold's cumulative total when calculating the IHT due on his estate at death.

Note: if Harold's grandson had sold the shares for £250,000, IHT on Harold's death would be calculated in the same way as above. If he had given them away, IHT would instead be calculated on the full value in 1993, ie £300,000.

ORDER OF GIFTS – SOME CONSIDERATIONS

Clients planning a number of gifts, some PETs and some immediately chargeable such as gifts to the trustees of a discretionary settlement, should be advised that the possible IHT consequences may differ depending upon the order of the gifts.

(1) Transfers made on the same day (IHTA 1984, s 266)

If a number of PETs are intended (but the client does not wish to make a discretionary settlement) and all are made on the same day there is, of course, no IHT payable. If the donor should die within 7 years so that IHT becomes payable it is charged on each PET on a pro rata basis. Had the gifts been made on separate days, the earlier gifts would benefit from the donor's nil rate band whereas the donees of later gifts would suffer IHT once the nil rate band was exceeded.

(2) PETs and discretionary settlements (immediately chargeable transfers – LCTs)

Here the order of gifts is important. There is an advantage if the discretionary settlement is made before (or at the latest on the same day as) the PETs. If the PETs come first and later become chargeable, they will be taken into account when calculating IHT payable by the trustees during the life of the discretionary settlement. This liability of the trustees is considered in Chapter 10. If the client intends creating more than one settlement, the gifts to the discretionary trustees should be made on different days so as to avoid the settlements being treated as 'related settlements' (IHTA 1984, s 62). The effect of related settlements on the calcualtion of the trustees' IHT liability is considered at **10.2.4**.

(3) PETs and LCTs – the donor's nil rate band exceeded

Again, the order of gifts can have a significant effect on the overall IHT liability, particularly where the donor dies more than 3 years but less than 7 years after his gifts as illustrated in the examples which follow. No annual exemptions are available.

Example 1: PET precedes LCT

			IHT £
(i)	PET	£220,000	nil
(ii)	LCT	£400,000	
	first	£215,000 – nil	
	balance	£185,000 @ 20%	37,000

(iii) Donor dies after 6 years.

PET	£220,000 – £215,000 = £5,000	
	£5,000 @ 40% × 20% (taper relief)	400
LCT	£400,000 @ 40% × 20% (taper relief)	32,000
	credit (tax already paid – no refund)	(37,000)

no IHT due

Total IHT – £37,400

Example 2: LCT precedes PET

			IHT £
(i)	LCT	£400,000	
	first	£215,000 – nil	
	balance	£185,000 @ 20%	37,000
(ii)	PET	£220,000	nil

(iii) Donor dies after 6 years.

LCT	£400,000	
first	£215,000 – nil	
balance	£185,000 @ 40% × 20% (taper relief)	14,800
	credit (tax already paid – no refund)	(37,000)

no IHT due

(iv)	PET	£220,000 @ 40% × 20% (taper relief)	£17,600

Total IHT – £54,600

Lifetime transfers – transfers on death

Clients who are estate planning through a combination of lifetime giving and gifts by will should be aware of the effect of PETs. Lifetime gifts which become chargeable on death have first call on the deceased's nil rate band and this may result in unexpected IHT being payable on property passing under the will.

Example

Year 1: Oswald makes a will leaving a nil rate band legacy of £215,000 to his children and the residue to his wife.

Year 2: He makes a PET gift of £100,000 to his eldest son.

Year 3: Oswald dies

Step 1: The PET becomes chargeable but as Oswald had made no previous lifetime transfers (other than £3,000 per annum to his children) the £100,000 is covered by his nil rate band.

Step 2 : The £100,000 is cumulated with his death estate and means that only the remaining £115,000 of the nil rate band is available to set against the legacy to his children. The balance (£100,000) is taxable at 40% (subject to grossing up); the residue is exempt.

Use of a 'formula clause' limiting the legacy to the amount available of the nil rate band at death (here £100,000) when drafting the will can anticipate and avoid this problem (see **11.5.1**).

USING THE RELIEFS

Property which attracts business property relief or agricultural property relief (especially at 100 per cent) should, where possible, be given to non-exempt beneficiaries as otherwise the relief may be lost (see **4.3.6** for an example). However, as the majority of gifts are PETs, the value of the relief will only become available should the donor die within 7 years, and then only if the relevant conditions remain satisfied at that time. Alternatively, and in view of the 100 per cent relief (effectively an exemption from IHT), consideration should be given to leaving the property attracting the relief by will to a non-exempt beneficiary.

EXCLUDED PROPERTY

IHT

Section 5 of the IHTA 1984 defines a person's estate as including everything 'to which he is beneficially entitled . . . but does not include excluded property'. By IHTA 1984, s 48 a reversionary interest (with three anti-avoidance exceptions – see below) is excluded property. Section 47 defines any future interest under a settlement as a reversionary interest, whether the interest is vested or contingent, and includes the interest expectant on the termination of an interest in possession, ie the interest which falls into possession on the death of a life tenant. The interest of a beneficiary under a discretionary settlement is not, therefore, within the definition.

Because a reversionary interest is not included in an individual's estate, it can be given away as part of estate planning without liability to IHT (and without CGT liability, see below).

Perhaps the most common example of excluded property is 'an interest in remainder' (see further LPC Resource Book *Wills, Probate and Administration* (Jordans, 1997)).

Example

S ——— settled property ———▶ Angela for life

remainder to Bernard

While Angela is alive Bernard has an 'interest in remainder'. Bernard is wealthy and has a house, shares and cash totalling £400,000. He is a widower and intends to leave everything to his daughter Davina.

(1)   If Bernard does nothing.

On Angela's death the trust fund, then valued at £250,000, is taxable as part of Angela's estate (her residuary estate is exempt).

Assume IHT of £14,000 is paid.

Bernard receives £236,000.

When Bernard dies his estate is £236,000 + £400,000 and Davina will pay IHT of £168,400.

(2)   If Bernard gives his interest in remainder to Davina whilst Angela is still alive there will be no IHT (IHTA 1984, s 5) and no CGT on the gift (see below; TCGA 1992, s 76).

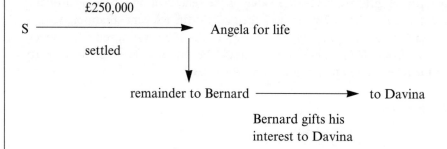

On Angela's, death, Davina will receive £236,000 (as Bernard did in (1)).

When Bernard dies his estate is £400,000 as the trust fund no longer forms part of his taxable estate. Davina will now pay IHT of £74,000 on her father's estate. This represents a tax saving of £94,400, ie IHT at 40% on the £236,000 trust fund.

The three exceptions within s 48 where the reversionary interest is not excluded property are:

(1)   Where the interest was purchased for money or money's worth.
(2)   Where the interest is one to which the settlor or his spouse is beneficially entitled.
(3)   Where it is the lessor's interest expectant on the ending of a lease granted for life; where such a lease for life is granted a settlement exists for IHT.

CGT

No gain arises for CGT where a beneficiary disposes of his beneficial interest under a settlement provided that it had never previously been acquired for a consideration in money or money's worth (other than consideration consisting of another interest under the settlement, for example on a 'swap' of interests by beneficiaries). Once any consideration in money or money's worth has been given, all future disposals of the interest will attract CGT (TCGA 1992, s 76).

If in the previous example Bernard had sold his interest to Davina, no CGT would be payable by him (assuming no prior consideration had been given for the interest) because s 76 would apply. On Davina's later disposal (by sale or by gift) she would be liable to CGT on any gain she realises.

Capital gains tax

Although a gift may not result in an IHT charge it may attract an immediate charge to capital gains tax. A gift is a disposal by the donor and if it is of a chargeable asset CGT will be calculated in the usual way (subject to appropriate reliefs and exemptions).

Example

Susan gives quoted shares worth £60,000 to her daughter Tina and cash of £50,000 to her son Vernon.

Both gifts are PETs for IHT purposes and the cash is not a chargeable asset for CGT.

Susan will pay CGT on the difference between the purchase price of the quoted shares and their open market value at the date of the gift to Tina, after taking into account the indexation allowance and annual exemption.

Where the gift is of a business asset hold-over relief will be available (for the definitions and conditions, see **4.4.5**) but, if the donor's annual exemption is available or he has unused losses, it may be better not to claim the relief.

Example

William gives his 10% shareholding in O Ltd to his daughter Yasmin. William acquired the shares for £100 and they are currently worth £6,700. Yasmin expects to sell the shares within the next 2 years. Last year, William made capital losses of £2,000.

(1) Hold-over relief claimed.

William pays no CGT and retains losses of £2,000

Yasmin acquires the shares at £100 (ignore indexation).

In 2 years' time she sells the shares for £7,600.

CGT is payable on any chargeable gain (ignore indexation).

	£
Disposal consideration	7,600
less Acquisition cost	100
	7,500
less Annual exemption	6,500
Chargeable gain	1,000

(2) Hold-over relief not claimed (ignore indexation).

William's gift is a disposal of a chargeable asset.

	£	£
Disposal consideration	6,700	
less Acquisition cost	100	
		6,600
Part of unused losses	100	
Annual exemption	6,500	
		6,600
William's chargeable gain		nil

When Yasmin sells:

	£	£
Disposal consideration		7,600
less Acquisition cost	6,700	
less Annual exemption (part)	900	7,600
Yasmin's chargeable gain		nil

INSTALMENTS (TCGA 1992, ss 280, 281)

January 31 following the end of the tax year of the disposal is the normal date for payment of a CGT liability. In limited circumstances, the tax may be paid by equal yearly instalments starting on 31 January. Interest is payable on the outstanding tax.

CGT may be paid by instalments if:

(1) Sales (s 280) – if the consideration is payable over a period exceeding 18 months and the Inland Revenue is satisfied payment of the tax in a lump sum would cause hardship. The instalment period is 8 years (or the payment period if the consideration is payable over a shorter period).

(2) Gifts or deemed disposals by trustees (s 281 – see **10.2.7**) – where the property is land, a controlling shareholding in either a quoted or an unquoted company or a minority holding in a company whose shares are unquoted, provided that hold-over relief was not available under either TCGA 1992, s 165 or s 260, ie neither the asset (s 165) nor the occasion (s 260) was appropriate to enable hold-over relief to be claimed. Failure to make the appropriate election for hold-over relief will not mean that the tax can then be paid by instalments. When available, the CGT may be paid by 10 equal annual instalments.

4.6.3 Post-death disclaimers and variations

Where a parent leaves assets by will to a wealthy adult child, that child may in turn decide to give that property to his own children. A post-death alteration of the will may be the most tax effective way of passing inherited property to the next generation (see Chapter 12).

4.6.4 Gifts into trust

The practical advantage of a gift into trust over an outright gift is flexibility. By using a settlement the settlor (the person making the gift into the trust) can determine who will benefit, when and how. Conditions can be imposed, for example 'To Ben if he attains 21 years of age' so that Ben will only receive the trust fund (gift) if he reaches his 21st birthday; or to limit the amount of the gift received, for example 'the income to Carol during her life and on her death the income and capital to Doreen'. This is not possible with an outright gift.

In estate planning the most common types of trust are:

(1) A 'bare trust' for minor children (see below).
(2) An accumulation and maintenance trust for children and/or grandchildren.
(3) A discretionary trust.
(4) An interest in possession trust.

Each trust has its own particular uses and conditions and those in (2) to (4) are considered in more detail in Chapter 5. Trusts with trustees resident outside the UK also play a considerable role in tax and estate planning. These are considered in Chapter 14.

Parental settlements (including outright gifts) for minor children

Settlements can be set up by parents for their children. Despite the obvious practical advantage, there is a potential tax problem if the children are unmarried and under 18 years when the settlement is created. Income tax rules state that any income (more than £100) paid to or for the benefit of an unmarried minor child from a settlement created by his or her parent will be taxed as though it is still the parent's income (ICTA 1988, s 660B). This is deliberate policy to prevent a parent who pays tax at 40 per cent from using a settlement to benefit his child who pays income tax at lower rates or possibly is not a tax payer at all. As will be seen in Chapter 13 the maximum rate of income tax in settlements is 34 per cent (for 1997/98) and often all this tax paid can be reclaimed from the Inland Revenue.

An outright gift by parents to their minor children is also caught by s 660B so that any income on the property given away is still a part of the parents' taxable income. In effect, income of any property settled for the benefit of a minor child or produced by the property given to the minor child is taxed as though it still belongs to the parents. The actual 'ownership' of the income does not belong to the parents even though it is 'deemed' the parents' for income tax purposes. The parent/settlor has a right of reimbursement from the trustees or beneficiaries to whom income is paid for the extra tax suffered because the income has been deemed to be his for income tax purposes. Normally, the trustees will have paid tax at 34 per cent so if the settlor pays tax at 40 per cent he will be able to recover the difference of 6 per cent. Once the child attains 18 or marries, s 660B ceases to apply. The income is then taxed as his, not his parents'.

BARE TRUSTS

A bare trust (a simple declaration of trust) offers a way of avoiding the deeming provisions of s 660B while, at the same time, allowing use to be made of the beneficiary's, income tax personal allowances and so recover tax paid by the trustees. There is some uncertainty, but the Inland Revenue appears to accept the following position. The property must be transferred to trustees to hold on an irrevocable bare trust for the minor beneficiary who is absolutely entitled, ie who has a vested interest in the property. Provided the trustees retain the property and accumulate its income, ie do not apply it for the benefit of the minor beneficiary, s 660B will not apply. The income will be taxed as income of the beneficiary, not the parents; further, the trustees will not be assessed to tax at 34 per cent. Assuming the beneficiary has total income not exceeding his personal allowance, the tax deducted at source by the companies or the building societies where the trust fund is invested can be recovered on the beneficiary's behalf by the trustees. The refund of tax should be retained in the trust and not paid to or applied for the beneficiary.

In a bare trust the minor beneficiary has a vested interest in both the capital and the income. It is for this reason that the income is treated as his during his minority. Furthermore, if the trust assets are sold by the trustees and the proceeds re-invested, for example on rearrangement of the trust portfolio, any capital gains tax liability will be assessed as the beneficiary's. A full annual exemption of £6,500 will be available and any resulting gain will be taxed at the beneficiary's own income tax rate.

There are disadvantages associated with bare trusts which can put parents off using them. These include:

(1) At majority, the beneficiary can demand the trust property from the trustees. The bare trust ends once he becomes 18. If the trust funds are likely to be substantial, parents may not be too enthusiastic for an 18-year-old to gain possession of the property. Settlements of a smaller capital sum initially might be appropriate.

(2) If the minor beneficiary dies under 18 his estate will include the capital value of the settled property. IHT may become payable on the property after which it will pass on the beneficiary's intestacy (he being too young to make a valid will). It is likely that the property may revert to his parents, although a post-death variation made within 2 years of the death might then be appropriate to re-direct the trust property elsewhere (see further Chapter 12).

PARENTAL SETTLEMENTS – OTHER CONSIDERATIONS
For parents who nevertheless wish to settle property on their children there are other possibilities to consider.

(1) If one parent is not a higher rate tax payer that parent should create the settlement or make the gift.

Example
Eric and Fiona are married with two children aged 8 and 5 years on whom they want to settle £100,000. Eric has assets in excess of £500,000 and pays income tax at 40% on most of his income. Fiona has assets of £200,000 and pays income tax at 23%.

The settlement should be made by Fiona as any income then paid out of the settlement to or for the benefit of her children will be taxed as though it is her income and so at 23%.

If Fiona had insufficient assets to create a settlement, the spouses' estates could have been equalised in advance.

(2) Unless the child needs an income from the trust, the trust fund could be invested in non-income producing assets, ie assets where the emphasis is placed entirely on capital growth at the expense of income. The trustees would need express power to permit them to invest in this way. As there would be little or no income, no real income tax disadvantage would be suffered by the parent.

4.6.5 Gifts with a reserved benefit (FA 1986, s 102 and Sch 20)

No estate planning involving gifts can take place without at least a brief consideration of the rules governing 'reservation of benefit'. Anybody, whether parent, grandparent, uncle etc making a gift must ensure that the donor does not continue to have any interest (with minor exceptions) in the subject matter of the gift or the gift will be ineffective for IHT purposes. This principle applies to outright gifts and gifts into trust and is illustrated by the following examples.

Example 1
Gina says to Henry 'I give you the Matisse which hangs in my drawing room but it must remain where it is'.

Example 2

For many years, Ian has owned a country cottage in which he spends his holidays. Ian transfers the ownership of the cottage to his son John but insists on spending his holidays there as before.

In both examples, there has been a valid gift for succession and CGT purposes (the latter because of the disposal by way of gift giving liability to the donor in the usual way). However, the Inland Revenue will not fully recognise the gift for IHT purposes because the donor has reserved a benefit in the property to himself: the continued enjoyment of the Matisse and the occupation of the cottage. Each gift is a PET for IHT purposes. The death of the donor within 7 years can attract IHT in the usual way. As the gift is caught by the 'reservation of benefit' provisions, the property will also be taxable as part of the donor's IHT estate at death. This prima facie double liability is, to an extent, alleviated by the Inheritance Tax Double Charges (Relief) Regulations 1987, SI 1987/1130.

If the reservation ends before the donor's death, he is treated as making a PET at that time. Again, the 1987 Regulations provide relief should each PET (the original gift and the ending of the reservation) be within 7 years of the donor's death.

The reservation of benefit provisions apply where an individual disposes of any property by way of gift and either:

(1) full possession and enjoyment of the property is not bona fide assumed by the donee at or before the beginning of the relevant period (s 102(1)(a)); or
(2) at any time in the relevant period the property is not enjoyed to the entire exclusion, or virtually to the entire exclusion, of the donor by contract or otherwise (s 102(1)(b)).

The relevant period means the period ending on the date of the donor's death and beginning 7 years before that date, or if it is later, on the date of the gift.

Example 1

David gives away (ie transfers the legal title to) his house to his only child Ella.

(1) If Ella moves in and David dies 2 years later – full possession and enjoyment at the beginning of the relevant period (of 2 years) – no reservation.
(2) If Ella moves in and David dies 8 years later – as before, no reservation.
(3) If after a year David resumes occupation for 6 months to write his autobiography the property is no longer enjoyed to the entire exclusion of David – gift with reservation.

Example 2

Fiona settles a property on discretionary trusts naming herself as one of the discretionary beneficiaries. Even though she has no more than an expectation of benefiting as a beneficiary of a discretionary settlement, all the trust property will remain taxable as part of her estate on death.

Section 102(1)(b), above, requires that 'the property' is 'enjoyed to the exclusion ...' etc. Identifying the property given is not normally difficult but is obviously essential before the rules can be applied appropriately. It also requires 'virtually entire exclusion' from the gifted property. Some continued enjoyment of the property is therefore possible. There is no statutory definition but the Inland Revenue interprets the phrase as meaning (and therefore including) 'cases in which benefit to the donor is insignificant in relation to the gifted property' (IR Tax Bulletin No 9, November 1993). Flexibility is applied by the Inland Revenue when applying the interpretation so that a donor can have limited access to the property given away.

The following are some of the situations which in the Inland Revenue view will not bring the rules into play.

(1) A house which becomes the donee's residence but where the donor subsequently:

   (i)   stays, in the absence of the donee, for not more than 2 weeks each year, or
   (ii) stays with the donee for less than one month each year.

(2) Social visits, excluding overnight stays, made by a donor as a guest of the donee, to a house which he had given away. The extent of the social visits should be no greater than the visits which the donor might be expected to make to the donee's house in the absence of any gift by the donor.

(3) A temporary stay for some short-term purpose in a house the donor had previously given away, for example:

   (i)   while the donor convalesces after medical treatment;
   (ii) while the donor looks after a donee convalescing after medical treatment.

(4) A house together with a library of books which the donor visits less than five times in any year to consult or borrow a book.

(5) A motor car which the donee uses to give occasional (ie less than three times a month) lifts to the donor.

(6) Land which the donor uses to walk his dogs or for horse riding provided this does not restrict the donee's use of the land.

Conversely, the following are instances (in the Inland Revenue view) where the rules may apply.

(1) A house in which the donor then stays most weekends, or for a month or more each year.

(2) A second home or holiday home which the donor and the donee both then use on an occasional basis.

(3) A house with a library in which the donor continues to keep his own books, or which the donor uses on a regular basis, for example because it is necessary for his work.

(4) A motor car which the donee uses every day to take the donor to work.

Inland Revenue Bulletin No 9 also provides some guidance on the meaning of the exclusion provided by FA 1986, Sch 20, para 6(1)(a). By this provision, if land or chattels are given away and the donor provides full consideration for his future enjoyment of the property the reservation provisions do not apply. What constitutes full consideration for the use has caused estate planners problems. Would anything less than full consideration be fatal? In the context of rent payable for the future use of property the Inland Revenue view is:

> 'While we take the view that such full consideration is required throughout the relevant period – and therefore consider that the rent paid should be reviewed at appropriate intervals to reflect market changes – we do recognise that there is no single value at which consideration can be fixed as 'full'. Rather, we accept that what constitutes full consideration in any case lies within a range of values reflecting normal valuation tolerances, and that any amount within that range can be accepted as satisfying the para 6(1)(a) test.'

Further aspects of the reservation rules and the family home are discussed in **4.7.5**.

The reservation of benefit provisions do not apply (inter alia) to transfers qualifying for the four following IHT exemptions:

(1) the spouse exemption;
(2) the small gift exemption;
(3) the gift in consideration of marriage exemption; and
(4) the gifts to charity exemption.

4.7 THE FAMILY HOME

Ownership of the main residence offers a number of tax-saving opportunities for the home owner, most notably mortgage interest relief (continued for 1997/98 to be restricted to relief at 15 per cent) and the CGT private residence exemption. As a substantial asset in its own right, home owners will frequently raise questions about gifts of the home, or at least an interest in it, as part of estate planning with a view to saving, principally, IHT on its value at death. There are many problems associated with gifts of this type, some of which are discussed later.

4.7.1 Mortgage interest relief

Mortgage interest relief where the loan is obtained from one of the major lenders has been discussed at **2.6.3** Income tax relief is available through the MIRAS (mortgage interest relief at source) scheme in most cases. If not, the relief is taken as a reduction in the tax payable by the borrower in his income tax calculation.

4.7.2 Insurance cover

It is sensible to provide insurance cover designed to repay the mortgage debt. In the case of property owned jointly by a husband and wife the policy will normally mature on the death of the first spouse to die leaving a mortgage-free property for the survivor. Various types of policy are available and are discussed in Appendix 2 (21). Often the choice of policy is limited by the financial resources available to the borrower; in addition to the mortgage interest payments the policy premiums can be too expensive. Because of this, the mortgage and the policy should be viewed as two separate but closely linked transactions. A mortgage protection policy alone may be sufficient; an endowment policy (with profits) can be a good investment as well as providing cover to repay the mortgage, but the premiums may be expensive.

4.7.3 Joint tenancy and tenancy in common

Joint tenancy and tenancy in common have already been discussed (see **4.5.1**) as the two common ways property is held by spouses. For IHT purposes there is no distinction made between joint tenancy and tenancy in common; it is the beneficial interest behind the trust for sale of the legal estate that is important when considering the 'estate' of each spouse. The differences between joint tenancy and tenancy in common from a succession point of view have also been considered earlier.

4.7.4 Capital gains tax private residence exemption (TCGA 1992, ss 222–226)

Gains made on the disposal by sale or by gift of an individual's dwelling house used as his only or main residence, including grounds of up to 0.5 hectares (or such larger area as is reasonably required for its enjoyment), are exempt. It is a question of fact in each case as to what constitutes a dwelling house. A caravan was held to be a dwelling house in *Makins v Elson* [1977] 1 All ER 572 but not in *Moore v Thompson* [1986] STC 170 (the caravan not having its own water or electricity supply).

Problems can also arise in deciding whether separate buildings can constitute the tax payer's residence. For example, a separate bungalow occupied by a caretaker and situated in the grounds of the tax payer's house was within the exemption when sold, ie physical separation of the buildings did not deny the tax payer the exemption (*Batey v Wakefield* [1982] 1 All ER 61). Later cases (where CGT was payable) show that the separate building must be physically close to the main building so as to enhance the tax payer's enjoyment of it (*Markey v Saunders* [1987] 1 WLR 864 – bungalow 130 metres away) or within the 'curtilage' of the main building (*Lewis v Lady Rook* [1992] 1 WLR 662 – cottage 200 yards away).

Land and residence sold separately

The order of sales can be important where the tax payer plans to sell land used with the main residence and the main residence itself. Land of up to 0.5 hectares (or a permitted larger area) is within the exemption if used in connection with the residence. Thus, sale of the residence with its grounds will be exempt but gains on the later sale of the retained land will be chargeable (*Varty v Lynes* [1976] 2 All ER 447).

Part business user

Use of part of the house exclusively for business purposes will mean that part of the gain on the disposal is chargeable. Exclusive user can easily be avoided, for example by having a television set in a room otherwise used as an office for a business run from home.

More than one residence

A taxpayer with more than one residence can elect for one to be treated as his main residence. This avoids difficult questions as to which of two or more residences is the only or main residence for the purposes of the relief. The election should be made within 2 years of acquiring the second residence. Failure by the taxpayer to elect will mean that the Inspector of Taxes will do so. The relative CGT liability on each property will generally influence the election of a particular property for treatment as the taxpayer's main residence.

A husband and wife can only have one main residence between them. When a couple marry, each owning a residence, the election for treatment as their main residence must be made within 2 years of the marriage.

Periods of absence

Exemption is available if a taxpayer occupies a property as his only or main residence throughout the period of ownership. Periods of absence will therefore cut back the exemption so that a proportion of the gain on disposal is chargeable.

Certain periods of absence can be ignored (so not prejudicing the exemption):

(1) The first 12 months' ownership due to delay in building or alteration (Statement of Practice D4).
(2) Periods not exceeding 3 years in total.
(3) Periods of employment overseas.
(4) Periods of up to 4 years when the owner was employed elsewhere and so could not occupy the property.

(5) The last 3 years of ownership, for example where the owner moves into new property and has delay in selling the former.

Note: for (2) to (4) above, absences are ignored only if there was no other available residence and the property was occupied before and after the periods of absence.

Private residences occupied under the terms of a trust (s 225)

If the trustees sell a dwelling house occupied by a beneficiary as his main residence under the terms of the trust, their capital gain is exempt. The exemption will apply where the beneficiary has an interest in possession, ie he is entitled to occupy under the terms of the settlement. It will also apply if he occupies as a result of the exercise of a discretion, for example where he is a beneficiary of a discretionary trust and the trustees exercise a power in the settlement to permit him to occupy (*Sansom v Peay* [1976] 3 All ER 375). In this latter situation the Inland Revenue will often argue that, following the exercise of their discretion, the beneficiary has acquired an interest in possession, ie the right to occupy the property (Statement of Practice 10/79). The IHT consequence which flows from this is that the 'estate' of the beneficiary will include the value of the underlying property, the value of the private residence, so that on his death IHT is calculated as if it was an interest in possession settlement.

4.7.5   Estate planning and the family home

The dilemma here is, on the one hand, the wish to give away part or all of the value of the home to save IHT; on the other hand, the necessity to maintain a roof over the donor's head. Saving tax in relation to the home (bearing in mind its value in the client's estate) is an obvious consideration but the best advice is often 'don't let the tax tail wag the dog', ie it is frequently better not to enter into arrangements just to save IHT. Joint tenancy between a husband and wife may often be the most practical approach for spouses.

Normally, IHT planning considerations will revolve around a gift of the house, or of an interest in it, to another individual who will usually be the donor's child. It is possible to give the house to trustees – and retain a right of residence – but this course is unlikely to be followed in most cases.

The gifts with reservation of benefit provisions (FA 1986, s 102) discussed at **4.7.5** present the main obstacle to estate planning where the family home is involved. A number of 'schemes' have been evolved to avoid the reservation rules and some rely on exemptions; only some of these are mentioned below.

'Occupation virtually to the entire exclusion of the donor' (s 102(1)(b))

A gift of the home to a child followed by occasional visits (as interpreted by the Inland Revenue in Tax Bulletin No 9, November 1993) should have no adverse IHT consequences.

'Occupation resulting from change of circumstances of the donor' (FA 1986, Sch 20, para 6(1)(b))

A gift of land which is subsequently re-occupied by the donor following unforeseen and unintentional change in his circumstances is excluded by para 6 provided: (i) the donor is through age or infirmity unable to maintain himself; (ii) the re-occupation is reasonable provision by the donee for the care of the donor; and (iii) the donee is a relative of the donor or his or her spouse. The scope of this exemption is clearly limited as shown in the following example.

Example

A father on his retirement gives to his daughter the family bungalow. He later returns to live there following serious ill health. No IHT consequences should follow from the re-occupation.

'Occupation of land and possession of a chattel for full consideration in money or money's worth' (FA 1986, Sch 6, para (1)(a))

A gift of the home and the arrangement of a right of continued occupation through a lease or licence should have no adverse IHT consequence. Full consideration is required throughout the period of occupation so that a full rent, reviewed regularly, will be essential (see the Inland Revenue's view as to this published in Bulletin No 9, referred to at **4.6.5**). A scheme using this paragraph will reduce the donor's estate for IHT but requires the donor to have sufficient income to pay the rent in full and regularly.

'Co-ownership' between the parents (donors) and the children (donees)

It is attractive to consider an inter vivos gift of such a beneficial interest as a means of reducing an estate for IHT. For example, a husband and wife could contemplate a gift of an interest as tenant in common in the family home to their eldest (adult) child. A gift of the beneficial interest as tenant in common is a PET and carries with it the right to occupy the entire property with the other co-owner(s). The all-important question which arises is whether the continued occupation by the donor(s) is by virtue of the co-ownership, and not through reservation of benefit? If it is the former, the scheme might be effective; if the latter, it will not. Although schemes of this sort may work, and there is considerable doubt, then the practical result is shared ownership and occupation with other (younger) members of the family. Often this will make such schemes unattractive. In view of the legal and practical uncertainty, the best advice is probably not to 'tax plan' in this way with the matrimonial home.

4.8 GIFTS TO CHARITY

In addition to, or perhaps instead of, gifts to family and friends, a taxpayer may wish to make gifts to his favourite charity or charities.

Although not always considered part of estate planning, such gifts can be achieved in a number of tax-efficient ways and the method chosen will normally be determined by the timing and anticipated amount of the gift.

4.8.1 Inheritance tax

All gifts to a charity, whether made inter vivos or by will, and regardless of the amount, are exempt from IHT (IHTA 1984, s 23). A wealthy client may well make sizeable lifetime gifts to charity. These will be exempt and never enter his cumulative total.

Many clients will not be able to afford or wish to make such lifetime donations but will make provision for a charity in their will. This may take the form of a legacy or a gift of residue. The amount given must be deducted as an exemption in the calculation to find the deceased's total chargeable estate.

The will or intestacy of a deceased person may also be varied (see Chapter 12) to provide an exempt gift to charity.

4.8.2 Capital gains tax (TCGA 1992, s 256)

The most common form of charitable gift is of cash and therefore CGT is not relevant.

Where, however, a taxpayer is transferring chargeable assets to a charity, the gift will be at no gain no loss (the rule works in a similar way to inter-spouse transfers, see **4.4.5**).

For property left to charity by will, the organisation will receive the property at its probate value and, as with inter vivos gifts, the property should be exempt from CGT on a subsequent disposal.

4.8.3 Income tax

For small and/or regular inter vivos payments to charity there are a number of accepted schemes which are income tax effective for the donor and which should, therefore, be especially attractive to higher rate tax payers.

Deeds of covenant (ICTA 1988, ss 660A(9)(G), 347A(7))

Deeds of covenant are a popular method of making regular annual payments to a charity, for example where the payment is an annual membership fee to charities such as the National Trust.

The covenant should be made in writing and signed and dated by the taxpayer. It must be capable of lasting for a period of more than 3 years, hence many charities have a standard form of covenant to last for 4 years (or the life of the donor if shorter) which the taxpayer can complete.

The effect of the covenant is that the taxpayer has a charge on his income, so reducing the amount of his taxable income. An example showing the tax relief for the payer and the machinery for collection of tax appears at **2.6.3**.

A 'deposited covenant' couples an ordinary covenant with an immediate loan of the full amount payable under the covenant to the charity. The advantage is the early receipt of the total sum by the charity while giving annual tax relief for the individual. Each year, as the annual amount falls due under the covenant, a corresponding sum is deducted from the total sum payable under the covenant.

> *Example*
> £1,000 (net) pa is payable to a charity for 5 years. The charity receives £5,000. In the first year, £1,000 attracts income tax relief for the payer and the total due under the covenant is reduced to £4,000. A similar process occurs in each of the following 4 years after which the covenant ceases and the payer is no longer entitled to tax relief.

Payroll giving (ICTA 1988, s 202)

The payroll giving scheme was introduced by the Government in 1988 with the sole purpose of encouraging charitable giving. Employers are encouraged to operate a scheme whereby part of an employee's wages or salary is deducted by the employer who pays that sum to an approved charitable agent. The agent then distributes the sum to the charity or charities of the employee's choice. Employees do not have to be involved and must expressly join the scheme if they want to make payments. The maximum contribution per employee is £1,200 per annum and it is deducted from the employee's gross pay so reducing the amount of his taxable income.

Gift aid (FA 1990, ss 25–26)

Gift aid is another government-initiated scheme to encourage charitable gifts. Whereas payroll giving is aimed at encouraging small regular annual payments, gift aid is aimed at larger 'one-off' gifts to charity paid out of the tax payer's income. The scheme is particularly popular, for example in the year to March1996, charities benefited to the extent of £330 million.

The minimum gift is generally £250; there is no upper limit as such but, effectively, the maximum is the total income of the individual in the tax year of the gift.

The tax payer will make the donation net of basic rate tax and thereby obtains relief at that rate. The tax payer obtains his higher rate tax relief on the gross amount received by the charity by making a claim in his tax returns. The charity reclaims the tax deducted from the Inland Revenue.

Example

Roger makes a payment of £1,540 net of basic rate income tax to his favourite charity. The Inland Revenue will receive £460. The charity obtains a refund of this £460 and so receives £2,000 in total.

Roger's actual outlay is £2,000, ie £1,540 paid to the charity and £460 (basic rate tax on £2,000) paid to the Inland Revenue. The cost to Roger (after tax relief) is considerably less than £2,000. If he is a higher rate taxpayer the cost is £2,000 – (£2,000 × 40%) = £1,200. He obtains £460 relief by deduction from his gross payment of £2,000 and £340 (higher rate relief) through his tax return. His total relief is, therefore, £800.

4.9 STAMP DUTY

No estate planning should be undertaken without some consideration as to the stamp duty position. Ad valorem stamp duty on voluntary dispositions was abolished by the FA 1985, s 82 for documents executed after 25 March 1985. If the transaction was effected without a document, no stamp duty would in any event be payable – stamp duty is a tax on documents, not on transactions.

However, fixed 50p stamp duty remained as did the requirement that documents be sent to the stamp office for a formal 'adjudication' stamp. For documents executed on or after 1 May 1987 each of these requirements was removed by the Stamp Duty (Exempt Instruments) Regulations 1987, SI 1987/516 for documents mentioned in the schedule to the Regulations. These include the following categories relevant to estate planning:

A   The vesting of property subject to a trust in the trustees of the trust on the appointment of a new trustee, or in the continuing trustees on the retirement of a trustee.

B   The conveyance or transfer of property the subject of a specific devise or legacy to the beneficiary named in the will.

C   The conveyance or transfer of property which forms part of an intestate's estate to the person entitled on intestacy.

D   The appropriation of property in satisfaction of a general legacy of money or of any interest of surviving spouse in an intestate's estate.

E   The conveyance or transfer of property which forms part of the residuary estate of a testator to a beneficiary entitled under the will.

F   The conveyance or transfer of property out of a settlement in or towards satisfaction of a beneficiary's interest, not being an interest acquired for money or money's worth, in accordance with the provisions of the settlement.

G   The conveyance or transfer of property on and in consideration only of marriage to a party to the marriage or to trustees to be held on a marriage settlement.

H   The conveyance or transfer of property in connection with divorce etc.

I to K   (*not relevant to estate planning*)

L   The conveyance or transfer of property as a voluntary disposition inter vivos.

M   The conveyance or transfer of property by a post death variation.

To be exempt, the document must be certified as coming within one or more of the categories. The certificate can be included in or endorsed on the document; it is usually found printed on the reverse of a stock (share) transfer form. A solicitor can sign the certificate in the name of his firm on behalf of the transferor (if as usual it is not signed by the transferor personally).

Form of certificate

I/we hereby certify that this instrument falls within Category .... in the Schedule to the Stamp Duty (Exempt Instruments) Regulations 1987.

4.10   CONCLUSION

Financial planning is concerned with maximising the wealth (capital and income) of the individual. Estate planning is concerned with the passing on of that wealth within the family. This can be achieved by lifetime transfers or by will or a combination of the two. Each client is unique and requires a personal plan. The task of the solicitor is to identify the possibilities for estate planning. However much the solicitor believes in a course of action, the decision whether or not to take it is the client's alone.

Tax avoidance through the use of available reliefs and exemptions as in the previous paragraphs is a legitimate activity. However, some schemes designed for tax payers by their advisers have been so contrived, and the potential savings so great, that legislation has been enacted to combat their effectiveness. The Inland Revenue has successfully challenged some schemes in the courts. Where the tax saving is achieved through a series of artificial steps carried out as a tax-saving measure only the Inland Revenue may be able to ignore the intervening steps and therefore negate the effect of the scheme. All practitioners need to be aware of the anti-avoidance legislation and cases (eg ICTA 1988, s 674A, ss 703–728, and s 776; IHTA 1984, s 268; and a series of cases beginning with *Ramsay (WT) Ltd v IRC* [1982] AC 300 and *Furniss v Dawson* [1984] AC 474) in putting forward tax-saving schemes).

Chapter 5

INTRODUCTION TO SETTLEMENTS

5.1 SETTLEMENTS

The term 'settlement' has a variety of meanings depending upon the context in which it is used. In the private client department, the term is commonly used to include any arrangement whereby an individual 'settles' property of any kind upon trust for a beneficiary or group of beneficiaries. The term 'settlement' refers to the whole arrangement; the 'trusts' are the terms upon which the property is held.

Contrast the following statutory uses of the term.

(1) In the concept of the Settled Land Act 1925, a 'settlement' or 'strict settlement' is a trust of land where no trust for sale is imposed. Technical provisions of the Settled Land Act ensure that in such a case the beneficiary who has the right to enjoy the land (the tenant for life) has many of the powers over the property which would normally be vested in the trustees (eg the power to sell the land). Such settlements are rarely encountered in practice, being avoided by the imposition of a trust for sale. The TLA 1996 prevents the creation of any new strict settlements (but does not prevent the use of a trust for sale).

(2) In tax statutes, the term 'settlement' is frequently used and is defined in a variety of different ways. For example, a parental 'settlement' for income tax purposes includes not only a settlement upon trust, but also an outright gift (see **4.6.4**).

5.1.1 Trusts background – some reminders

Fixed interest trusts

When an individual ('the settlor') settles property upon trust he may wish to determine precisely the extent to which his chosen beneficiaries are to enjoy the settled property in the future. He may, for example, divide their enjoyment of the property by creating successive interests or he may prevent beneficiaries from obtaining access to the capital before a certain age by giving them contingent interests.

Where capital or income is to be divided between a group of individuals, the settlor may determine the extent of each beneficiary's share. Allowance may be made for future generations by describing the beneficiaries rather than naming them (eg my grandchildren) provided that the description is sufficiently clear to enable the beneficiaries to be identified with certainty.

The settlor who creates such a trust gives fixed equitable interests to the beneficiaries. Each beneficiary has a bundle of rights resembling an interest in property which he may sell or give away (provided that any such assignment complies with s 53(1)(c) of the LPA 1925).

If the beneficiaries are between them entitled to the whole equitable interest and are all sui iuris, they may by agreement put an end to the trust, calling for the trustees to distribute the capital between them in such shares as they may agree (the rule in *Saunders v Vautier* – see **10.1.3**). The rule does not apply if any beneficiary is a minor, or if there are potential beneficiaries who may be born in the future, although the court has power to consent on behalf of such beneficiaries under the Variation of Trusts Act 1958 (see **12.2.3**).

The period during which the settlor may dictate how the property is to be held is limited by the rule against remoteness of vesting; interests which do not vest within the perpetuity period will fail (see **6.2.7**). If the trusts in the settlement should fail for this or any other reason, the property will revert to the settlor (or his estate if he is dead).

Discretionary trusts

Where the settlor does not wish to determine in advance the precise extent of each beneficiary's entitlement, he may nominate a category of beneficiaries and give his trustees the power to determine how much (if anything) each potential beneficiary should receive.

The trustees' discretion may simply concern the distribution of income. If the trustees are obliged to distribute the income, the trusts are said to be 'exhaustive'. Alternatively, the settlor may widen the trustees' discretion to allow them to retain (or accumulate) the income if they think fit ('non-exhaustive' trusts). The period during which a power to accumulate income may continue is limited by the rule against accumulations (broadly, to 21 years – see **6.2.8**).

A discretion over the distribution of income may be combined with fixed interests in capital.

Alternatively, the trustees' discretion may extend to capital as well as income, giving the trustees the power to distribute capital to one or more of the designated class of beneficiaries at any time (and thus if they think fit bring an end to the trust).

A beneficiary under a discretionary trust cannot claim any property as of right. He has only a hope that the trustees will exercise their discretion in his favour. Although in principle the rule in *Saunders v Vautier* would allow all the potential beneficiaries to end the trust by agreement, this is unlikely to be possible in practice as the class will be too widely drawn.

Any discretion over income or capital must be limited to the perpetuity period in order to comply with the rule against remoteness of vesting. A fixed period of 80 years is usually specified in the trust instrument and the trustees will normally distribute the whole fund within that period. If, however, all members of the class of beneficiaries should die before the trustees have distributed the capital, the trusts will fail and the property will revert to the settlor (or his estate if he is dead) on resulting trust. For tax reasons, it is important to avoid any possibility of 'reverter to settlor' (see **6.2.10**) and so an 'ultimate default' provision is usually included (see **7.4**).

Students of trusts will recall the difficult distinction between a power of appointment and a discretionary trust or 'trust power'. A trust power arises where the settlor's overriding intention is to benefit a particular class of beneficiaries, giving a power of selection to his trustees. A power of appointment involves no such overriding intention: if it is not exercised, the property will pass in default of appointment. Since the assimilation of the tests for certainty of objects applicable to powers of appointment and discretionary trusts (*McPhail v Doulton* [1971] AC 424) the distinction is largely academic. In practice, the trustees' power of selection is commonly expressed as a widely drawn power of appointment enabling them not only to give capital outright to a beneficiary, but also to resettle it on new trusts for the benefit of particular members of the class (see Chapter 9 and Appendix 4, clause 5).

5.1.2 Settlements in practice

There are many rules of equity and statutory provisions which have a practical effect on the creation and use of settlements. The most important of these are the tax provisions which govern the treatment of the settlement for tax purposes on its creation, during its life and when it comes to an end. Settlements fall into three main categories for tax purposes: interest in possession settlements; discretionary settlements; and accumulation and maintenance settlements.

The purpose of this chapter is to introduce each of the three types of settlement and to explore:

(1) what can be achieved by using a settlement; and
(2) the taxation cost to the settlor;

with the aim of enabling the selection of the appropriate type of settlement for a particular client.

This and the following three chapters are concerned with inter vivos creation of settlements. Chapter 11 considers how to create settlements in wills and their tax effects.

5.2 SETTLEMENTS CREATING INTEREST IN POSSESSION TRUSTS

5.2.1 Introduction

An interest in possession has been defined as 'a present right to the present enjoyment of income': *IRC v Pearson* [1980] 2 All ER 479. Put more simply, it means the trustees have to pay the annual trust income to a beneficiary.

The simplest example of an interest in possession is a life interest.

> *Example*
> Adam gives £100 to trustees to hold on trust for Brenda for life with the remainder to Colin. Brenda has an interest in possession. She is entitled to all the income generated by the trust fund of £100. The trustees must pay that income to her.

The purpose of this type of settlement is to provide successive interests. There are various ways to achieve this.

(1) The settlor may want to benefit several people, one after the other.

> *Example*
> Diana wants to benefit her son and daughter-in-law by giving them extra income. She also wants to benefit her grandson. She might set up a trust giving:
>
> (a) the income to her son for life; and on his death
> (b) the income to her daughter-in-law (if still living) for life; and on the death of the survivor of her son and daughter-in-law
> (c) the capital to the grandson absolutely.

(2) The settlor may wish to give one person the right to income for a given time and then the capital to somebody else.

Example

Ernest wants to provide finance for his granddaughter while she studies to be an architect. He thinks she will need his support for about 8 years but ultimately he wants all his money to go to his favourite charity.

He might set up a trust giving:

(a) the income to his granddaughter for 8 years or until she qualifies as an architect, whichever is the shorter period; and then
(b) the capital to the charity absolutely.

(3) The settlor may want to stagger a beneficiary's entitlement to property.

Example

Fred wants to give a substantial sum of money to his grandson George who is 19. George is in urgent need of some money but Fred does not want him to receive everything immediately. Fred might set up a trust giving:

(a) the income to George until he is 25 years of age; and then
(b) the capital to George absolutely.

In each of the above examples, a beneficiary was receiving the income. If the trustees have the power to decide whether or not to pay income to a beneficiary, it is not an interest in possession trust.

5.2.2   Taxation on creation of settlements with an interest in possession

IHT

The creation of such a settlement is a transfer of value by the settlor, which will be a PET insofar as not exempt (IHTA 1984, s 3A). Where a settlor dies within 7 years of creating the settlement, the PET becomes chargeable. The tax is paid by the trustees from the settlement.

Example

Harriet sets up a trust for her brother for life with the remainder to her nephew. She transfers cash and shares valued at £271,000 to the settlement. Harriet dies 2 years later with 'free estate' of £130,000 which she leaves to charity (IHT exempt).

As the free estate is exempt, IHT is payable on the trust property only (no taper relief as Harriet died within 3 years of creating the settlement).

	£
Value transferred	271,000
Less: two annual exemptions	6,000
	265,000

IHT on the first £215,000 @ 0%   =   nil
On the balance of £50,000 @ 40% =   £20,000

The tax is due 6 months from the end of the month in which Harriet died and must be paid by the trustees from the trust fund, so reducing the present value of the trust fund by £20,000.

A settlor can avoid the fund being depleted by the tax if the transfer becomes chargeable by insuring his life for 7 years and writing the policy in trust for the trustees of the settlement to receive as additional trust property on his death (see Appendix 2 for term assurance).

Example
After creating the settlement in the previous example Harriet insures her life for £20,000.

	£
On Harriet's death trustees receive £20,000 from the insurance policy	
Value of trust fund £271,000 + £20,000 =	291,000
Less: IHT as result of Harriet's death	20,000
Value of fund remains	271,000

There may be subsequent charges to IHT within the settlement if the interest in possession ends, for example, the person with the interest in possession dies or gives up the right to the income for any other reason (see **10.1**).

CGT

The transfer of property by a settlor to trustees is a disposal (TCGA 1992, s 70). If chargeable assets are settled, a chargeable gain (or allowable loss) may result. The gain (if any) will be the settlor's and he will bear the tax.

Example
Ilyana (a 40% income taxpayer) settles her quoted shares worth £35,500 acquired for £8,500 and cash of £30,000. She has made no other disposals in that tax year. The beneficiaries are her daughter for life with remainder to her grandchildren.

Calculate the CGT on the disposal.

Cash is exempt

		£
Shares:	Market value at disposal	35,500
less:	acquisition cost	8,500
		27,000
less:	indexation allowance (say)	500
		26,500
less:	annual exemption	6,500
	Chargeable gain	20,000

CGT @ 40% on £20,000 = £8,000

Calculate the cost of the settlement to Ilyana.

	£
Value of shares	35,500
Cash	30,000
CGT	8,000
	73,500

The acquisition cost of the shares to the trustees for the purpose of any future capital gains on a disposal by them is £35,500.

If the settlor settles business property, the gain may be held-over at the election of the settlor only (TCGA 1992, s 165 – see **4.4.5**). The effect is that the trustees take the business property at the settlor's acquisition cost (plus indexation) and this becomes the trustee's acquisition cost for any subsequent disposal.

Once the settlement has been created, any sales of trust assets by the trustees (see Chapter 13) or a transfer of the trust fund, or part of it, to a beneficiary (see **10.1.4**) may give rise to a CGT charge.

The creation of the settlement is also a PET for IHT purposes of £59,500, ie £65,500 (minus 2 × £3,000 annual exemptions). The reduction in Ilyana's estate of £8,000 CGT is ignored for IHT purposes, ie this reduction does not also reduce the estate when calculating the IHT bill.

Income tax

The creation of a settlement should have no income tax consequences for the settlor (other than saving of income tax on any actual loss of income). All dividend and savings income arising after the settlement has been created will be taxed at 20 per cent and any other income at 23 per cent in the hands of the trustees (see Chapter 13).

5.3 SETTLEMENTS CREATING DISCRETIONARY TRUSTS

5.3.1 Introduction

Settlements creating discretionary trusts are settlements in which there is no interest in possession, ie trusts where no beneficiary has a present right to the present enjoyment of income.

The settlor identifies the beneficiaries whom he wishes to benefit but leaves it to the trustees to select which of these beneficiaries is to benefit and how and when. Discretionary trusts are the most flexible type of settlement because the decision as to beneficial entitlement can be deferred and does not have to be determined at the time the trusts are created. The discretion is normally given over both the capital and income of the trust fund.

Example

Barry wishes to benefit his grandchildren, Cora, Doris and Edward. All three are aged under 5 years and he does not know how they will develop and whether their needs will be the same. He settles £50,000 on discretionary trusts.

Twenty years later Cora has just qualified as a lawyer; Doris is a hairdresser and single parent; Edward is a bank clerk and physically disabled as a result of an accident several years ago. The trustees decide to distribute the money unevenly between the three beneficiaries.

5.3.2 Taxation on the creation of discretionary settlements

IHT

THE LIFETIME CHARGE (IHTA 1984, ss 1–3)
A transfer of property to a discretionary settlement is a lifetime chargeable transfer insofar as not exempt and taxable at the time it is made. The rate of tax is one half of the death rate.

> *Example 1*
> John (who has made gifts of £3,000 per annum in this and the preceding tax year) settles £75,000 on discretionary trusts.
>
> IHT is charged at 0% on £75,000 = nil

> *Example 2*
> Karen settles £271,000 on discretionary trusts on the basis that any IHT is paid out of the trust fund. She has made no previous transfers.
>
> | | £ |
> |---|---|
> | Value transferred | 271,000 |
> | *Less*: two annual exemptions | 6,000 |
> | | 265,000 |
>
> IHT on the first £215,000 @ 0% = nil
>
> On the balance of £50,000 @ 20% = £10,000.

THE CHARGE ON THE DEATH OF THE SETTLOR
If the settlor dies within 7 years of making the transfer, IHT is recalculated at the death rates with credit being given for tax already paid.

> *Example 3*
> The facts are the same as Example 2 above but Karen dies 18 months later leaving her free estate to her husband.
>
> | | £ | |
> |---|---|---|
> | IHT is payable on £265,000 | | |
> | IHT on first £215,000 @ 0% = | nil | |
> | on balance £50,000 @ 40% = | 20,000 | |
> | | 20,000 | |
> | *Less*: IHT already paid | 10,000 | (as per Example 2) |
> | Additional IHT payable as a result of Karen's death (taper relief not available) | 10,000 | |

GROSSING UP

In the above examples, it has been assumed that the tax will be paid by the trustees, ie that the tax will be deducted from the amount going into the settlement. In Example 2, Karen's discretionary settlement will have an initial trust fund of £261,000 (£271,000 – £10,000) and in Example 3, Karen's death will reduce the fund by a further £10,000.

Where the settlor intends the settlement to retain the full amount of the transfer he must pay the IHT. Since IHT is calculated on the fall in value in the transferor's estate, tax will be charged on the value of the gift and on the IHT on the gift. This requires the transfer to be grossed up.

Example

Karen wants the full £271,000 to go into the discretionary trust. This is a net gift. IHT on the gross gift will be calculated as follows:

Step 1: Deduct available exemptions to find the value transferred, ie £271,000 – £6,000 = £265,000

Step 2: Gross up the value transferred at the appropriate tax rates.

net		*gross equivalent*
£215,000	=	£215,000
£50,000 × $\frac{100}{80}$	=	£62,500
		£277,500

The settlement receives £271,000 (ie including the £6,000 covered by Karen's annual exemption).

The Inland Revenue will receive IHT of £12,500 from Karen (£277,500 – 215,000 = £62,500 at 20%).

Any charge which arises as a result of Karen's death within 7 years will be based on a value transferred of £277,500.

SUBSEQUENT EVENTS (IHTA 1984, ss 58–69)

Once the discretionary settlement has been created there is a potential IHT charge on the trust fund every 10 years. There is also an 'exit' charge, for example, when any part of the capital of the trust fund is given to a beneficiary or an interest in possession arises (see **10.2**).

CGT (TCGA 1992, s 260)

The disposal of property by a settlor into a discretionary settlement is a chargeable event (unless cash is being settled). Hold-over relief is available:

(1) irrespective of the nature of the asset being settled, therefore including land and quoted shares; and

(2) irrespective of whether any IHT is actually payable.

Only the transferor need make the election (see **4.4.5**).

Example 1

Lesley settles on discretionary trusts her country cottage which she bought for £50,000 and is now worth £80,000. She has made no previous transfers.

IHT will be payable but at 0% because the £80,000 falls within Lesley's nil rate band.

CGT hold-over relief is available.

Example 2
Morris settles quoted shares purchased for £1,000 and now worth £6,000 on discretionary trusts. He has made no other transfers but has made chargeable gains this year of £8,000 on disposal of other assets.

The transfer to the discretionary settlement is a transfer of value but for IHT purposes the value transferred is nil because of Morris's unused annual exemptions.

CGT hold-over relief is available.

Sales by the trustees after the settlement has been created will be subject to CGT subject to exemptions and reliefs. Transfers of capital from the trust fund to a beneficiary may also attract CGT, although hold-over relief may be available, see Chapter 10.

Income tax
The usual rate of income tax on all trust income is 34 per cent (see Chapter 13).

5.4 SETTLEMENTS CREATING ACCUMULATION AND MAINTENANCE TRUSTS

Settlements creating accumulation and maintenance (A & M) trusts can only be set up to benefit young people under the age of 25 years when the settlement is created. They are settlements without an interest in possession but, provided they comply with the rules in the IHTA 1984, s 71, are afforded special IHT treatment (see **5.4.2**). If a settlement does not comply with s 71, it cannot be an A & M settlement.

5.4.1 The requirements
Section 71 lays down three requirements all of which must be satisfied:

(1) One or more beneficiaries . . . will, on or before attaining a specified age not exceeding 25, become entitled to, or to an interest in possession in, the settled property.
(2) No interest in possession subsists in the settled property and the income from it is to be accumulated so far as it is not applied for the maintenance, education, or benefit of such a beneficiary.
(3) Either:

   (i) not more than 25 years have elapsed since the day on which the settlement was made ...; or
   (ii) all the ... beneficiaries ... are grandchildren of a common grandparent... or [are] children, widows or widowers of such grandchildren who were themselves beneficiaries but died before becoming entitled as . . . [in (1) above].

Each of these requirements will be considered in turn.

At least one beneficiary will become entitled to the trust property, or an interest in possession in it, on or before his 25th birthday

This requirement gives the settlor a choice. He may give an entitlement to the capital of the trust fund on or before 25 years, or he may give an entitlement to income on or before that age.

CAPITAL ENTITLEMENT

A & M trusts create contingent benefits. In a simple settlement, a beneficiary will only be entitled to the capital of the trust fund, or a portion of it, if he reaches the specified age.

Example 1

£10,000 is settled on trust for Adam if he attains 18 years of age.

If Adam reaches 18 years (ie satisfies the contingency) the trustees must give him the £10,000.

If Adam dies, say aged 15 years, the trust will fail. The £10,000 will not form part of Adam's estate.

Example 2

Year 1: Property is settled for Brian (now aged 17) and Clare (now aged 15) if they attain 21 years of age, and if both reach 21, in equal shares.

Year 4: Brian attains 21 and he will receive half the trust fund.

Year 6: Clare is now 21 and receives the other half of the trust fund.

If Clare had died in Year 5, she would not have satisfied the contingency and neither she nor her estate would have any right to the trust fund. In those circumstances, Brian would receive the other half.

The words 'will become entitled' should be read as if meaning 'will become entitled if at all on or before 25'. Therefore, the death of all the intended beneficiaries before the specified age does not prevent the settlement being an A & M settlement (see further *Inglewood (Lord) v IRC* [1983] STC 133).

INCOME ENTITLEMENT

On occasion the settlor will not want the beneficiary to receive the capital of the trust fund on or before his 25th birthday but will want the contingency delayed to a later age, say 30. This need not be fatal to the settlement being an A & M settlement. Section 71 requires a beneficiary to become entitled to the settled property or 'an interest in possession in it' on or before 25 years.

A beneficiary has an interest in possession in a trust fund if he has a right to income from the fund.

Section 31 of the TA 1925 provides that a minor beneficiary who is contingently entitled to capital of a fund nevertheless has the right to the income from that fund from his 18th birthday.

Example

Property is settled on trust for Dora if she attains the age of 30 years.

At first sight, this is not an A & M settlement because Dora will not acquire the capital of the fund until after she is 25. But, assuming s 31 of the TA 1925 applies to the settlement, she will acquire the right to the income in the fund at the age of 18. As her interest in possession arises on or before 25, ie at 18 years, this satisfies this part of s 71.

Trust draftsmen will often modify s 31 of the TA 1925 or replace it with an express clause. In such circumstances, care must be taken to ensure that, if the right to capital is delayed beyond the age of 25, the right to income is given on or before the beneficiary's 25th birthday (see Chapter 8).

No beneficiary may have an interest in possession when the trust is created and any income not applied must be accumulated

As with the first requirement, there are two aspects, namely no interest in possession and the accumulation of income. Both are normally satisfied while the beneficiary is a minor by the effect of s 31 of the TA 1925.

NO INTEREST IN POSSESSION

Because of this requirement, if any beneficiary has an immediate right to the income of the trust fund, it will not be an A & M settlement.

Section 31 of the TA 1925 applies to all settlements unless it is expressly excluded or overridden. Where s 31 applies, a beneficiary has no right to any of the income of the trust fund (ie to an interest in possession) until he attains his 18th birthday.

Example 1
Property is settled on Ella and Francis contingent on their attaining the age of 25 years and, if more than one, in equal shares. Section 31 of the TA 1925 applies.

At the time the property is settled, Ella is 9 and Francis 4. As a result, neither is entitled to the income until 18 years of age. Therefore, this part of s 71 of the IHTA 1984 is satisfied.

Example 2
Property is settled on Gina (aged 22) contingent on her attaining the age of 30. Section 31 of the TA 1925 applies to the settlement.

Section 31 gives Gina an immediate right to the income from the trust fund and so prevents this being an A & M settlement. (It is an interest in possession settlement whereby Gina is to receive the income until she is 30 and then the capital absolutely (see **5.2**).)

Example 3
Property is settled on Harry (aged 19) to receive both the capital and income contingent on his reaching 25 years of age (ie s 31 of the TA 1925 has been suitably modified). This requirement of s 71 of the IHTA 1984 is satisfied.

Example 4
Property is settled on Ian (aged 21) and Susan (aged 17) contingently on their attaining 25 years of age. Section 31 of the Trustees Act 1925 applies. Section 71 of the IHTA 1984 is satisfied so far as Susan is concerned but not Ian. There is an A & M settlement for Susan (if all the other conditions are also satisfied). Ian has an interest in possession in one half of the settled property.

ACCUMULATION

Section 71 of the IHTA 1984 provides that the income of the trust fund is to be accumulated so far as not applied for the maintenance, education or benefit of a beneficiary.

Section 31 of the TA 1925 gives trustees the power to apply income for the maintenance education or benefit of a minor beneficiary and requires them to accumulate the balance of the income.

> *Example*
> Property is settled on Keelash (aged 9) contingent on her attaining the age of 18 years. Section 31 of the TA 1925 applies. Every year the trustees apply some of the trust income towards Keelash's education and her annual holiday and accumulate the balance. Section 71 is not breached.

The trust must not last for more than 25 years or all the beneficiaries must have a common grandparent (or be the children, widows or widowers of such beneficiaries)

Where the beneficiaries do not share a common grandparent, the settlement must not last for more than 25 years. If it does, a charge to IHT may then arise (see **10.3.2**).

The grandparent must be common to all the beneficiaries but need not have any blood tie to the settlor.

This requirement is designed to prevent more than one generation from benefiting from A & M trusts. A second generation can nevertheless benefit because the provisions permit substitution where an original beneficiary has died.

5.4.2   Taxation on the creation of an A & M settlement

IHT (IHTA 1984, s 3A)

The creation of an A & M settlement is a PET (insofar as not covered by an exemption) by the settlor. If the settlor dies within 7 years any tax will be paid from the trust fund.

Therefore, if the amount being settled exceeds the settlor's nil rate band (after deducting all available reliefs and exemptions) consideration should be given to insurance. The insurance can be effected either by the settlor insuring his own life and writing the insurance policy in trust for the settlement or by the trustees of the settlement insuring the settlor's life (see **5.2.2**).

IHT SUBSEQUENTLY (IHTA 1984, s 71(4)

The main advantage of an A & M settlement over other settlements without an interest in possession, (eg discretionary settlements) is its IHT treatment.

Apart from the potential charge on creation, there should be no IHT charges levied on an A & M settlement either during its life or on its termination (see further Chapter 10 and **11.6.2**, where an A & M settlement is created by will).

CGT

The transfer of property by a settlor to an A & M settlement is a chargeable event for CGT purposes. CGT is calculated in the normal way and paid by the settlor. Consideration could be given to settling cash thereby avoiding CGT or where appropriate assets such as business property, which attract hold-over relief (TCGA

1992, s 165), can be settled. Hold-over relief under TCGA 1992, s 260 is not available since a PET occurs when the settlement is created (see **4.4.5**).

Subsequent dealings with the trust property, such as sales or distributions to beneficiaries, may attract a charge to CGT (see Chapter 10).

5.5 FURTHER TAX IMPLICATIONS OF CREATING SETTLEMENTS

Any settlor who is thinking of creating a settlement should consider the overall tax position, before and after its creation, both for himself and for the settlement. Tax should not be the only reason for creating a settlement but it will always be one of the most important factors. The type of settlement which is chosen may be governed by its particular tax treatment.

5.5.1 IHT

A settlor who is proposing to make more than one inter vivos settlement must be aware of the cumulative effect of IHT on his second (and subsequent) settlements as well.

Cumulation

Because of the way cumulation works, a taxpayer who makes a lifetime chargeable transfer (eg settles property on discretionary trusts) has to survive for 14 years before it ceases to have any impact.

Example

Year 1: Jake settles £165,000 on discretionary trusts.

Year 5: Jake makes a gift of £50,000 to his sister Susan.

Year 6: Jake settles £165,000 on A & M trusts for his grandchildren.

Year 9: Jake dies.

Ignore annual exemptions.

Step 1:

The discretionary settlement was an immediately chargeable lifetime transfer (LCT) made more than 7 years before death and so no further tax is due on it but it is within the cumulative total of chargeable transfers relevant to the calculation of IHT on the gift in Year 5.

Step 2:

The gift was made less than 7 years ago and so the PET becomes chargeable; a failed PET. Look back 7 years from the gift to see if there are any chargeable transfers. If so they must be cumulated with the gift. The LCT's existence reduces the nil rate band available when calculating IHT on the failed PET.

	£	£
Gift – PET now chargeable		50,000
Cumulative total – LCT	165,000	
Nil rate band (part)	165,000	
Nil rate band (balance)		50,000
		nil

IHT on failed PET – nil

Step 3:

The A & M settlement was a PET when made but has also become chargeable. It must be cumulated with all chargeable transfers made in the preceding 7 years. In this case the cumulative total of chargeable transfers is £215,000 and so exhausts the nil rate band.

	£	£
A & M – PET now chargeable		165,000
Cumulative total – the failed PET and the LCT	215,000	
Nil rate band	215,000	
Nil rate band (balance)		nil
		165,000

IHT on £165,000 @ 40% payable by the trustees. Taper relief is available only if 3 years have elapsed since the creation of the A & M settlement.

Step 4:

Jake's estate on death is cumulated with the two failed PETs (the gift and the A & M settlement). As these together give a cumulative total of chargeable transfers of £215,000, Jake's estate is prima facie taxable at 40%. The discretionary settlement was made more than 7 years ago and drops out of the cumulation.

Order of gifts and same day transfers (IHTA 1984, ss 62, 66 and 68)

Where a client is proposing to create a discretionary settlement and to make a PET, it is advisable to transfer the property to the settlement before making the PET. Further, a client should be advised against making more than one transfer on the same day, especially if one transfer will be a lifetime chargeable transfer (see further **4.7.2**).

5.5.2 CGT

Provided neither the settlor nor his spouse has an interest in the settlement (in which case CGT would be paid at his income tax rate of 20 per cent, 23 per cent or 40 per cent, see **6.2.10**), CGT on any disposal by the trustees is paid at 23 per cent if an interest in possession settlement; 34 per cent if a discretionary or accumulation and maintenance settlement. Normally, this is the same rate as income tax within a settlement, for example if any income is charged at 34 per cent, CGT will also be paid at 34 per cent (see Chapter 13).

Trustees have an annual exemption of half that available to an individual, ie £3,250 per annum. Where a settlor has created more than one settlement the annual exemption is divided between them.

> *Example*
> Albert creates four separate settlements. Each settlement will have an annual exemption of £812.50 (£3,250 ÷ 4).

This rule is subject to a minimum exemption per settlement of £650.

Chapter 6

DRAFTING SETTLEMENTS: SOME COMMON POINTS

6.1 INTRODUCTION

This chapter and the following two chapters concentrate on the drafting of settlements containing discretionary and A & M trusts. Interest in possession trusts are not considered in detail here having been dealt with in the LPC Resource Book *Wills, Probate and Administration* (Jordans, 1997).

As each client is unique, the available 'standard' precedents may not be appropriate for his requirements. In modifying an existing deed or drafting from scratch, a draftsman must be aware of the effect of every clause he includes and the effect of excluding a particular clause. In addition, he should aim for a consistency of style and not use both 'modern' and 'traditional' styles in the same trust instrument.

The basic structure of each settlement differs very little as the following comparative example shows. The clauses shown do not provide a definitive list of what can or should be included in a settlement but are the most important types of basic clauses. The main differences between the two settlements are the trusts of the beneficial interests, as the purposes of discretionary and A & M settlements are different. The drafting of the trusts of the beneficial interests is considered in Chapters 7 and 8. Additional powers required by trustees and their use are examined in Chapters 9 and 10. The administrative provisions are discussed in Chapter 13 but are broadly similar to those in will drafting. These and other provisions are often placed in Schedules.

Discretionary settlement	*Accumulation and maintenance settlement*
Date	Date
Parties	Parties
Recitals	Recitals
Definitions	Definitions
Perpetuity period	Perpetuity period
Accumulation period	Accumulation period
Trust (for sale)	Trust (for sale)
Trusts of the beneficial interests	Trusts of the beneficial interests
Trustee powers over the beneficial interests	Trustee powers over the beneficial interests
Administrative provisions	Administrative provisions
Appointment of new trustees	Restrictions on trustee's powers, so as not to take the settlement outside IHTA 1984, s 71
Exclusion of settlor and spouse	Appointment of new trustees
Stamp duty certificate	Exclusion of settlor and spouse
Schedules	Stamp duty certificate
Signatures	Schedules
	Signatures

6.2 DRAFTING COMMON CLAUSES

6.2.1   The date and opening words

It is usual for the date on which the settlement was made to be set out at the beginning of the trust instrument. In modern style settlements, this may be preceded by a table of contents (see **6.2.4**). The date may be important for subsequent time-limits and the chronology of events where a settlor has made more than one settlement. Some settlements are known by titles which include their dates, for example, 'Mrs Brown's Grandchildren Settlement of 4 April 1990'.

Sample clause

> **THIS SETTLEMENT is made the   day of   One thousand nine hundred and ninety**

6.2.2   Parties

The settlor and the initial trustees must be clearly identified. How this and the opening words are set out will also determine the style for the rest of the document, ie is it to be modern (Clauses 1 and 2) or traditional (Clause 3)?

Sample clause 1

> **BETWEEN**
> **(1) DAVID SMITH of [address] ('the Settlor')**
> **(2) TONY TUBBS of [address] and TOM THOMAS of [address] ('the Trustees') which expression shall where the context admits include the trustee or trustees for the time being of this Settlement**

Sample clause 2

> **PARTIES:**
> **(1) [   ] (the 'Settlor'); and**
> **(2) [   ] (the 'Trustees').**

Sample clause 3

> **BETWEEN DAVID SMITH of [address] (hereinafter called 'the Settlor') of the one part and TONY TUBBS of [address] and TOM THOMAS of [address] (hereinafter called 'the Trustees' which expression shall where the context so admits include the trustee or trustees for the time being of the Settlement) of the other part**

The definition of the trustees may instead come later in a clause which collects together all definitions used in the settlement.

6.2.3   Recitals

Recitals appear immediately after the parties and in traditional style settlements are introduced by the word 'Whereas'. The numbers or letters to the recital clauses are normally placed in brackets which distinguishes them from 'operative' clauses, ie the clauses declaring the beneficial interests.

Recitals explain the background to the settlement: why it has been created and the settlor's intentions.

A declaration that the settlement is to be irrevocable means that the settlor cannot subsequently change his mind about having created the settlement and demand his money or property back from the trustees. Whilst revocable settlements are possible, they are uncommon because of their unfavourable tax treatment. Where there is a power to revoke the trusts the result is that the fund may revert to the settlor or his spouse (see **6.2.10**).

Sample clause

> **WHEREAS**
> **(1) THE Settlor wishes to make this Settlement and has transferred or delivered to the Trustees the property specified in the Schedule**
> **(2) IT is intended that this Settlement shall be irrevocable.**

6.2.4   Table of contents, clause headings, definitions and Schedules

Table of contents

Because settlements are often long and complex, modern precedents generally start by setting out in a table of contents the constituent parts of the settlement, showing the operative parts separately from the administrative provisions. While this simplifies the use of the settlement it is important that a further clause ensures that the use of the table does not affect its meaning (see 'Clause headings' below).

Clause headings

Some draftsmen like to give each clause a heading as this enables a person who is reading the trust instrument to see quickly and clearly what each clause concerns. This can be particularly useful once the settlement is in use. For example, a trustee may want to know what powers of investment the trustees have. Rather than having to read every clause until he finds the investment clause he need only look at the clause headings to identify the one he needs to study. It is a matter of personal preference as to whether or not clause headings are used but they should either be used for every clause, or not at all. Where headings are used, it should be made clear by an additional clause that they are only for administrative convenience, ie they do not affect the construction of the trust instrument.

Sample clause

> **Clause headings**
> **THE clause headings are included for reference only and do not affect the interpretation of this Settlement**

Definitions

Many descriptions and phrases will need to be repeated, often several times, in drafting a settlement. It is, therefore, convenient to give these descriptions and phrases a 'name' by which they can be identified throughout the trust deed.

> *Example*
> Adam is settling a house, some cash and several holdings of quoted shares on discretionary trusts.
>
> Reference needs to be made to these assets being held on trust, being available for distribution, being invested and so forth.

Unless a 'name' is used, each time reference is made to them the trust deed will have to read: 'The Trustees shall hold the freehold house known as [address], £x cash, 500 shares in A plc etc upon trust ...'.

It is much neater and simpler to call the combined assets 'The Trust Fund' so that the clause would read: 'The Trustees shall hold the Trust Fund upon trust ...'.

It is good practice to give the first letter of the 'names' a capital letter to indicate to the reader that they are definitions.

There is a choice of where to record the definitions of the 'names':

(1) Definitions can be dealt with as and when they arise in the body of the deed, for example:

> **The Trustees shall hold the Trust Fund upon trust for such of them, David, Sue and Charles (hereinafter together called 'the Beneficiaries') as shall attain 18 years of age and if more than one in equal shares**

The problem with this approach is finding the definition when subsequently using the trust instrument. For example, Brenda is a trustee of an A & M settlement. She wants to know if the trustees have a power to apply income for the maintenance of a particular beneficiary. A glance through the clause headings shows her that she needs to study clause 18. In reading this clause, she comes across the expression 'the Accumulation Period'. She has no idea what it means and will have to read all the preceding clauses until she finds where the expression was used for the first time.

(2) Definitions can be contained in a schedule to the deed. A person reading the trust instrument who comes across a 'name' such as 'the Beneficiary' will know to turn to the schedule whenever he meets a 'name'.

(3) All the definitions can be set out in Clause 1 of the trust instrument. This is common practice in modern style settlements.

Sample clause

(1) Definitions

IN this deed where the context so admits
(a) 'the Trust Fund' shall mean ...
(b) 'the Beneficiaries' shall mean ...

Schedules

Schedules can serve a useful purpose in keeping the various parts of the settlement deed separate. Most settlements will contain at least one Schedule and some draftsmen like to consign everything but the clauses directly related to the trusts of the beneficial interests to Schedules.

Example

The 1st Schedule: definitions.

The 2nd Schedule: details of the trust property.

The 3rd Schedule: the necessary administrative provisions.

The 4th Schedule: miscellaneous clauses etc.

6.2.5 The trust fund

The settlement needs some property to be the subject-matter of the trusts from the outset. The settlor may add to the original trust property from time to time and other people may also transfer property to the settlement. All the trust property will be defined as the 'trust fund' and will be set out in detail in a Schedule.

When property is transferred from the settlor to the trustees, the correct mode of transfer must be used or the transfer will be ineffective. For example, shares must be transferred by signed stock transfer form and land by deed.

6.2.6 Trust or trust for sale?

Before the TLA 1996, it was usual practice for the trustees of inter vivos settlements to hold property on an express trust for sale. This ensured that a strict settlement under the SLA 1925 could not arise where land was settled property. The TLA 1996 prevents any new strict settlements being created after 31 December 1996 but does not prevent continued use of a trust for sale. Such use is likely only to continue where the settlor wishes the trustees to be under a duty to sell. If, instead, a power of sale is considered sufficient, the trustees will be directed to hold the settled property 'on trust' and will be given power of sale in the administrative provisions of the settlement. This approach is already adopted in some modern style settlements drafted before the TLA was enacted.

If a trust for sale is used, it has five constituent parts as shown in the sample clause.

Extracts from sample clause – trust for sale

1   **The Trustees shall hold the Trust Fund upon trust as to investments or property other than money in their absolute discretion to sell, call in or convert into money all or any of such investments or property**

2   **But with power to postpone such sale, calling in or conversion**

3   **To permit the same to remain as invested**

4   **Upon trust as to money with the like discretion to invest the same in their names or under their control in any of the investments authorised by this Settlement or by law**

5   **With power at the like discretion from time to time to vary or transpose any such investments for others so authorised**

6.2.7 Perpetuity – the trust period

Perpetual trusts

English law does not allow a private trust (as opposed to a charitable trust) to be perpetual. It must come to an end and the capital vest in a beneficiary within a limited period of time. The time from the creation of the settlement to the moment when the capital must vest is called 'the perpetuity period'.

Property does not have to vest in possession provided it has vested in interest by the end of the perpetuity period.

Example 1

Property is settled on Agnes for life with the remainder to Bert. Agnes has an immediate interest in possession (ie the right to the income) and Bert is guaranteed the capital although the actual receipt of the capital will be delayed until Agnes dies.

Agnes's interest is vested in possession.

Bert's interest is vested in interest.

Example 2

Property is settled on Connie for life with the remainder to David if he attains 25 years of age.

At the time the settlement is created, David is 5 years old. David will only become entitled to the settled property *if* he attains 25 years. Until then Connie's interest is vested in possession and David's interest is contingent.

David must fulfil the contingency, if he is to do so, within the perpetuity period. If he only attains 25 years *after* the perpetuity period has expired the trusts in his favour will be void.

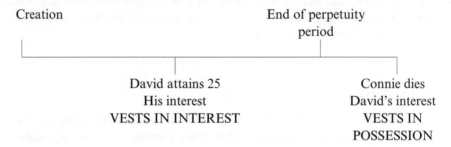

The trust is valid. There has been no breach of the perpetuity rules.

Contrast the following, where a short perpetuity period applies (see later).

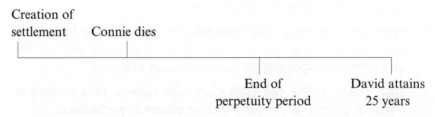

David has not obtained any vested rights before the perpetuity period expired. The trusts in his favour therefore fail.

The perpetuity period is, therefore, relevant when looking at A & M settlements where the gifts to children are contingent upon them reaching a specified age as in the previous example.

The perpetuity period also applies to discretionary settlements. Trustees select the beneficiary from within a class of beneficiaries and decide how much of the trust property to give that beneficiary. They must exhaust the trust fund, ie give a vested interest in the trust property, within the perpetuity period. A failure to do so will render void the trusts over any remaining property.

Example

£10,000 is settled on discretionary trusts for the children of X.

There are 3 children: Rose, Arthur and Kate. The stated perpetuity period is 10 years.

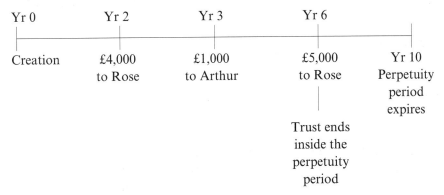

Selection of a perpetuity period

The settlor chooses the perpetuity period which is to apply to his settlement. It will be defined in the settlement as the 'trust period'. There is a common law period which is a life in being plus 21 years, but today most settlors and their professional advisors use the Perpetuities and Accumulations Act 1964 (PAA 1964) and adopt a fixed period of anything up to 80 years. The chosen number of years must be expressly stated in the trust instrument as the perpetuity period. If no mention of a perpetuity period is made in the trust instrument the common law rules will apply.

Sample clause – the trust period

THE Trust Period shall mean the period ending on the last day of the period of eighty years from the date of this Settlement which period shall be the applicable perpetuity period

6.2.8   Accumulations

Meaning of accumulations

Discretionary and A & M settlements are settlements without an interest in possession. However, the fact that no beneficiary has a right to the trust income does not mean that the trust property is not earning income. Where income is not being paid out to a beneficiary, it is retained by the trustees within the trust. Such retained income is said to be 'an accumulation'.

Accumulation periods

There is a limit to the number of years during which income can be accumulated. The PAA 1964 sets out a choice of maximum periods for which income can be accumulated. Most trust draftsmen specify that income can be accumulated for a fixed period of 21 years from the date of the settlement. Although this period is possibly shorter than the PAA 1964 would allow, a fixed period provides for certainty. The specified accumulation period must not exceed the perpetuity period applicable to the settlement. At the end of the accumulation period, all income arising in each future year must be paid out to the beneficiaries unless the beneficiary is a minor (see below).

Example

Property is settled on discretionary trusts for the benefit of Susan, John and Harry. The accumulation period is 21 years. The trust income is £300 per annum.

		Susan	John	Harry	Accumulated
Accumulation	Yr 1	100	–	–	200
	r 7	–	300	–	–
	r 8	100	100	100	–
period	Yr 15	–	–	–	300
After accumulation period ends	Yr 22	100	200	–	–
	Yr 23	100	100	100	–
	Yr 24	150	–	150	–

Extension of accumulation period

Where a beneficiary is a minor at the end of the accumulation period, s 31 of the TA 1925 allows the income of the minor's share of the trust fund to continue to be accumulated until he is 18 years of age.

Example

Three brothers were the beneficiaries of a discretionary settlement. The two older boys both died leaving Adam (aged 16) the only beneficiary. The settlement's accumulation period has just ended. The trustees may accumulate income for a further 2 years.

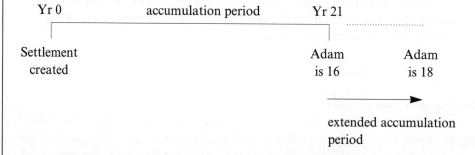

Sample clause

THE Accumulation Period shall mean the period of twenty-one years from the date of this Settlement or the Trust Period if shorter

As in **6.2.7**, the trust period means the perpetuity period applicable to the settlement.

6.2.9   Appointment of new trustees

If a new trustee needs to be appointed because, for example, one of the original trustees has died or wishes to retire, in the absence of anything to the contrary in the trust instrument, the choice and appointment rests with the continuing trustee(s). Under the TLA 1996 (unless expressly excluded by the trust instrument) beneficiaries of certain settlements can direct the retirement and appointment of trustees (see further **13.4.2**).

A settlor who wishes to continue to exercise sole control over the selection of trustees during his lifetime can do so only if the trust instrument gives him the appropriate power (see **13.4.2**).

Sample clause

> **DURING the lifetime of the Settlor the power of appointing new trustees shall be vested in the Settlor**

6.2.10 Exclusion of settlor (and spouse)

To prevent settlors using settlements to obtain an unfair tax advantage for themselves there are a number of anti-avoidance provisions in the tax legislation. Broadly, for each of the three main taxes these provisions require that neither the settlor nor his spouse has 'an interest in the settlement'. The phrase is directly relevant to income tax and CGT; for IHT the 'reservation of benefit' provisions discussed at **4.6.5** are relevant.

The general income tax avoidance rules (ICTA 1988, Part XV)

These complex, wide-ranging provisions are intended to prevent a higher rate tax payer from avoiding income tax on income by transferring the property which produces it to another person who either pays no income tax or pays at a rate lower than the transferor.

The rules apply to 'settlements'. These are defined (ICTA 1988, s 660G) to include 'any disposition, trust, covenant, agreement or arrangement or transfer of assets'. Thus, although they can in theory apply to any type of settlement, they are effectively restricted to two main areas. They apply to settlements 'where the settlor retains an interest in the settled property' (s 660A) and they apply specifically to settlements by parents for the benefit of their infant unmarried children (s 660B is discussed at **4.6.4**).

Section 660A is particularly wide-ranging. The income of the settled property 'shall be treated . . . as the income of the settlor and not as the income of any other person'. To avoid this income tax treatment, the settlor must show that the income is 'from property in which the settlor has no interest'. Any 'strings attached' whereby the settlor or his spouse could or might benefit from the settled property or its income in the future will be fatal to the settlor's tax-saving purpose.

Typically (but not exclusively), s 660A will apply where:

(1) The settled property will revert to the settlor, for example where the property is settled on A for life the remainder to the settlor. Such a settlement might be considered if a settlor wished to provide an elderly relative with an income but at the same time wanted to ensure return of the settled property when the relative died.

(2) The settlement contains a power of revocation whereupon the settled property would revert to the settlor or his spouse.

(3) The settlement contains a discretionary power to benefit the settlor or his spouse, ie they are among the objects of the trustees' discretion.

> *Example*
>
> Thomas created a discretionary settlement during his lifetime under which he and his wife Agatha may benefit because they are included in the class of beneficiaries, ie they are among the objects of the trust. Even if neither Thomas

nor Agatha actually benefits, for example because the trustees of the settlement accumulate the income or apply all of it for other beneficiaries, all of the income of the settled property will be taxed as though it belonged to Thomas.

Where the rules apply, the income of the property in the settlement is 'treated' as belonging to the settlor for all income tax purposes, although generally he can recover from the trustees any tax he has to pay on the income. If the settlor is a higher rate tax payer, the plan to save tax through using the settlement will not be achieved. Although the rules treat the income in a particular way for income tax purposes, they do not affect the entitlement of the settlement trustees to receive the income and to use it for the beneficiaries.

CGT where the settlor has an interest in the settlement

Where the settlor and the trustees are UK resident or ordinarily resident, anti-avoidance provisions (TCGA 1992, ss 77 and 78) similar to the income tax provisions (see above) prevent a settlor who would otherwise pay CGT at 40 per cent from using the settlement to realise his gains and pay tax at a relatively lower rate. These provisions apply where the settlor or his spouse has an 'interest in the settlement' and are widely defined. They apply (inter alia) 'if the settled property or its income will or may become applicable for the benefit of the settlor or his spouse'. In such cases, all gains are deemed made by the settlor and not by the trustees. The settlor, and not the trustees, must therefore pay tax on the settlement gains at the rate appropriate to the settlor, ie 20 per cent, 23 per cent or 40 per cent depending on his income tax position. As in the case of income tax, there is a right of reimbursement from the trustees for any CGT paid by the settlor.

Reservation of benefit and IHT

Although the phrase 'an interest in the settlement' is not found in FA 1986, s 102 nonetheless the concept lies behind the reservation of benefit provisions. These have been discussed at **4.7.5**. If settled property is subject to reservation of benefit for the settlor or his spouse, s 102 will apply with the result that the property is still within the settlor's estate for IHT.

Drafting the settlement

Where a settlor could or might benefit from income or capital the settlement is ineffective for tax purposes, ie the trust property is still taxed for income tax, CGT and IHT, as if it still belongs to the settlor. It is therefore essential that a settlor has no interest in the trust property. Because of the wording of the anti-avoidance provisions, the settlor's spouse must also be excluded from benefiting although it is permissible for a widow or widower of the settlor to be included as a beneficiary.

So as not to fall foul of these provisions a discretionary settlement will normally contain two references to the exclusion of the settlor and spouse; the first, in relation to the power to add new beneficiaries and the second in relation to the exercise of the administrative powers (see Appendix 4, clauses 3(3) and 15). Only the general exclusion in exercise of the administrative powers appears in an accumulation and maintenance settlement (see Appendix 5, clause 14) since a power to add beneficiaries is inappropriate to such settlements.

A settlor or his spouse does not have to be named as a beneficiary to be deemed to have an interest in the settlement. If the trust property will, or might, revert to the settlor at the end of the trust period he has an interest in the settlement.

The trust instrument may give the trustees very wide powers and discretions over the trust fund (see Chapter 9). For example, if the trustees can use their powers to benefit the settlor or his spouse, even though the power is never used, the settlor is deemed to have an interest in the trust property.

In drafting a settlement, therefore, it is essential to ensure that the beneficial interests are fully disposed of and that in no circumstances can the settlor or his spouse be said to have an interest in the settlement – see **7.4** and **8.4**. In addition, a clause should be included in the settlement deed to the effect that the settlor and his spouse cannot and must not benefit from the trust. This clause serves as a prohibition against trustees ever exercising a trust power in favour of the settlor or his spouse.

Sample clause

> **No discretion or power conferred on the Trustees by this Settlement or by law shall be exercised and no provision in the Settlement shall operate, directly or indirectly so as to cause or permit any part of the capital or income of the Trust Fund to become in any way payable to or applicable for the benefit of the Settlor or the spouse of the Settlor**

6.2.11   Stamp duty certificate

Stamp duty is a tax which is payable on some dealings with property involving documents or instruments. A settlement deed evidences that property has been voluntarily transferred (ie without consideration) from the settlor to the trustees. The Stamp Duty (Exempt Instruments) Regulations 1987 provide a list of categories of instruments which are now exempt from stamp duty and this list includes voluntary settlements (see **4.10**). The deed should contain a statement (certificate) to that effect.

Sample clause

> **IT is hereby certified that this instrument falls within Category L in the Schedule to the Stamp Duty (Exempt Instrument) Regulations 1987**

6.2.12   Signatures

A trust instrument is a deed and must be signed as such by the settlor, and the trustees as well to show their acceptance of the trusts. One witness is required to each signature.

Sample clause

> **SIGNED as a deed and delivered**
> **by [name of Settlor] in the**
> **presence of**

Chapter 7

DRAFTING DISCRETIONARY TRUSTS

7.1 INTRODUCTION

The aim of this chapter is to introduce drafting of the clauses which ensure that the settlement creates discretionary trusts. It should be read in conjunction with Chapters 5 and 6.

The settlement deed will begin with the identification of trustees, recitals and, if used, a definitions clause. The perpetuity period will normally be stated as being 80 years and the accumulation period 21 years from the date of the settlement. The settlement will also require trustee powers.

7.2 BENEFICIARIES

The major requirement of the definition of 'beneficiaries' is that it provides certainty, ie that the trustees can clearly identify who is within the class of beneficiaries. This may be achieved by naming the beneficiaries. However, this is not possible if the identity of potential beneficiaries is not yet known, for example, unborn children or the spouses of people who have not yet married. In such circumstances the beneficiary must be identified by description.

Sample clause

> **'The Beneficiaries' shall mean the following persons (whether now in existence or who come into existence during the Trust Period)**
>
> **(i) the settlor's children and remoter issue and the spouses widows and widowers (but not such widows or widowers as have remarried) of such children and remoter issue**

Example
Aisha created a settlement with a trust period of 80 years and the above clause 20 years ago. When she set up the trusts, she had three adult children, Ben, Cora and Deirdre, and one grandson, Edwin. The trustees wish to know who are the current beneficiaries.

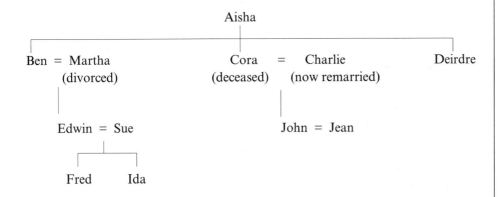

The beneficiaries are:

(1) Ben, Deirdre, Edwin, John, Fred and Ida because they are the issue of the settlor; and

(2) Sue and Jean because they are the spouses of the settlor's issue.

Martha and Charlie have been within the class of beneficiaries, but are now excluded. Martha's divorce from Ben means she is no longer his spouse; although Charlie was the spouse and then widower of the settlor's child, he has remarried.

If a person who was within the class of beneficiaries is subsequently excluded, because of a change in status, he does not have to pay back to the settlement any previous benefit he may have received from it.

Example
The facts are the same as in the previous example. After Cora's death the trustees gave Charlie £5,000. Charlie remarried 2 years later. He does not have to repay the £5,000 but is precluded from receiving anything more from the settlement.

7.3 THE DISCRETIONARY TRUSTS

The discretionary trusts apply to both income and capital of the trust fund. There are separate clauses for each. The component parts of these clauses are discussed at **7.3.1** and **7.3.2**. A full precedent of the clauses is found in Appendix 4.

7.3.1 Discretionary trusts of income

The primary trust
The primary trust enables the trustees to decide how to distribute the income of the trust fund amongst the beneficiaries.

Sample clause

> **The Trustees shall pay or apply the income of the Trust Fund to or for the benefit of such of the Beneficiaries as shall for the time being be in existence, in such shares and in such manner generally as the Trustees shall in their discretion from time to time think fit**

The clause gives trustees the choice not only of which beneficiaries to benefit, but also how to provide that benefit.

Example
Property is settled on discretionary trusts for the settlor's two grandchildren, Adam and Debbie. The annual income is £100 net. Adam is at university, reading medicine; Debbie is 16, at school and wants to be an actress.

For the last 2 years the trustees have made an outright payment of £100 per annum to Adam as he is not managing on his grant.

This year the trustees decide to buy one year's membership to the local theatre club for Debbie at a cost of £80 and pay the insurance premium (£20) on the bicycle she has bought herself to save bus fares.

Power to accumulate income

Trustees may not wish to distribute all the income every year. The PAA 1964 limits the length of time income can be accumulated. The accumulation period applicable to the settlement must be stated (see **6.2.8**) and without the need for a further clause the effect of stating the accumulation period is that during the period the trustees may exercise their discretion by retaining rather than distributing some or all of the annual income.

Example

Property is settled on discretionary trusts for Roger, Sally and Thomas. The stated accumulation period is 21 years and the annual income £120 net.

	Roger	Sally	Thomas	Accumulate
Year 1	40	70	10	–
Year 5	–	–	–	120
Year 6	40	40	–	40
Year 7	–	10	20	90
etc				

At the end of the accumulation period, all future income must be fully distributed each year.

Example

	Roger	Sally	Thomas	Accumulate
Year 20	30	40	20	30
Year 21	–	–	–	120
Year 22	40	60	20	
Year 23	40	40	40	
Year 24	–	120	–	
etc				

Power to use accumulated income

As a general rule, income received during the accumulation period and accumulated becomes part of the capital of the trust fund and so unavailable as income of future years.

The settlor may wish to give the trustees more flexibility.

Sample clause

> **The Trustees may under sub-clause [ ] apply the whole or any part of the income accumulated as if it were income arising in the then current year.**

The effect of this clause is that during the accumulation period any income retained from previous years can be made available to increase the income available in the current year.

Example

Property is settled on discretionary trusts for Gail and Martin. The accumulation period is 21 years and the annual income £100 net.

	Gail	Martin	Accumulate	Total of Accumulated Income
Year 1	75	25	–	nil
Year 2	–	–	100	100
Year 3	90	–	10	110
Year 4	60	60	–	90
etc				

Accumulated income at the end of the accumulation period

Where the trustees are given a discretion over the accumulated income, the settlement must direct what is to happen to any undistributed income at the end of the accumulation period.

Extract from clause

. . . and subject to sub-clause [   ] shall hold such accumulations as an accretion to capital

The power to accumulate and to use accumulated income to increase the available annual income can last only for the accumulation period. Any accumulated income which has not been spent by the end of the accumulation period is added to the capital of the trust fund.

Example

£5,000 is held on discretionary trusts for Penny and Nick. The accumulation period is 21 years and the annual income £100 net.

	Penny	Nick	Total of Accumulated Income	Capital
Year 20	90	–	320	5,000
Year 21	100	100	220	5,000
Year 22	60	40		5,220
Year 23 etc	50	50		5,220

7.3.2 Discretionary trusts of capital

The trusts over capital enable the trustees to decide how, when and to which beneficiaries to distribute the capital of the trust fund. The trustees will give effect to their decision by the exercise of a power of appointment.

The primary trust

Sample clause

> **The Trustees may pay or apply the whole or any part of the capital of the Trust Fund to or for the benefit of all or such of the Beneficiaries in such shares and in such manner generally as the Trustees shall in their discretion think fit**

Example

£10,000 is settled on discretionary trusts for Alice and Bertram.

Year 1:   Trustees decide not to pay out any capital.

Year 2:   Bertram is buying a car and the trustees decide to give him £2,000.

Year 15:   For 13 years the trustees exercised their power by not distributing any capital but this year gave £1,000 to Alice to help towards the cost of looking after her new baby and £5,000 to Bertram for alterations to his house.

Year 16:   The trustees decide that the costs of running the settlement outweigh its benefits and so bring it to an end by giving £1,000 each to Alice and Bertram.

Transfers on to other trusts

Sample clause

> **The Trustees may, subject to the application (if any) of the rule against perpetuities pay or transfer any income or capital of the Trust Fund to the trustees of any other trust, wherever established or existing, under which any Beneficiary is (whether or not such Beneficiary is the only object or person interested or capable of benefiting under such other trust) if the Trustees in their discretion consider such payment or transfer to be for the benefit of such Beneficiary**

The trustees may feel it appropriate to benefit a particular beneficiary by 'resettling' property on new trusts of which he is a beneficiary. This clause enables them to do so. The exercise of such a power is considered in Chapter 10.

7.4   ULTIMATE DEFAULT TRUSTS

All the capital and income of the trust fund must be fully distributed or be subject to vested interests by the end of the trust (perpetuity) period so that the trusts are not void for perpetuity. If for any reason the trustees have not distributed everything, the property remaining in the trust fund will revert back to the settlor. Even though in practice this never happens because the trustees do distribute fully, the fact that it could happen means that the settlor has an interest in the settlement and suffers adverse tax consequences (see **6.2.10**).

To ensure that 'reverter to settlor' can never happen, the settlement should contain an ultimate default trust, ie a clause directing who should receive any surplus left in the trust at the end of the trust (perpetuity) period.

This ultimate beneficiary must be living or in existence (eg a charity) and be given a vested interest in the trust fund at the date of the settlement. A settlor will often choose a charity as the ultimate default beneficiary.

Sample clause

> **SUBJECT as above and if and so far as not wholly disposed of for any reason whatever by the above provisions, the capital and income of the Trust Fund shall be held in trust for [name] absolutely**

Example

Many years ago, property was settled on discretionary trusts for the settlor's children and remoter issue with a charity as ultimate default beneficiary. The trust (perpetuity) period is 80 years. The settlor had one child (Tracy) when the trust was set up. Tracy had two sons Wayne and Calvin.

Since the settlement was created the trustees have distributed £170,000 of the trust fund but Wayne died when he was 6 years old, Tracy died 3 years ago and Calvin has just died having never had any children.

There is no other issue of the settlor and a surplus of £30,000 remains within the trust. The trustees must transfer this to the charity and bring the trust to an end.

Chapter 8

DRAFTING ACCUMULATION AND MAINTENANCE TRUSTS

8.1 WHAT ARE ACCUMULATION AND MAINTENANCE TRUSTS?

Settlors and testators often wish to settle property on contingent trusts, for example, 'on trust for X if he attains 25' or 'on trust for such of my grandchildren X, Y and Z as attain 21 and if more than one equally between them'. These are A & M trusts.

Although taking the form of a 'no interest in possession trust', A & M trusts permit contingent trusts to be established which do not attract the usual IHT charges associated with discretionary settlements, ie the periodic charge and the distribution (exit) charges will not apply. It is for these reasons that A & M trusts have become known as 'favoured category' or 'harmless' trusts for IHT since no liability will arise (apart from possible liability to IHT on creation). There is no equivalent treatment for income tax and CGT so that ordinary principles of liability will apply (see **13.5**).

8.1.1 The statutory straitjacket: IHTA 1984, s 71

The structure of an A & M settlement is not dissimilar from a discretionary settlement (see Chapters 5 and 7) but the particular skill required by the draftsman is to ensure that the settlement complies with the three requirements of s 71 of the IHTA 1984 (see **5.4.1**). These requirements impose a discipline on the draftsman not present when drafting interest in possession settlements or discretionary settlements. If the tax advantage is to be derived from the opportunities offered by s 71, the settlement (whether arising on death or inter vivos) must comply with all three requirements from the outset. Further, any possibility that the settlement may fail to comply with the requirements in the future will deny the settlement the IHT advantages which the settlor expected, ie A & M trusts will not have been established in the first place. Particular care is needed when drafting powers for the trustees. If any power is capable of exercise in a manner which is in breach of the requirements of s 71, an A & M settlement will not be created; the fact that the power is not actually exercised by the trustees does not matter. Restrictions on the manner of exercise of the trustees' powers are therefore commonly inserted in A & M trusts (see Appendix 5, clause 10) in order to ensure so far as possible the trust's A & M status is not prejudiced.

8.1.2 Trustee Act 1925, s 31

It appears that the parliamentary draftsman had the provisions of the TA 1925, s 31 in mind when drafting the provisions of s 71 of the IHTA 1984. In the case of the most basic A & M trust, the provisions of the TA 1925 automatically satisfy the requirements of the IHTA 1984. The consequence is that many contingent gifts on death, by will or under the intestacy law, to minor children and/or grandchildren are A & M trusts. The relevance of s 31 to contingent gifts by will to minors in the context of s 71 is considered in **11.6**.

8.1.3   Inter vivos A & M settlements

Clearly, the draftsman of an inter vivos A & M settlement must ensure that its trusts comply with the provisions of s 71 of the IHTA 1984. He may do so by drafting provisions as illustrated in **5.4** and by placing reliance upon s 31 of the TA 1925.

The trust mentioned earlier 'on trust for such of my grandchildren X, Y and Z as attain 21 and if more then equally between them' satisfies the three requirements of s 71 since:

(1)   self-evidently the capital entitlement arises at 21 but income entitlement arises earlier at 18 (s 31), ie the beneficiary becomes entitled on or before 25; and

(2)   income not applied by the trustees for maintenance, education or benefit must be accumulated (s 31), ie there is no subsisting interest in possession; and

(3)   again self-evidently all the beneficiaries have a common grandparent.

Although a settlement drafted in this manner provides the trustees with considerable discretion (through the provisions of the TA 1925, ss 31 and 32) and, therefore, flexibility, many settlors prefer to build greater flexibility into their settlements. If so, the draftsman is required to draft a settlement which complies with s 71 but which contains wider powers and discretions for the trustees.

8.1.4   The objectives of this chapter

The remainder of this chapter considers drafting A & M trusts containing an added degree of flexibility beyond that contained in the settlement described above. However, before proceeding further with this chapter, the explanation of s 71 of the IHTA 1984, and the examples provided in **5.4** should be reconsidered. A precedent for the principal clauses of an A & M settlement is in Appendix 5.

8.2   DRAFTING AN INTER VIVOS SETTLEMENT

8.2.1   The date, opening words, etc

The formal parts, ie the appointment of the original trustees and the recitals will follow the usual pattern (see Chapter 6). Within the definitions clause there will be statements as to the perpetuity period (normally an 80-year period) and the accumulation period (normally a period of 21 years from the date of the settlement); the beneficiaries will also be identified (see **8.2.2**).

8.2.2   The beneficiaries

The trust instrument must clearly identify the beneficiaries. For an A & M settlement to comply with s 71 of the IHTA 1984 there must be at least one beneficiary in existence at the date of the settlement.

It is normal practice to include each beneficiary's date of birth since this enables the trustees to calculate the beneficiary's age and to know the date when his interest will vest, ie in the income and capital of the trust fund. This may be important if steps are to be taken by the trustees in the future to avoid CGT liabilities (see **10.3.2**).

Sample clauses

The 'Primary Beneficiaries' shall mean:

(a)   The existing [grand]children of the Settlor namely

[   ] who was born on [   ];

[   ] who was born on [   ];

[   ] who was born on [   ]; and

[   ] who was born on [   ]; and

(b)   every other [grand]child of the Settlor born after the date of this Deed and before the Closing Date.

The 'Closing Date' shall mean whichever shall be the earlier of:

(a)   the date on which the first Primary Beneficiary to do so attains the age of 25; and

(b)   the date on which the Trust Period shall determine.

References to the children, grandchildren and issue of any person shall include his children, grandchildren and remoter issue, whether legitimate, legitimated [, illegitimate] or adopted [, but shall exclude any illegitimate person and his descendants].

Commentary on the clauses

If a settlor anticipates the possibility of further grandchildren being born after the settlement has been made, he may provide for them to be added to the class of beneficiaries. However, in this clause or separately within the definitions, the date on which the class is to close should be specified as the date when the first beneficiary attains a vested interest in the capital of the trust fund, ie when the contingency is first satisfied, or the end of the trust if this is earlier. If the class was to remain open beyond the date when the earliest vesting occurs, and if the trustees had distributed funds to a beneficiary whose interest had vested, the trustees would have paid out settled funds too early, ie before the class had closed. This would amount to a breach of trust by the trustees.

Example

Property is settled on A & M trusts for the grandchildren of Adam contingent upon them reaching 21 years of age. When the settlement is created Adam has two grandchildren: Belinda (16) and Charles (12). By the time Belinda becomes 21, no further grandchildren have been born. David, a grandson, is born 3 years later.

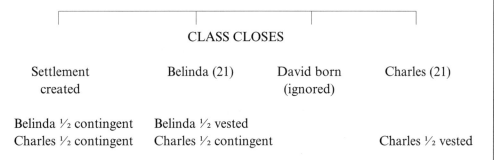

Settlement created	Belinda (21)	David born (ignored)	Charles (21)
Belinda ½ contingent	Belinda ½ vested		
Charles ½ contingent	Charles ½ contingent		Charles ½ vested

CLASS STAYS OPEN

Settlement created		
Belinda ½ contingent	Belinda (21)	David born
Charles ½ contingent	½ vested (but class is still open)	Belinda ⅓ vested
	Charles (17)	Charles (20)
	½ contingent	⅓ contingent
		David ⅓ contingent

It is possible to stipulate an age greater than 25 years as the closing date in the sample clause. If so, it will be important to provide elsewhere in the trust instrument that a beneficiary must attain a vested entitlement to income on or before 25 years, ie reliance can be placed on the alternative provision within the first requirement of s 71 of the IHTA 1984, see **5.4.1**.

The expression 'child or grandchild' etc always includes adopted and legitimated (grand) children and those whose parents are not married to each other. If the settlor wants to exclude any such person, a clause to that effect (eg as in the sample clause) should be included.

Where, as here, all beneficiaries are the 'grandchildren of a common grandparent' the settlement complies with the third requirement of s 71. Thus, the IHT advantages of the A & M settlement will not be limited to a 25-year period since the date of its creation (see **5.4.1**); they will remain available for however long the settlement may continue.

8.2.3 The principal trusts

The primary intention of the settlor should be stated in this clause, namely that the capital of the trust fund is to be held by the trustees for the beneficiaries until they attain the specified age. That age, in terms of s 71, may not exceed the age of 25 years. The age may relate to either the income entitlement or to the capital entitlement. Thus, at the very least, a beneficiary must become entitled to an interest in possession in the income on or before 25 years, even if the capital entitlement is deferred.

Sample clause

> **The Trust Fund shall be held upon trust for such of the Primary Beneficiaries as:**
>
> **(a) attain the age of 25 before the end of the Trust Period; or**
> **(b) are living and under that age at the end of the Trust Period**
>
> **and, if more than one, in equal shares absolutely.**

Commentary on the clause: capital provision

PERPETUITY RULES
To comply with the perpetuity rules, the contingent interests created by the A & M trust must vest within the perpetuity period chosen for the trust; this will normally be a period of 80 years.

This trust provides contingent gifts which are to vest in beneficiaries at the age of 25 years. Any beneficiary attaining that age within the trust period, ie the perpetuity period of the trust, will have a vested entitlement. Any beneficiary who is still under the age of 25 years when the trust period ends will nonetheless then immediately acquire a vested entitlement to a share of the trust fund. The perpetuity period is, therefore, complied with and the trusts are not void for perpetuity.

Example
Georgina settled property on A & M trusts for her grandchildren contingent upon them attaining 25 years of age. The perpetuity period was stated as 30 years. When the settlement was created there were two grandchildren in existence: Clara aged 10 years and Sara aged 3 years. A third grandchild, Petra, was born 6 years later.

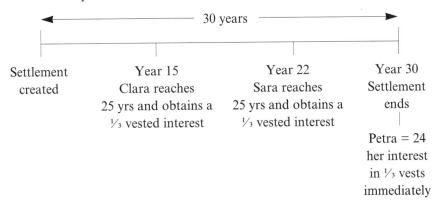

CAPITAL TO VEST AT 25 YEARS (OR SOONER)
It is usual for a settlor to provide that a beneficiary's entitlement to capital will vest at or before 25. A settlement drafted in this manner will clearly comply with the age requirements of s 71 of the IHTA 1984. The sample clause in the previous paragraph illustrates a provision of this type.

DELAYING THE RIGHT TO CAPITAL BEYOND 25 YEARS
If he chooses, a settlor may delay the age at which the beneficiary's capital entitlement is to vest. If he does so, the draftsman must then insert the appropriate age within the sample clause. Where capital entitlement is to vest beyond 25 years the settlement will (prima facie) not qualify as an A & M settlement. However, it can still be drafted to qualify based on the alternative aspect of the first requirement of s 71, ie an income entitlement on or before the beneficiary's 25th birthday (see below).

TRUSTEES ACT 1925, s 32
Section 32 of the TA 1925 gives the trustees power to apply capital for the advancement or benefit of a beneficiary who has an interest in the capital of the settlement. The power may be exercised where the beneficiary has a contingent interest even though the beneficiary may never satisfy the contingency, for example, because he dies before the age stipulated for the vesting of the capital. In the absence of contrary provision, s 32 will automatically apply to an A & M settlement to enable the trustees to advance up to one half of a beneficiary's presumptive, ie contingent entitlement to capital irrespective of the age to which the right to the capital has been delayed by the terms of the settlement. Its existence does not prejudice the A & M settlement.

The implied power may be modified when drafting the A & M settlement to enable the trustees to advance up to the whole of a beneficiary's presumptive entitlement in the same way as the power is often extended when drafting a will. The status of the settlement as an A & M settlement will not be prejudiced by an extension of the power in this way.

Commentary on the clause: income provision

INCOME ENTITLEMENT AT 18 YEARS

This clause contains no express reference to income. In particular, the clause has not attempted to vary the implied provisions of s 31 of the TA 1925 by substituting a later age of up to 25 years for the statutory age of 18 years. Income entitlement of the primary beneficiaries and the trustees' duty to accumulate surplus income must therefore be determined in accordance with s 31 of the TA 1925.

TRUSTEE ACT 1925, s 31

Unless expressly excluded, s 31 of the TA 1925 will automatically apply to the settlement. It serves a twofold purpose in the context of an A & M settlement:

(1) It ensures an income entitlement on attaining the age of 18 years (or any later age (not exceeding 25 years) which may be stipulated), ie the beneficiary has an interest in possession on or before the age of 25 years as required by s 71 of the IHTA 1984 (see **5.4.1**); and

(2) Until the age of 18 years (or later age) is reached the trustees have discretion to apply the income of the beneficiary's share for his maintenance, education or benefit and they are directed by the section to accumulate (by addition to the capital) any income which they have not applied. This direction to accumulate satisfies a further requirement of s 71 (see **5.4.1**).

Conclusion

The effect of the principal trusts considered above is to give the beneficiaries an entitlement to capital at an age which may exceed 25 years but an entitlement to income at 18 years. Until the age at which the income entitlement arises, the trustees have discretion to apply income for the maintenance, education or benefit of a beneficiary and a duty to accumulate any unapplied income (TA 1925, s 31). Accumulated income can be used as income in future years whilst the interest in capital is contingent. Any undistributed accumulations thereafter are added to the capital (TA 1925, s 31(2)). In addition, the trustees may apply capital under TA 1925, s 32.

8.3 WIDENING THE PRINCIPAL TRUSTS

An A & M settlement will frequently be drafted so that it provides the trustees with a greater degree of flexibility than the trust described above but which at the same time continues to satisfy the requirements of s 71 of the IHTA 1984. This can be achieved by widening the principal trusts which apply to the income and capital of the beneficiary's contingent share in the trust fund. In the sample clause which follows, the principal trust discussed at **8.2.3** is repeated (sub-clause (a)) and is extended by sub-clause (b).

Sample clauses

(a) The Trust Fund shall be held upon trust for such of the Primary Beneficiaries as:

    (a) attain the age of 25 before the end of the Trust Period; or

    (b) are living and under the age at the end of the Trust Period

    and, if more than one, in equal shares absolutely.

(b) The provisions of clause [ ] shall apply to the share of the Trust Fund to which any of the Primary Beneficiaries is or may become entitled under sub-clause [ ]. In those provisions, such share is called the 'Share' and that one of the Primary Beneficiaries who is primarily interested in the Share is called the 'Primary Beneficiary'.

Commentary on the clauses

Sub-clause (a) gives a beneficiary a contingent interest in the trust capital and the income which it generates. The wording ensures that beneficiaries will have a right to the income at 18 years (TA 1925, s 31) and the capital at 25 years and, therefore, satisfies s 71 of the IHTA 1984.

Sub-clause (b) establishes that a beneficiary's share of the trust fund is subject to further trusts (set out in later clauses of the trust instrument) which are exercisable by the trustees until the beneficiary's interest vests. The nature of these additional trusts over income and capital are considered below. In this way the trustees can be given additional flexibility over the trust income and its capital similar to the powers of the trustees of discretionary settlements (see Chapter 7).

Example

Property has been settled on A & M trusts for Sheila (16) and Ruth (14) contingent upon their attaining 25 years. Sheila will be absolutely entitled to half the property when she attains her 25th birthday. Until then, her interest in both the trust capital and any income it generates is contingent (see sub-clause (a)).

In the language of sub-clause (b), Sheila is the primary beneficiary of half of the trust fund, ie the 'Share' and so sub-clause (b) applies to create additional trusts over Sheila's contingent interest in half of the trust fund (see below).

8.3.1   Additional trusts applying to income

Sample clauses

(a) The Trustees may pay or apply any income of the Share to or for the maintenance or education or otherwise for the benefit of the Primary Beneficiary, or any other Primary Beneficiaries who are for the time being living and under the age 25.

(b) ... [applies to capital, see 8.3.2]

(c) Subject as above, the income of the Share shall, during the Accumulation Period, be accumulated as an accretion to the capital of the Share. Any such accumulations may, at any time, be paid or applied in the manner set out in sub-clause 5.1 as if they were income of the Share arising in the then current year.

(d)　Subject as above, s 31 of the Trustee Act 1925 (as modified below) shall apply to the income of the Share.

Commentary on the clauses

By sub-clause (a) the trustees may at their discretion apply income of a share of the trust fund for any primary beneficiary, ie they are not limited to applying the income for any particular primary beneficiary. The trustees have, in effect, a discretion to apply the income (for the stated purposes) for any of the beneficiaries.

Insofar as income is not applied, sub-clause (c) directs accumulation of the surplus income as an accretion to the share of the primary beneficiary, ie it is to be treated as part of the capital of that share and not of the whole trust fund. This sub-clause provides a duty to accumulate surplus income and so satisfies the requirement of s 71 of the IHTA 1984.

Sub-clause (d) merely reminds the trustees that s 31 of the TA 1925 applies to the trusts of the settlement but that where its effects are contrary to the express income provisions included in the settlement, ie sub-clauses (a) and (c), the express provisions take precedence.

Example 1

The trust fund in Sheila and Ruth's settlement consists of quoted shares and some cash on deposit with the bank. Trust income consists of dividends paid on the shares and interest on the deposit account. The net income of the trust fund in year 1 is £200. Sheila has the chance to go on a school activity holiday costing £80.

Her share of the trust fund is one half, so the trustees can apply up to £100 for her education.

Example 2

The income of the trust fund in year 2 is £100 net. Sheila and Ruth's interests are still contingent. Ruth would like music lessons which will cost £90. This is more than one half of the annual income. The clause allows the trustees to pay the income from Sheila's share for Ruth so that this year they may pay for Ruth's music lessons.

Example 3

Income of the trust fund in year 3 is £150 net. No income is applied by the trustees who must, therefore, accumulate it by adding £75 to each share of the trust fund still held for Sheila and Ruth.

8.3.2　Additional trusts applying to capital

Sample clause

The Trustees may also pay or apply any capital of the Share to or for the maintenance, education, advancement or otherwise for the benefit of the Primary Beneficiary. No capital may be so applied in a way which would or might prevent the Primary Beneficiary from becoming entitled to it, or to an interest in possession in it, on or before attaining the age of 25 ...

Commentary on the clause

The trustees may use some or all of the capital of the beneficiary's share of the trust fund before he satisfies the contingency. Unlike the additional trusts which apply to the income, the capital which can be made available is limited to the share, ie the capital of the share of other primary beneficiaries is not available. The effect of the implied power in s 32 of the TA 1925 is modified by this clause since the trustees may advance up to the whole of the capital.

The purpose of the limitation in the second sentence of the clause is to ensure that the trustees are not able to exercise their discretionary powers over the capital of the trust fund in such a way as to prevent a beneficiary's interest in the income or capital arising at or before his 25th birthday. The mere possibility of this happening would mean the settlement would not satisfy s 71 of the IHTA 1984, and so it would not be an A & M settlement.

The trustees may 'apply any capital of the Share for the . . . benefit of the Primary Beneficiary'. The trustees may consider it appropriate to exercise this power by resettling the beneficiary's share of the trust fund. They can do this provided the 'new' settlement does not infringe s 71 (see above and see further Chapter 10).

Example 1

Property is settled on Sylvie and Alison contingent upon them attaining 25 years of age. When Sylvie attains 22 years of age, she decides to buy a flat for £50,000. The trust fund is currently valued at £120,000.

Sylvie's contingent share is one half, ie £60,000 and so the trustees could apply £50,000 now. She would receive a further £10,000 when she attains 25 years.

Had the flat cost £80,000, the maximum the trustees could have applied would have been £60,000, and if they had given this amount to Sylvie it would have extinguished her right to any further capital.

Example 2

£10,000 has been settled on Ken (15) and Wayne (13) contingent on their attaining 18 years and, if they both attain that age, equally between them. Just before Ken's 18th birthday the trustees decide that he is too immature to be able to handle his share of the trust fund. Therefore, the trustees transfer £5,000 to the trustees of a new trust, the terms of which are that the capital and income of the trust fund are to be held on trust for Ken until he attains 25 years of age.

8.4 ULTIMATE DEFAULT TRUSTS

It is essential for tax reasons that the trust property can never revert to the settlor (see Chapter 6). A clause should, therefore, be included in the trust instrument which gives the capital (including accumulated income) to a named individual (or charity) absolutely. Such a clause would take effect only if the principal trusts fail for some reason, ie the trust property is not fully distributed to the intended beneficiaries.

Sample clause

> **In the event of the failure or determination of the above trusts, the capital and income of the Trust Fund shall be held upon trust for [such of the Primary Beneficiaries as are living at the date of this Deed, and if more than one, in equal shares] absolutely.**

Example

Property is settled on trust for Adam (14) and Lucinda (12) until they attain 18 years of age and, if they both attain that age, in equal shares.

Adam and Lucinda are killed in a car crash 2 years later. The trust property will revert back to the settlor unless a settlement contains a default trust.

8.5   RESTRICTIONS ON POWERS OF TRUSTEES

The trustees have wide powers which they can exercise over the settled property. They are given these by the settlement, by the general law or (commonly) by a combination of the two. There is the risk that the width of these powers could prevent the settlement from complying with s 71 of the IHTA 1984 and so never become an A & M settlement. To prevent this a clause placing restrictions on the trustees' powers is always inserted in the settlement deed.

Sample clause

> **In this clause, 'qualifying property' means any part of the Trust Fund which is for the time being property to which s 71 of the Inheritance Tax Act 1984 (or any statutory modification or re-enactment of such section) applies.**

> **Where the Trust Fund or any part of it would (in the absence of the restrictions imposed by this sub-clause) fail to be qualifying property by reason only of powers conferred on the Trustees by this Deed or by law, those powers shall be capable of being exercised only in a manner which does not prevent the Trust Fund or that part of it from being qualifying property.**

8.6   SUMMARY

Drafting an A & M settlement calls for continuous attention to the requirements of s 71 of the IHTA. Any clause which the draftsman uses should be very closely examined to ensure that its terms do not prevent the settlement from declaring A & M trusts. This is particularly important when the settlor requires as much flexibility as possible for his trustees.

Chapter 9

TRUST ADVANCES AND APPOINTMENTS

9.1 WHAT ARE ADVANCES AND APPOINTMENTS?

Dispositive powers of trustees over the trust capital

The result of exercising a power of advancement or appointment is generally the same. The trust property, or some part of it, will become subject to different beneficial interests. The property will either become the absolute property of a beneficiary, ie it ceases to be subject to the trusts of the settlement, or it will remain settled property subject to the trusts of the original settlement or of a new settlement. The trustees' powers may be sufficiently wide for them to 'declare new trusts' over some part of the trust property. The manner of the exercise of these powers is discussed further in Chapter 10.

A power of advancement may be available to the trustees as a statutory power (ie the power to advance trust capital under the TA 1925, s 32) or as an express power through provision in the trust instrument. Powers of appointment have no statutory form and so must appear, if at all, as express powers. Modifying the statutory power of advancement by express provision and the drafting of express powers are considered at **9.4** and **9.5**.

9.2 LEGAL SIMILARITIES AND DIFFERENCES

9.2.1 Similarities

Both powers are fiduciary powers and are dispositive in nature. Either can be exercised to create new beneficial interests for the beneficiaries of the trust under which the powers are exercisable. Generally, the powers are exercisable by the trustees for the benefit of beneficiaries who have been selected by the settlor of the settlement.

9.2.2 Differences

There are differences which relate to the existence of the powers and the manner of their exercise.

Existence of the powers

Only the power of advancement is statutory. Section 32 of the TA 1925 will be implied into every settlement but its effect may be extended or restricted by express provision in the settlement depending on the instructions given by the settlor at the time the settlement was created. If the power is to be exercised, careful consideration must first be given to the extent of the power available to the trustees. Section 32 of the TA 1925, and its possible modification, are considered at **9.4**.

A power of appointment can exist only if created by express provision in the trust instrument. A power which is widely drafted may permit advancements of the type permitted by s 32 and so render that provision superfluous. Drafting powers of appointment is considered further at **9.5**.

Exercise of the powers

POWER OF ADVANCEMENT

By exercising a power of advancement the trustees are effectively anticipating the beneficiary's entitlement under the settlement. For example, the trust property may be held by the trustees for a beneficiary contingently on his attaining 25 years. If the trustees exercise the power in the TA 1925, s 32 (or an equivalent express power) and advance capital to the beneficiary when he is aged 21, they anticipate his entitlement by bringing forward the time when he becomes absolutely entitled to the property.

POWER OF APPOINTMENT

The exercise of a power of appointment may have an effect similar to the exercise of a power of advancement provided the power is sufficiently wide in its terms. Alternatively, the exercise of the power of appointment may create a change of beneficial entitlement in the trust property while leaving the property subject to trusts. Those trusts may be the trusts established in the original trust instrument or they may be new trusts specifically created by the instrument which exercises the power.

> *Example*
> Trustees are holding property on trust for the settlor's grandchildren. There is a wide power of appointment over the settled property and its income enabling the trustees to appoint the property among the beneficiaries at such times and in such proportions and for such purposes as they think fit. In default of appointment, the trust property will pass equally to such of the settlor's grandchildren living at the date of the settlement who attain 18.

The trustees may exercise a power of this nature:

(1) to provide capital for the absolute benefit of any single beneficiary, or group of beneficiaries, even before the age of 18 years. They must exercise their powers in proper manner having regard to their fiduciary nature;

(2) to provide capital for one or more of the beneficiaries on their attaining 21 years, ie the power of appointment is executed to create new trusts in favour of beneficiaries selected from the class beneficiaries. If the power is exercised in this way, care must be taken to observe the perpetuity period applicable to the settlement (see **6.2.7**).

9.2.3   General and special powers of appointment

Powers of appointment are generally characterised as either special or general powers of appointment.

General powers

These powers permit the trustees to appoint to any person they may choose and are, therefore, uncommon. The settlor will generally wish to select the class of beneficiaries among whom the trustees may exercise the power. For this reason most settlements contain special powers of appointment.

Special powers

These permit the trustees to appoint to beneficiaries within a class chosen by the settlor. Two areas in particular require prior consideration before the trustees exercise a special power of appointment.

THE OBJECTS OF THE POWER

No power may be exercised in a manner which exceeds any limitations laid down by the settlor in the settlement. The exercise of the power of appointment must, therefore, be for the benefit of a member or members of a class of beneficiaries selected by the settlor. Although the settlor and his spouse may be within the class of beneficiaries, generally they will be excluded for tax reasons (see **6.2.10**).

THE PERPETUITY PERIOD

The property must vest in interest in the beneficiary in whose favour the power is to be exercised before the perpetuity period relevant to the settlement expires. In the case of special powers, this period is the period established by the settlement and which starts to run from the date of creation of the settlement (see **6.2.7**).

Example

The facts are the same as in the example at **9.2.2**. The perpetuity period is 80 years. Fifteen years after the settlement is created, the trustees appoint one quarter of the trust funds on trusts for two of the settlor's grandchildren, Hannah (aged 3) and Millie (aged 1) if they attain 21 years and equally between them if both do so.

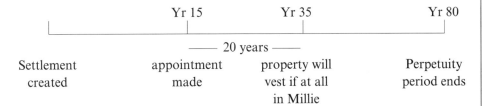

	Yr 15	Yr 35	Yr 80
	—— 20 years ——		
Settlement created	appointment made	property will vest if at all in Millie	Perpetuity period ends

As the property appointed by the trustees vests within the perpetuity period, the power is properly exercised.

9.3 PRACTICAL SIMILARITIES

The exercise of a power will require the execution by the trustees of a deed of advancement or a deed of appointment depending on the method selected by the trustees. However, a power of appointment is generally drafted in particularly wide form and will often allow the trustees to achieve by appointment all and more than they may be able to achieve by advancement under the statutory power in s 32 of the TA 1925. In such cases, the trustees will normally be advised to exercise their power of appointment and not the power of advancement. Careful consideration of the objectives and of the powers available to achieve them will be necessary before the appropriate deed can be prepared for execution.

The initiative for the exercise of the power will generally come from one or more of the beneficiaries, normally because they need money. The trustees must, on each occasion, consider whether they have adequate powers to satisfy the beneficiary's request and, if so, whether they wish to exercise those powers.

Any exercise of a power pursuant to such a request will have taxation implications. These should be fully considered before any power is exercised. Taxation aspects of the exercise of powers are considered in Chapter 10.

On occasion, the trustees rather than the beneficiaries will take the initiative as to the need to exercise a power and so begin discussion with the beneficiaries on the manner and method of exercise of the power. This usually happens where the trustees foresee a particularly disadvantageous tax position developing within the settlement and so propose a course of action, involving use of their powers, to circumvent it or at least to reduce the liability to tax. These aspects of the use of the trustees' powers are considered further in Chapter 10.

The exercise of either power may cause settled property to cease to be subject to trusts. In such cases the trustees will need to consider the method of transferring the trust property to the beneficiary. Similarly, if property becomes subject to new trusts, the trustees of the original settlement may need to transfer the property to the trustees of the new settlement. If the property remains subject to the original trusts, generally there will be no need for the property to be transferred to new trustees. The manner of vesting trust property in beneficiaries or new trustees is considered at **13.4.3**.

9.4 THE STATUTORY POWER OF ADVANCEMENT

9.4.1 The power of advancement

Section 32 of the TA 1925 states:

'(1) Trustees may at any time or times pay or apply any capital money subject to a trust, for the advancement or benefit, in such manner as they may, in their absolute discretion, think fit, of any person entitled to the capital of the trust property or of any share thereof, whether absolutely or contingently on his attaining any specified age or on the occurrence of any other event, or subject to a gift over on his death under any specified age or on the occurrence of any other event, and whether in possession or in remainder or reversion, and such payment or application may be made notwithstanding that the interest of such person is liable to be defeated by the exercise of a power of appointment or revocation, or to be diminished by the increase of the class to which he belongs:

Provided that –

(a) the money so paid or applied for the advancement or benefit of any person shall not exceed altogether in amount one half of the presumptive or vested share or interest of that person in the trust property; and

(b) if that person is or becomes absolutely and indefeasibly entitled to a share in the trust property the money so paid or applied shall be brought into account as part of such share; and

(c) no such payment or application shall be made so as to prejudice any person entitled to any prior life or other interest, whether vested or contingent, in the money paid or applied unless such person is in existence and of full age and consents in writing to such payment or application.

(2) This section applies only where the trust property consists of money or securities or of property held upon trust for sale calling in and conversion, and such money or securities, or the proceeds of such sale calling in and conversion are not by statute or in equity considered as land, or applicable as capital money for the purposes of the Settled Land Act 1925.

(3) This section does not apply to trusts constituted or created before the commencement of this Act.'

9.4.2 Commentary on the statutory power

The power is discretionary: the trustees 'may'
Beneficiaries cannot compel trustees to exercise the power. Before exercising this power, the trustees must ensure their intended use of the power is for a legitimate purpose. If not, it will be an improper exercise of the power which will be invalid and which may cause the trustees personal liability for loss suffered by the trust fund.

Interest in capital of the trust fund (or part)
Only beneficiaries with an interest in the capital may benefit from exercise of the power. However, the interest may be any of the following:

(1) absolute or contingent (on attaining any age or on any other event occurring);
(2) in possession, remainder or reversion.

It does not matter that a beneficiary's interest is liable to be defeated or diminished by the occurrence of a future event, for example, because the beneficiary may die at a young age and never reach the age at which the interest vests. As a principal beneficiary of a discretionary settlement has merely a hope of benefiting by the exercise of the trustees' discretion, he has no interest in the capital of settlement within s 32.

> *Example*
> Trustees are holding £10,000 on trust for Saul contingent upon his attaining the age of 25 years (if he dies under the age of 25 the money is to go to charity). On his 18th birthday, the trustees advance £2,500 to enable Saul to go to university. This is a proper exercise of the power even though Saul may die before his 25th birthday.

Limitations on the exercise of the power
The trustees may exercise their power only where it is for 'the advancement or benefit' of the beneficiary. 'Advancement' is normally considered to cover capital payments designed to 'set the beneficiary up in life (often in a business)' or payments made on the occasion of marriage. 'Benefit' has a particularly wide meaning. It has been held *Pilkington v IRC* [1964] AC 612 to have a meaning wide enough to permit the trustees to exercise their power of advancement (a 'Pilkington advance') by creating new trusts in relation to settled property if such is for the benefit of the beneficiary.

> *Example*
> Trustees are holding £100,000 on A & M trusts for Martha when she attains 25 years. She is now aged 24, is wealthy and has two children aged one and 3 years. She would prefer the funds transferred to trustees for her children so that IHT may be avoided if she should die soon after her 25th birthday. The trustees may exercise their power and advance some of the settled funds onto accumulation and maintenance trusts for Martha's children.

The statutory power limits the trustees to paying or applying 'not more than one half' of a beneficiary's presumptive or vested share. If the power is exercised, the amount paid or applied must be 'brought into account' if the beneficiary later becomes entitled to a share in the trust property, ie hotchpot applies to the sum advanced.

Prior life or other interests

The statutory power can be exercised only if consent is obtained from a beneficiary with a prior interest. For example, if property is held on trust for a beneficiary for life and then for other beneficiaries in remainder, the trustees could not exercise their power in favour of the remaindermen without the consent of the life tenant.

9.4.3   Modifying the statutory power

Normally, only minor amendments, as discussed below, need to be made to the statutory form of the power. They are similar to those made when drafting a will for a testator. As mentioned at **9.2.2**, it is often the case that a settlement contains a wide power of appointment. If so, the trustees may prefer to exercise this power rather than the statutory power, even in modified form.

The alterations made by express provision to the statutory power of advancement are normally:

(1)   to permit the trustees to pay or apply up to the whole (not merely one half) of a beneficiary's presumptive or vested share;
(2)   to remove the requirement that hotchpot will apply on distribution of the settled property.

It is unnecessary to consider extending the circumstances in which the statutory power can be exercised by the trustees. The phrase 'advancement or benefit' is generally considered sufficiently wide, especially in view of the particularly wide meaning of the word 'benefit'.

9.5   DRAFTING POWERS OF APPOINTMENT

As there is no statutory power of appointment, all powers must be drafted as express powers in a trust instrument. The precise form which the power takes will depend upon the particular settlement which is to be drafted. Powers of appointment are considered at **7.3.2** and **8.3** in connection with drafting discretionary settlements and accumulation and maintenance settlements.

9.6   TAXATION ASPECTS OF THE EXERCISE OF POWERS OF ADVANCEMENT AND APPOINTMENT

As each power is exercisable in relation to the trust capital, ie the property in the settlement, it follows that only the IHT and CGT aspects of the exercise of the power need be considered by the trustees before the power is actually exercised. These are discussed in Chapter 10.

Chapter 10

THE EXERCISE OF POWERS OF ADVANCEMENT AND APPOINTMENT

10.1 INTEREST IN POSSESSION SETTLEMENTS

10.1.1 The nature of the trusts and the powers

Settlements with an interest in possession are more often created by will than by inter vivos disposition. When created by will, the testator is normally seeking to provide his spouse with an income for life and to control the devolution of the capital thereafter by his own will, often by providing that the capital shall pass to children of an earlier marriage. A settlor who is contemplating a lifetime settlement will be better able to achieve his objectives through the use of either a discretionary settlement or an A & M settlement combined with careful selection of trustees and the use of a 'letter of wishes' written to the trustees (see further **13.4.1**).

However, many interest in possession settlements created by will do exist and not infrequently the trustees, after the death of a testator, are asked to exercise powers in relation to the capital of the trust.

Property settled on interest in possession trusts (as well as on other trusts) will normally be held by the trustees upon a trust for sale. The beneficial trusts provide the life tenant with an income for life and the remainderman with an interest which vests in possession on the life tenant's death.

Example
Trustees hold settled property worth £200,000 on trust to pay the income to Aida for life, thereafter for Carmen in remainder. Aida has an interest in possession, ie the right to income produced by the trust property. Carmen has the right to receive the trust property when Aida dies.

Carmen's interest in the example, is an interest in remainder but is often called (albeit incorrectly) 'a reversionary interest'. It is a valuable asset which can be professionally valued, ie a value can be placed on Carmen's right to receive the trust property when Aida dies. Since Carmen has the right to receive the trust property only when Aida dies, the value of the interest in remainder may be significantly less than the current value of the settled property. The value will be influenced (inter alia) by the prospective life expectancy of Aida. Carmen's interest in remainder is an asset which she may consider selling or possibly giving away as part of her estate planning arrangements (see **4.6.2**).

Example
If Carmen waits until Aida dies, she will receive the full trust fund (currently valued at £200,000). Carmen, however, is in need of some money immediately and decides to sell her interest in remainder to David:

(1) Assuming Aida is 84 years old, David might pay Carmen £175,000 for the right to receive the trust fund when Aida dies.

(2) Assuming Aida is 35 years old, David might pay Carmen £40,000 for that right.

If Carmen's sale is for full value, no IHT nor CGT would be payable by her. If, instead, she gave her interest in remainder to David, no tax would be payable (see **4.6.2**) because:

(1) her interest in remainder is 'excluded property' for IHT purposes, ie it is not in Carmen's 'estate' and so may be given away free of IHT, and
(2) as a beneficial interest in settled property acquired without any payment by Carmen, it is exempt from CGT on a disposal whether by sale or gift.

The trustees' power to advance capital in s 32 of the TA 1925 applies to an interest in possession settlement although it may have been modified by express provision in the trust instrument. Any exercise of the statutory power to pay or apply trust property would, unless also suitably modified, require the prior consent of the life tenant.

10.1.2 Provision of capital for the beneficiaries of an interest in possession settlement

Apart from capitalisation of a life interest on an intestacy, there are three methods of providing the beneficiaries with capital from the trust:

(1) By the exercise of an express power of advancement. Only if the trust instrument contains express provision can the trustees advance capital to or for the benefit of the life tenant.
(2) By the exercise of the statutory power in s 32 of the TA 1925 in favour of the remainderman (with consent of the life tenant). The decision to exercise either of these powers is a matter for the trustees. Their decision will generally follow an approach by the beneficiary with a request for the advance of some money. The trustees' decision should be formally recorded either:

    (a) by a minute in the trustees minute book for the trust (if any); or
    (b) by signing a separate notice to the effect that, in exercise of a power contained in the settlement or in s 32 of the TA 1925 certain property is advanced from the settlement to a named beneficiary. This notice should be retained with the trust instrument and records.

(3) By partitioning the trust fund between the life tenant and the remainderman (see **10.1.3**).

10.1.3 Partitioning the trust fund

In the absence of an express power to advance capital to a life tenant, capital may be provided by 'breaking the trust' under the rule in *Saunders v Vautier* (1841) 4 Beav 115. 'Trust busting' under this rule allows beneficiaries who are sui juris and together entitled to the whole beneficial interest in the trust fund to bring the settlement to an end and to direct the trustees to transfer the property as they wish.

If the beneficiaries decide to end the trust in this way, they will need to reach agreement as to the value of their respective beneficial interests, ie a value needs to be placed on the life tenant's right to receive income for life and on the remainderman's right to receive the capital of the trust on the life tenant's death. Agreement may be reached informally between the beneficiaries or by formal valuation by an actuary instructed to act on their behalf.

Example

Trustees hold £10,000 on trust for Mary for life, William in remainder. Mary and William agree that their respective interests are worth 40% and 60% of the settled property. They may direct the trustees to sell the trust property and to divide the sale proceeds between them in the agreed proportions.

Instead of directing the trustees to sell the trust property as in the example, the beneficiaries may prefer to direct the trustees to divide the assets between them so that each beneficiary receives the appropriate proportion of the trust fund. This method of division will require each asset to be valued separately. It may be necessary for the trustees to use cash to achieve exactly the correct proportions of the funds for each beneficiary.

Example

The facts are the same as in the previous example. The £10,000 trust fund is made up of shares in A plc valued at £5,000, shares in B plc valued at £4,000 and £1,000 cash.

William will receive:
– £3,000 A plc shares;
– £2,400 B plc shares;
– £600 cash.

Mary will receive:
– £2,000 A plc shares;
– £1,600 B plc shares;
– £400 cash.

Before the settled property is actually distributed among the beneficiaries, the trustees must first consider the taxation implications.

10.1.4   Taxation implications of provision of capital for the beneficiaries

The exercise of the statutory or express power of advancement has capital tax implications which the trustees must consider before releasing the formerly settled property from their control. The trustees must ensure that they have retained control over sufficient of the trust property where they become personally liable for tax as a result of the exercise of a power. Normally they will retain some of the trust property in their own names until all liabilities have been discharged.

IHT

The 'estate' of an individual is defined (IHTA 1984, s 5) for IHT purposes as 'all the property to which he is beneficially entitled' and this includes property in which he has an interest in possession. This is the position of a life tenant.

Example

Edwin is the life tenant in a trust with a fund of £100,000. He also owns a house and shares worth £80,000, Edwin's estate for IHT purposes is £180,000.

The inter vivos termination of an interest in possession is a PET provided the property is then held for (inter alia) one or more of the beneficiaries absolutely, ie the settlement has come to an end. Tax (calculated in the normal manner where there is a 'failed' PET) will only be payable if the former life tenant dies within 7 years of termination of the settlement (IHTA 1984, ss 52(1) and 3A). IHT may, therefore, become payable where a power is exercised to provide capital to beneficiaries in the three ways mentioned below. If IHT is payable, it is the trustees of the settlement who must pay it to the Inland Revenue and who should therefore reserve funds for the purpose.

EXPRESS POWER OF ADVANCEMENT

If the trustees exercise a power to advance all of the capital to the life tenant, his interest in possession will determine in the capital advanced. However, no IHT will be payable. This is because there is no fall in the value of his estate since for IHT purposes he is deemed already to own that property which is actually being advanced (IHTA 1984, s 53(2)).

Example

Trustees hold trust property valued at £50,000 on trust for Leonard (an adult) for life, and subject thereto for Rachel in remainder. The trustees advance the whole fund to Leonard whose free estate is worth £100,000.

Before the advance:

Leonard's estate	£100,000	
Trust fund	£ 50,000	£150,000

After the advance:

Leonard's estate £100,000 + £50,000 advanced = £150,000.

STATUTORY POWER OF ADVANCEMENT

If the life tenant consents to the trustees exercising their power to advance the capital to the remainderman, his interest in possession ends in that part of the settled property. A PET is made by the life tenant which becomes chargeable only if he dies within 7 years of the advance (IHTA, ss 52(1) and 3A).

Example

Trustees are holding £100,000 for Lionel for life, and subject thereto for Rowland in remainder. Lionel consents to an advance to Rowland of £10,000. If the PET becomes chargeable, any IHT payable on £10,000, ie the value of the property in which Lionel's interest in possession has ended, is payable by the trustees from the trust fund.

PARTITION OF THE TRUST FUND

If, by agreement, the fund is partitioned, the life tenant's interest in possession ends in the trust property which passes to the remainderman. This too is a PET made by the life tenant. IHT is payable by the trustees on that portion of the trust fund if the life tenant dies within 7 years of the partition (IHTA 1984, s 52(2)).

Example

Trustees are holding £100,000 for Linda for life, and subject thereto for Rowena in remainder. Linda and Rowena agree to partition the fund between them in the proportions 30:70. Linda makes a PET of £70,000 (£100,000 − £30,000 = £70,000). IHT is payable by the trustees (if Linda dies within 7 years of the partition) on the proportion of the funds which pass to the remainderman.

CGT

Liability to CGT can occur only if there is a disposal of chargeable assets. Disposals may be actual or deemed. No actual disposal occurs on the exercise by the trustees of their power of advancement. However, in each case there is a deemed disposal. Actual disposals by trustees are considered in Chapter 13.

DEEMED DISPOSALS (TCGA 1992, S 71)

A deemed disposal occurs when an individual becomes 'absolutely entitled' to settled property against the trustees, for example, on any of the occasions mentioned in **10.1.2**. The trustees are deemed to dispose of each item of settled property at its market value and to re-acquire it immediately at the same value as nominees for the beneficiary, ie they continue to hold the property in their names as bare trustees for the beneficiary. The property is no longer settled property but belongs to the beneficiary whose acquisition cost of the property is the market value when the re-acquisition occurred.

> *Example*
> Trustees appoint 1,000 ABC plc shares worth £10,000 to Lindsay, the life tenant of an interest in possession settlement. A deemed disposal occurs. The shares were worth £2,000 when the settlement was created.

Disposal consideration	£10,000
Less: acquisition cost	£ 2,000
	£ 8,000
indexation allowance (say)	£ 1,000
gain	£ 7,000

Lindsay's acquisition cost of the shares is £10,000.

RELIEFS, EXEMPTIONS AND RATE OF TAX

If any tax is due, it is calculated at 23 per cent of the chargeable gain and is payable by the settlement trustees. As their deemed disposal gave rise to the gain, any tax is their liability. They pay the tax from the settled funds. If a loss occurs, the trustees can claim relief for it by setting the loss against their gains on other disposals of trust assets in the same or future tax years.

Before calculating their liability to tax, the trustees may deduct an annual exemption of £3,250, ie one half of the exemption available to individuals.

On the joint election of the trustees and beneficiaries hold-over relief will be available when assets leave a settlement if:

(1) the settled property comprises business property (see **4.4.5**); or
(2) the occasion gives rise to an immediate liability to IHT, ie it is not a PET. This is not the case where property ceases to be subject to an interest in possession settlement (but see **10.2.7** and **10.3.2** for discretionary settlements and accumulation and maintenance settlements).

10.1.5   Drafting a deed of partition

Heading and date

Sample clause

DEED OF PARTITION

DATE: [   ]

Parties

Normally, there will be three parties:

(1)   the life tenant (who gives up the right to income in part of the trust fund); and
(2)   the reversioner (who gives up the right to part of the capital of the trust fund); and
(3)   the trustees.

Sample clause

> **(1) [name] ('the Life Tenant');**
> **(2) [name] ('the Reversioners'); and**
> **(3) [name] ('the Trustees')**

Recitals

A number of recitals will be included to explain the background circumstances giving rise to the partition.

Sample clause

RECITALS

(A) This Deed is supplemental to the settlement (the 'Settlement') [and to the other documents and events] specified in the First Schedule.

(B) The Trustees are the present trustees of the Settlement.

(C) Under and by virtue of the Settlement and in the events which have happened, the Life Tenant is entitled to the income of the Trust Fund for life and, subject thereto, the capital and income of the Trust Fund is held upon trust for the Reversioners [in equal shares] absolutely.

(D) The Trust Fund presently consists of the property described in Parts 1 and 2 of the Second Schedule.

(E) It has been agreed between the Life Tenant and the Reversioners that the Trust Fund shall be partitioned so that [   ] per centum as described in Part 1 of the Second Schedule ('the Life Tenant's Share') shall be held for the Life Tenant absolutely and the balance remaining being [   ] per centum as described in Part 2 of the Second Schedule (the 'Reversioners' share'), shall be held for the Reversioners in equal shares absolutely.

(F) The Trustees have agreed, following the joint request of the Life Tenant and the Reversioners, to release the Trust Fund to the parties respectively entitled under the above agreement.

[(G) This partition is carried out following and in accordance with actuarial advice.]

The clauses assume that there is more than one reversioner and that the reversioners agree to divide their share equally between them. Amendment will be needed for the case where there is only one reversioner. If actuarial advice as to value has not been obtained, clause G should be deleted.

The operative part

Normally, there will be two clauses, one each for the life tenant and the reversioner, whereby they respectively assign and surrender to the other their interest in the income or capital of the trust fund. The consequence is that the trust property is freed from the trust and may be transferred by the trustees in accordance with the arrangement mentioned in the recitals.

Sample clause

OPERATIVE PROVISIONS

1. Definitions and construction
In this Deed, where the context admits, the definitions and rules of construction contained in the Settlement shall apply.

2. Assignment by Life Tenant
The Life Tenant hereby assigns [his/her] interest in the Reversioners' share to the Reversioners in equal shares absolutely, to the intent that such interest shall merge and be extinguished in the reversion and that the Reversioners shall become entitled to the Reversioners' share [in equal shares] absolutely.

3. Assignment by Reversioners
The Reversioners hereby assign their respective interests in the Life Tenant's Share to the Life Tenant absolutely, to the intent that the life interest and the reversion shall merge, the life interest shall be enlarged and the Life Tenant shall become entitled to the Life Tenant's Share absolutely.

4. Payment of tax
Without prejudice to the provisions contained in clause 5, it is hereby agreed and declared that any inheritance tax occasioned by the partition in respect of the Reversioners' Share shall be borne by that share and any capital gains tax occasioned by the partition shall be borne by the Life Tenant and the Reversioners in the same proportions as they become absolutely entitled to the Trust Fund.

5. Trustees' lien
Nothing in this Deed shall prejudice or impair in any way any lien to which the Trustees are entitled in respect of any claim for costs, charges or expenses or in order to protect themselves against any tax liabilities.

Clauses 4 and 5 above deal with liability to IHT and CGT which may arise following the partition and the position of the trustees who are liable for that tax. This has been considered at **10.1.4.**

Schedules

The first Schedule will give details of the settlement which is to be ended, ie the date and parties to it. A second Schedule will detail the division of the trust property between the life tenant and the reversioner in accordance with the agreement stated in the recitals.

10.2 DISCRETIONARY SETTLEMENTS

10.2.1 The nature of the trusts and the powers

Whereas a life tenant of an interest in possession trust has a right to enjoy the income of settled property, a person who is among the class of beneficiaries of a discretionary settlement has no such right. As an object of the trustees' discretion, he has no right to capital or income unless and until the trustees exercise their discretion. He has a mere hope of benefiting.

Drafting the dispositive provisions of a discretionary settlement is considered in detail in Chapter 7. Generally, the trusts are drafted in as wide a form as possible. Such wording permits maximum possible flexibility for the trustees. They can pick and choose between beneficiaries. They have power to appoint absolute interests or to make trust appointments, ie to create new trusts in favour of the beneficiaries. Unless and until this power is exercised, the trust fund and its income will be subject to default provisions.

10.2.2 Taxation implications of exercising the power of appointment

The exercise of the power will affect the capital of the settlement. Before exercising it, the trustees must consider the IHT and CGT implications. Having done so, additional clauses may be inserted in the deed of appointment dealing with the payment of the tax (see **10.2.8**).

10.2.3 IHT

Settlements without an interest in possession (IHTA 1984, ss 58–69) are subject to their own regime. The concept of ownership of the settled property by the bene-ficiaries is not relevant. The settlement is a taxable entity in its own right. Rates of tax are limited to half the rates applicable on death, ie a maximum rate of 20 per cent applies, although tax is often charged at rates considerably less than 20 per cent (see **10.2.4**).

The regime charges IHT on 'relevant property', ie settled property in a settlement in which there is no qualifying interest in possession. A qualifying interest in posses-sion includes one to which an individual is beneficially entitled, for example, the life tenant in an interest in possession settlement.

There are a number of occasions when a discretionary settlement is charged to IHT (in addition to the charge which may have arisen when the settlement was created, see Chapter 5). These include the periodic charge and the distribution (exit) charge.

The periodic charge

This is an anniversary charge at 10-yearly intervals on relevant property in the settlement immediately before the 10th anniversary. The anniversary is calculated from the date of the settlement (or the date of death if the discretionary settlement was created by will).

Example

A discretionary settlement is created on 1 July 1993, the first 10-year anniversary charge falls on 1 July 2003 and the second on 1 July 2013, etc.

The distribution (exit) charge

A charge also arises when certain events occur. The most common occasion is when property leaves the settlement, for example, on the exercise of a power of appointment by the trustees. Another occasion is when property ceases to be subject to the discretionary trusts because an interest in possession has arisen in some part of the settled property, ie there is now a qualifying interest in possession. Such an interest may arise following the exercise by the trustees of a power of appointment whereby a beneficiary is given a right to income but not to capital (see also *Sansom v Peay* [1976] 3 All ER 353 – see **4.7.4**). This charge is based on the number of complete quarters (periods of 3 months) the property has been in the settlement since its creation or the previous periodic charge. There are 40 quarters in a 10-year period. If property has been in the settlement for 5 years, 20 quarters will be relevant.

10.2.4   The distribution (exit) charge before the first 10-year anniversary

A special provision operates to calculate the charge when property leaves a settlement before the first periodic charge.

To calculate the liability to IHT, it is necessary to calculate the settlement's rate of IHT and then to apply that rate to the fall in the value of the trust fund, for example, the fall in value when property leaves the settlement following the exercise of a power of appointment. The value of the trust fund when the charge arises is not relevant to this calculation. To calculate the exit charge, it is necessary to follow five steps:

Step 1: Ascertain the value of a hypothetical chargeable transfer

This is done by adding together:

(1)   the value of the trust property on creation; and
(2)   the value of property added to the settlement after its creation, if any (using the value when added); and
(3)   the value of property in any related settlement (ie the value at creation of any other settlement created by the settlor on the same day).

Step 2: Ascertain the tax on this hypothetical transfer

The rate of tax is ascertained from the current table of rates, ie 0 per cent and 40 per cent where the nil rate band is exceeded. Any chargeable transfers made by the settlor in the 7 years before the settlement was created are taken into account. Although the settlor's cumulative total is in this way relevant to the charge, no account is taken of any other transfers made on the same day as the settlement. Thus, if the discretionary settlement is created by a will, no account is taken of the deceased's estate (although his cumulative total of chargeable transfers will be relevant). Tax is calculated at 20 per cent, ie half the death rate, even if the discretionary settlement is created by will.

Step 3: Ascertain the settlement rate of tax

The tax calculated in Step 2 is converted to an estate or average rate. The rate at which tax is then charged, 'the settlement rate', is 30 per cent of this rate. Thus the maximum rate is 30 per cent × 20 per cent (Step 2) = 6 per cent.

Step 4: The charge to IHT

IHT is charged on the fall in value of the trust property, as a result of the exercise of the power of appointment, at the rate of one fortieth of the settlement rate for each complete quarter (3 months) between the setting up of the settlement and the event giving rise to the liability. If an appointment had occurred within the first quarter, there would be no liability.

Step 5: Paying the IHT

Example 1

A settlor settles £100,000 on discretionary trusts on 1 July 1995. On 1 February 1998 the trustees appoint £50,000 to a beneficiary.

Assume that at the time the settlement was created the settlor had made no previous transfers, ie he had no cumulative total.

Step 1:	Hypothetical chargeable transfer (ignore added and related property)		£100,000
Step 2:	Ascertain tax payable		
	Hypothetical transfer	£100,000	
	Less: nil rate band (part)	£100,000	nil
Step 3:	Ascertain settlement rate		nil
	IHT – nil		

Example 2

Assume that the settlor's cumulative total of chargeable transfers was £125,000 and that he paid the IHT when the settlement was created.

Step 1:	Hypothetical chargeable transfer (ignore added and related property)		£100,000
Step 2:	Ascertain tax payable		
	Settlor's cumulative total	£125,000	
	Nil rate band (part)	£125,000	
	Nil rate band (balance)		£ 90,000
			£10,000

IHT @ 20% × £10,000 = £2,000

Step 3:	Ascertain settlement rate

Average rate = $\dfrac{£\ 2,000}{£100,000}$ × 100 = 2%

Settlement rate = 30% × 2% = 0.6%

Step 4: Ascertain the charge to IHT
1 July 1995 – 1 February 1998 = 10 complete quarters

$\dfrac{10}{40}$ × 0.6% = 0.15%

0.15% × £50,000 (fall in value of the trust property) = £75

Step 5:   Paying the IHT
            If the beneficiary pays the IHT = £75
            If the trustees pay grossing up will apply.

Example 3
As above but the settlor had a cumulative total of £215,000, ie his nil rate band was already exhausted when the settlement was created.

Step 1:   Hypothetical chargeable transfer   £100,000
            (ignore added and related property)

Step 2:   Ascertain tax payable
            Hypothetical transfer   £100,000
            IHT @ 20% × £100,000 = £20,000

Step 3:   Ascertain settlement rate
            Average rate = $\frac{£\ 20,000}{£100,000}$ × 100 = 20%
            Settlement rate = 30% × 20% = 6.0%

Step 4:   Ascertain the charge to IHT
            1 July 1995 – 1 February 1998 = 10 complete quarters
            $\frac{10}{40}$ × 6.0% = 1.5%
            1.5% × £50,000 (fall in value of the trust property) = £750

Step 5:   Paying the IHT
            If the beneficiary pays the IHT = £750
            If the trustees pay, grossing up applies.

The effect of the settlor's cumulative total of chargeable transfers

If the settlor had made no chargeable transfers before making the settlement (and had created no related settlement nor added any property to the discretionary settlement), then the hypothetical chargeable transfer in Step 1 is a transfer of the trust property at its value on the creation of the settlement. If this value does not exceed £215,000, the value of the nil rate band, all exit charges before the first 10-year anniversary will be at a nil rate as the rate of tax established in Step 3 will be nil. Increases (or decreases) in the value of the trust fund since the creation of the settlement will not affect this position.

10.2.5 The first 10-year anniversary charge

This charge is on the value of the property in the settlement (including any accumulated income) immediately before the anniversary of the creation of the settlement.

Step 1: Ascertain the value of a hypothetical chargeable transfer

This is done by adding together:

(1) the current value of the relevant property in the settlement; and
(2) the value at creation of any property in a related settlement (if any); and
(3) the value at creation of other property (in the settlement (if any)).

Items (2) and (3) are anti-avoidance provisions which do not often apply. Thus, any charge will usually only relate to the current value of the settled property. For this purpose income will be included as relevant property once it has been accumulated.

Although this is not clear from the legislation, it is the view adopted by the Inland Revenue (see Inland Revenue Statement of Practice SP 8/86).

Step 2: Ascertain the tax on this hypothetical transfer (ignoring items (2) and (3) in Step 1)

The tax is ascertained from the table of rates. Two cumulative totals may be relevant to this. The settlor's cumulative total of chargeable transfers in the 7 years before the settlement was created, and the settlement's own cumulative total of chargeable transfers made in the first 10 years must be taken into account. Tax is calculated at 20 per cent, ie half the death rate (even if the settlement is created by will).

Step 3: Ascertain the settlement rate of tax

The tax calculated in Step 2 is converted into an estate or average rate. The settlement rate is 30 per cent of this rate.

Step 4: The charge to IHT

IHT is charged at the settlement rate applied to the property in the settlement at the anniversary date.

Step 5: Paying the IHT

Example 1

On 1 July 1995 a settlor settled £100,000 on discretionary trusts. The first 10-year anniversary charge falls on 1 July 2005 when the trust fund is worth £140,000 as a result of sound investment by the trustees. No income has been accumulated.

Assume that the settlor had no cumulative total when he created the settlement and no appointments have been made.

Step 1:	Hypothetical chargeable transfer	£140,000
Step 2:	Ascertain the tax payable on	
	the hypothetical transfer	£140,000
	Less: nil rate band (part)	£140,000
		nil
	IHT – nil	
Steps 3 – 5:	Need not be made.	

Example 2

Assume that in 1995 the settlor had a cumulative total of £125,000 from an earlier transfer of value.

Step 1:	Hypothetical chargeable transfer		£140,000
Step 2:	Ascertain tax payable		
	Settlor's cumulative total	£125,000	
	Nil rate band (part)	£125,000	
	Nil rate band (balance)		£ 90,000
			£50,000

IHT @ 20% × £50,000 = £10,000

Step 3:   Ascertain the settlement rate

Average rate = $\frac{£\ 10,000}{£140,000}$ × 100 = 7.14%

Settlement rate = 30% × 7.14% = 2.14%

Step 4:   The charge to IHT
2.14% × £140,000 = £2,996

Step 5:   Paying the IHT
The trustees pay the IHT from the settled funds.

Example 3

Assume that in 1995 the settlor had the cumulative total of £125,000 and that during the first 10 years of the settlement an appointment out of £50,000 was made to a beneficiary.

Step 1:   Hypothetical chargeable transfer   £140,000

Step 2:   Ascertain tax payable

Cumulative totals of:
(i) the settlor	£125,000	
(ii) the settlement	£50,000	
	£175,000	
Nil rate band (part)	£175,000	
Nil rate band (balance)		£ 40,000
		£100,000

IHT @ 20% × £100,000 = £20,000

Step 3:   Ascertain the settlement rate

Average rate = $\frac{£\ 20,000}{£140,000}$ × 100 = 14.29%

Settlement rate = 30% × 14.29% = 4.29%

Step 4:   The charge to IHT
4.29% × £140,000 = £6,006

Step 5:   Paying the IHT
The trustees pay the IHT from the settled funds.

The effect of cumulative totals of chargeable transfers of the settlor and the settlement

Each of these has the effect of reducing, or extinguishing, the nil rate band available to the settlement on the occasion of the anniversary charge. Uniquely, the settlor's own cumulative total at the time he made the settlement remains relevant to IHT calculations for as long as the settlement continues. It does not 'drop out' in the way it does for an individual after 7 years. The settlement's own cumulative total ceases to be relevant once an anniversary has passed, although subsequent exit charges will cause the settlement to acquire another cumulative total which will remain relevant until the next 10-year anniversary charge. These factors are particularly relevant to the trustees when considering whether to make distributions, ie appointments of settled property or to 'break' the settlement.

10.2.6   Subsequent distribution and anniversary charges

Later distribution (exit) charges are brought about by the same events as discussed previously. IHT is charged on the fall in the value of the settled property at a rate based on the rate at the previous 10-year anniversary charge. The number of quarters (periods of 3 months since then) will be relevant.

Example 3 (continued) – Exit charge
A discretionary settlement created on 1 July 1995 had a settlement rate of 4.29% on its first 10-year anniversary. On 1 January 2008 (10 quarters later) the trustees appoint £40,000 to a beneficiary. The rate will be one-fortieth of the settlement rate for each complete quarter since the first 10-year anniversary.

The rate of IHT will be 4.29% $\times \dfrac{10}{40} = 1.07\%$

IHT payable will be £40,000 $\times$ 1.07% = £428.

Later anniversary charges are calculated in the same way as the first anniversary charge. Any cumulative total of chargeable transfers of the settlor before he created the discretionary settlement are taken into account but only distributions out of the settlement since the last anniversary charge will be relevant.

Example 3 (continued) – Anniversary charge
The facts are the same as in the previous example. Calculate the anniversary charge in 2015 when the value of the trust fund has increased to £190,000 and no further distributions have been made.

Step 1: Hypothetical chargeable transfer   £190,000

Step 2: Ascertain the tax payable

Cumulative totals of:		
(i) the settlor	£125,000	
(ii) the settlement	£40,000	
	£165,000	
Nil rate band (part)	£165,000	
Nil rate band (balance)		£ 50,000
		£140,000

IHT @ 20% $\times$ £140,000 = £28,000

Step 3: Ascertain the settlement rate
Average rate = $\dfrac{£\ 28,000}{£190,000} \times 100 = 14.74\%$
Settlement rate = 30% $\times$ 14.74% = 4.42%

Step 4: The charge to IHT
4.42% $\times$ £190,000 = £8,398

Step 5: Paying the IHT
The trustees pay the IHT from the trust fund.

10.2.7 CGT

As in the case of interest in possession settlements, a deemed disposal by the trustees will occur on their exercise of a power of appointment whereby someone becomes 'absolutely entitled' to the settled property against the trustees.

Deemed disposals

Deemed disposals have been considered at **10.1.4** in relation to interest in possession settlements. The principles discussed apply equally to appointments by trustees from discretionary trusts in favour of individuals.

If the trustees by appointment create new trusts of which there are new trustees, these new trustees may likewise become absolutely entitled to the settled property as against the 'old' trustees. If so, a deemed disposal by the old trustees will occur with similar consequences. However, if the appointment leaves the property subject to the original trusts and trust instrument, there will be no deemed disposal. There is often a fine line between the two situations. This is considered further at **10.4**.

Reliefs, exemptions and rates

The rate of tax for discretionary trustees is 34 per cent of the chargeable gain. An annual exemption of £3,250 is available to the trustees.

Hold-over relief will generally be available when assets leave a discretionary settlement (see **10.1.4**). The relief can be claimed (inter alia) if the occasion which gives rise to the disposal is also an occasion of immediate liability to IHT. The relief will be available even if the rate at which IHT is charged is at nil per cent. This will occur where the nil rate band is available to the trustees when the property leaves the discretionary settlement (see the first example at **10.2.4**).

If the trustees and the beneficiaries agree to claim hold-over relief, it is convenient to add an appropriate clause to the deed of appointment containing the hold-over election. As a joint election of the beneficiaries and the trustees is required, they should all be made parties to the deed of appointment. If preferred, the election can be contained in a separate document.

> *Example*
> Trustees of a discretionary settlement appoint 5,000 DEF plc shares worth £20,000 to Johan. The shares were worth £5,000 when the settlement was created.
>
> | | | |
> |---|---|---|
> | Disposal consideration | | £20,000 |
> | *Less*: acquisition cost | £5,000 | |
> | | | £15,000 |
> | indexation allowance (say) | | £ 1,750 |
> | | gain | £13,250 |

(1) No hold-over relief election:

Trustees pay tax on £13,250 – £3,250 (annual exemption) = £10,000 @ 34% = £3,400. Johan acquires the shares at a cost of £20,000.

(2) Hold-over relief election:

There are two consequences:

(i) the trustees pay no CGT
(ii) Johan's acquisition cost is reduced

market value of shares at appointment	£20,000
less: held over gain	£13,250
Johan's acquisition cost	£6,750

Johan benefits from the trustees' indexation allowance but not from their annual exemption.

10.2.8 Drafting a deed of appointment

A deed should always be used even though an absolute appointment may be made less formally and could merely be recorded by the trustees in their records.

Heading and date

Sample clause

> **DEED OF APPOINTMENT**
>
> **DATE: [   ]**

Parties

There will be two parties to a deed if an absolute appointment is intended:

(1) the appointors, sometimes defined as 'the trustees'; and
(2) the beneficiary.

If an appointment on further trusts with the same trustees is to be made, the deed will normally be made by the appointors alone.

Sample clause

> **BETWEEN**
> **(1) [name] ('the Appointors')**
> **(2) [name] ('the Beneficiary')**

Recitals

The recitals should be used to explain the circumstances surrounding the exercise of the power. They will be confined to a brief statement that the trustees intend to exercise their power of appointment under the settlement in the manner indicated in the operative part of the deed.

Sample clause

> **RECITALS**
>
> **(A) This Deed is supplemental to the settlement (the 'Settlement') [and to the other documents and events] specified in the [First] Schedule.**
>
> **(B) The Appointors are the present trustees of the Settlement.**
>
> **(C) [   ] is a member of the class of Beneficiaries.**

(D) The Appointors wish to exercise their power of appointment under clause [   ] of the Settlement in the following manner.

The operative part

Sample clause

OPERATIVE PROVISIONS

1. Definitions and construction

In this Deed:

1.1 the 'Appointed Fund' shall mean [that part of] the Trust Fund [specified in the Second Schedule]; and subject thereto,

1.2 where the context admits, the definitions and rules of construction contained in the Settlement shall apply.

2. Appointment

The Appointors, in exercise of the power of appointment conferred by clause [   ] of the Settlement and of all other relevant powers, hereby [ir]revocably appoint and declare that the Appointed Fund shall henceforth be held upon trust for [   ] absolutely.

[3. Application of Settlement provisions

The trusts, powers and provisions contained in the Settlement shall continue to be applicable to the Appointed Fund so far as consistent with the provisions of this Deed.]

[4. Payment of tax and expenses

Any inheritance tax or capital gains tax and all other costs, expenses and other liabilities occasioned by the appointment contained in this Deed shall be borne by [the Appointed Fund] [the balance of the Trust Fund.]

5. Trustees' lien

Nothing in this Deed shall prejudice or impair in any way any lien or charge to which the Trustees are entitled in respect of any tax and other liabilities whatever for which they are or may become accountable.

[6. Capital gains tax hold-over relief

The parties claim relief under the provisions of s [165] [260] of the Taxation of Chargeable Gains Act 1992 in respect of the appointment contained in this Deed.]

[7. Power of revocation

The Trustees shall have power, at any time during the Trust Period, by deed or deeds wholly or partly to revoke the appointment contained in this Deed.]

Clause 7 will not be required if, as is usual, the appointment is irrevocable. Clause 3 will not be required if the appointment is both irrevocable and gives the beneficiary an absolute interest. If the appointment is onto trusts, Clause 3 can be used to indicate that the powers under the original settlement are to apply to the Appointed Fund (where those powers are considered suitable). Clause 3 will also be required where the appointment is revocable. Clause 4 deals with the division of capital tax liability where part only of the trust fund is appointed. If the whole fund is appointed, it can be omitted.

Clause 6 is a claim by the parties for hold-over relief on the basis that the appointment is an occasion of charge to IHT. An equivalent claim could be made under the TCGA 1992, s 165 if the assets appointed from the settlement were business assets. Hold-over relief is considered at **4.4.5** and see **10.14**.

Schedules

Schedules will give details of the settlement under which the appointment is made and of the trust fund (or part) which is being appointed.

10.3 ACCUMULATION AND MAINTENANCE SETTLEMENTS

10.3.1 The nature of the trusts and the powers

Accumulation and maintenance settlements are a particular type of settlement without an interest in possession. They are settlements where no beneficiary has a present right either to the income or the capital of the trust. However, the settlements differ from discretionary settlements in that they will only qualify as accumulation and maintenance settlements where it is certain, from the outset, that one or more of the beneficiaries will acquire either a right to the income of the settled property or to the property itself. Further, the beneficiary's acquisition of the right to income or capital must occur on or before the beneficiary attains 25 years of age. If the conditions (discussed in Chapters 5 and 8) are satisfied, the settlement will benefit from specific IHT reliefs. These are discussed in **10.3.2** but, broadly, the settlement is taken outside the discretionary settlement charging regime discussed in **10.2.2**.

A power of appointment may be inserted in an A & M settlement. However, considerable care is needed to ensure that neither the wording of the power, nor the manner in which it may be exercised, cause the settlement to fail to qualify from the outset as an A & M settlement and so lose the IHT advantages. If, through the existence of the power, there is any possibility, however remote, that an entitlement to income or capital will not be acquired on or before the beneficiary attains 25 years of age, the settlement will not qualify as an A & M settlement. Drafting the power so that it is not capable of exercise by the trustees in a way which could infringe the conditions is considered in Chapter 8.

10.3.2 Taxation implications of exercising the power of appointment

The exercise of the power by the trustees will affect the capital of the trust. Thus, before its exercise the trustees must consider the IHT and CGT implications as well as making provision for any tax for which they may become liable.

IHT

The exercise of the power of appointment shows the advantages of the A & M settlement.

Normally, the effect of the exercise of the power is that the property in the settlement is no longer held in a 'no interest in possession settlement'. The property may either become subject to an interest in possession settlement if the trustees exercise their powers to grant a beneficiary a right to income only, or if an absolute appointment is made, it will become the absolute property of a beneficiary. Under the normal discretionary settlement charging regime a distribution (exit) charge would arise (see **10.2.3**) but this is not so for A & M settlements.

Provided the A & M settlement is drafted to comply with the basic conditions, the exercise of a power of appointment will not give rise to an IHT liability. IHTA 1984, s 71(4) provides that tax shall not be charged under this section: (a) on a beneficiary's becoming beneficially entitled to, or to an interest in possession in, settled property on or before attaining the specified age or (b) on the death of the beneficiary before attaining the specified age (the specified age is an age not exceeding 25 years, as required by s 71(1)(a)).

Example

£100,000 is held by trustees on A & M trusts for such of Sanjay's grandchildren as attain 21 years. The trustees exercise a power to appoint £50,000 on interest in possession trusts for the benefit of the eldest grandchild. No IHT is payable. The grandchild has an interest in possession on or before 25 years as required by s 71 of the IHTA 1984. The property remains settled property subject to interest in possession trusts. The A & M settlement has ended in relation to the £50,000.

EXIT CHARGES AND ACCUMULATION AND MAINTENANCE SETTLEMENTS
An A & M settlement will end when the conditions in IHTA 1984, s 71 are no longer satisfied. Often this will occur following the exercise of a power of appointment. This occurred in the previous example where an interest in possession was created; a similar result would occur if an absolute entitlement was granted by the exercise of the power.

An A & M settlement will also end where the beneficiary satisfies the conditions for the vesting of income and/or capital contained in the settlement. For example, a settlement giving the right to income at 18 (TA 1925, s 31 applies) and capital at 25 will end once the beneficiary attains majority (condition (2) in **5.4.1** is no longer satisfied). Likewise a settlement giving the right to income and capital at 25 (TA 1925, s 31 modified appropriately) will end once the beneficiary attains 25.

No liability to IHT will arise in either of these circumstances (IHTA 1984, s 71(4)). However, if the settlement ends in other circumstances an exit charge can arise.

Example

Property is held by trustees on A & M trusts for the settlor's grandchildren. The settlor is dead. In default the property will pass to Tom, the only child of the settlor. Helen, the settlor's only grandchild and her mother die in a road accident. The trust continues for the benefit of any future born grandchildren of the settlor. Tom dies later having had no other children. The trust ends and the property passes to the default beneficiary. No IHT is payable on the value of the property in the settlement as a result of Helen's death. However, there will be an exit charge on the distribution to Tom's estate based on the value of the fund and the length of time it has been in the settlement.

A liability may also arise where the period of 25 years for the duration of the settlement expires (condition (3) in **5.4.1**) in a settlement where the common grandparent test was not used.

CGT

As in the case of interest in possession settlements and discretionary settlements, a 'deemed' disposal will occur when someone becomes 'absolutely entitled' to the trust property against the trustees.

DEEMED DISPOSALS

The principles discussed in **10.2.7** in relation to discretionary settlements apply equally to appointments by trustees from A & M settlements.

RELIEFS, EXEMPTIONS AND RATES

The rate of tax for A & M trustees is 34 per cent of any chargeable gain. An annual exemption of £3,250 is available to the trustees.

Hold-over relief may not always be available when the property leaves the settlement. The position is determined by the nature of the beneficial interests at the time of the deemed disposal by the trustees, and of the settled property. Hold-over relief is available if the settlement qualifies as an A & M settlement at the time of the deemed disposal (TCGA 1992, s 260) or if the assets disposed of are business assets (TCGA 1992, s 165) – see **4.4.5**. If the A & M settlement has ended before the deemed disposal occurs, relief will not be available, for example where the beneficiary of an A & M settlement becomes absolutely entitled as against the trustees, having earlier attained an interest in possession (the A & M settlement ended when that interest was acquired because IHTA 1984, s 71(1)(b) is then no longer satisfied). If the settled property is 'business assets', the relief will always be available (TCGA 1992, s 165). In the following examples, there are no business assets.

> *Example 1*
>
> Trustees of an A & M settlement hold property on trust for Rajid if he attains the age of 18 years. When he does so, the A & M settlement ends and Rajid becomes absolutely entitled to the settled property. Any gain made by the trustees on the deemed disposal on Rajid's 18th birthday may be held over on an election being made by the trustees and Rajid.

> *Example 2*
>
> Trustees of an A & M settlement hold property on trust for Amy contingently on her attaining the age of 25 years. At 18, Amy becomes entitled to the income of the settled property under s 31 of the TA 1925. The A & M settlement ends (because Amy now has a right to the income) but no deemed disposal occurs. This is not an event which affects the capital of the settlement.
>
> At 25, Amy becomes absolutely entitled to the settled property. A deemed disposal occurs and hold-over relief is not available since the A & M settlement ended when the interest in possession arose on Amy's 18th birthday.

> *Example 3*
>
> Assume the facts are as in Example 2, but Amy is entitled to both the capital and the income at 25. When the deemed disposal occurs on her 25th birthday, the A & M settlement ends. Any gain on the deemed disposal by the trustees may be held over on an election being made by Amy and the trustees since the A & M settlement continued until her 25th birthday.

By planning ahead the trustees may be able to overcome the potential loss of hold-over relief. If they consider it appropriate, they may be able to exercise either the statutory power of advancement (under the TA 1925, s 32) or an express power of appointment to coincide with the time when the beneficiary is to obtain an interest in possession. If the statutory power is exercised, only one half of the beneficiary's entitlement can be advanced to him (with the benefit of hold-over relief) leaving the beneficiary to become entitled to the remaining half of the entitlement on the vesting date provided by the settlement.

10.3.3   Drafting a deed of appointment

As the beneficial interests under an A & M settlement are similar to those under a discretionary settlement, a power of appointment by the trustees will be drafted in a similar manner to the deed discussed in **10.2.8**. As in that case, the trustees may create by appointment absolute interests or interests under new trusts.

The significant difference in the drafting of appointments is the limitation in the scope of the power in the context of the A & M settlement. The terms of the power will be limited so that its existence does not infringe the conditions for A & M settlements discussed in Chapters 5 and 8. Any exercise of the power will be confined by its terms to appointments creating absolute interests or interest in possession trusts to arise on or before the beneficiary attains 25 years. However, there may be other limitations. In all cases the power of appointment must be carefully examined before it is exercised.

10.4   RESETTLEMENTS

10.4.1   Absolute entitlement for CGT?

So far, this chapter has concentrated upon deemed disposals where an individual has become absolutely entitled to settled property against the trustees. Modern settlements, in particular discretionary settlements but also accumulation and maintenance trusts, are drafted in flexible form which generally includes fiduciary powers for the trustees to 'declare new trusts' in relation to some or all of the settled property. The possibility of exercising either a power of advancement or appointment in this way is mentioned in Chapter 9 (see **9.1**). Although the statutory power of advancement is s 32 of the Trustee Act 1925 is generally used to give an individual absolute entitlement to property freed from any continuing trusts, it has been held that the section may also be used to create trust advances, ie to advance property in such a way that it is to be held in trust for a beneficiary, see *Pilkington v IRC* [1964] AC 612 where a settled advance was for a beneficiary's 'benefit' within s 32 (see **9.4.2**).

The phrase 'absolutely entitled against the trustees' does not mean 'absolutely and beneficially entitled'. It is therefore possible that one set of trustees (whether they are the same people or not) may, following the exercise of a fiduciary power, become absolutely entitled against another set of trustees. However, this does not necessarily mean that there will be a separate settlement. If there is not, then the usual rule in TCGA 1992, s 69 that the trustees are a single and continuing body of persons will apply, ie there will be no deemed disposal and so there can be no question of liability to CGT arising.

If a fiduciary power is to be exercised, it is first necessary to address the question 'will there be absolute entitlement or not?', or (put differently) 'is there a separate settlement for CGT purposes, so that liability to tax must also be considered?' This is an area of some uncertainty although clarification has been provided through the Inland Revenue Statement of Practice (SP 7/84) following the decision in *Bond v Pickford* [1983] STC 517 (see **10.4.2** and **10.4.3**).

10.4.2   A separate settlement or not?

In *Roome v Edwards* [1982] AC 279, the leading case in this area, Lord Wilberforce suggested that the existence of separate trustees, trusts and trust property was not necessarily conclusive as to the existence of a separate settlement. In the following extracts from the judgment a distinction is drawn between a *special* power of appointment (its exercise being unlikely to create a separate settlement) and the exercise of a power in a wider form which may create a separate settlement because property may be removed from the original settlement.

Special power

> '. . . trusts declared by a . . . special power of appointment are to be read into the original settlement . . . If such a power is exercised, whether or not separate trustees are appointed, I do not think that it would be natural . . . to say that a separate settlement had been created, still less so if it were found that provisions of the original settlement continued to apply to the appointed fund, or that the appointed fund were liable, in certain events, to fall back into the rest of the settled property.'

Wider form power

> 'If such a power is exercised, the natural conclusion might be that a separate settlement was created, all the more so if a complete new set of trusts were declared as to the appropriated property, and if it would be said that the trusts of the original settlement ceased to apply to it. There can be many variations on these cases each of which will have to be judged on its facts.'

In *Bond v Pickford* there were three relevant powers in the settlement whereby the trustees could:

(1)   Pay or apply funds to or for the benefit of the beneficiaries.
(2)   Allocate funds to beneficiaries either absolutely or contingently on attaining a specified age.
(3)   Resettle funds for the benefit of the beneficiaries.

What was the effect of an allocation of funds for named beneficiaries on attaining 22 under (2) above: did it create a separate settlement? The Court of Appeal held that a new settlement had not been created and in doing so distinguished between powers in the 'narrower form' and powers in the 'wider form'. The former do not permit property to be freed from the original settlement; the latter do permit this. It is not so much the description given to the power in the trust instrument which is significant, it is what as a matter of construction it permits the trustees to do. The Court of Appeal held that the power in (2) above was a narrower form power in that it permitted a reorganisation internally within the original settlement and not the removal of funds from the settlement.

The manner of exercise of any given power is crucial. The mere fact that a wider form power may be exercised to free property from the original settlement does not necessarily mean it has been exercised in this way. It will be a matter of intention; the trustees may decide to exercise it in a narrower form way. If they wish to avoid a separate settlement, and the associated deemed disposal for CGT, they will exercise the power in a narrower way.

10.4.3   Statement of Practice (SP 7/84)

This Statement of Practice followed the Court of Appeal decision in *Bond v Pickford* and contains the following:

> '. . . the Board considers that a deemed disposal will not arise when . . . [powers in the wider form, which may be powers of advancement or certain powers of appointment, are] . . . exercised and trusts are declared in circumstances where:
>
> (a)   the appointment is revocable, or
> (b)   the trusts declared of the advanced or appointed funds are not exhaustive so that there exists a possibility at the time when the advancement or appointment is made that the funds covered by it will on the occasion of some event cease to be held upon such trusts and once again come to be held upon the original trusts of the settlement.
>
> Further, when such a power is exercised the Board considers it unlikely that a deemed disposal will arise when trusts are declared if duties in regard to the appointed assets still fall to the trustees of the original settlement in their capacity as trustees of that settlement . . . Finally, the Board accepts that a power of appointment or advancement can be exercised over only part of the settled property and that the above consequences would apply to that part.'

By this Statement of Practice the Inland Revenue accepts that a new settlement can only be created if a wider form power is exercised. There are, however, limitations when a new settlement would not be created, ie where the exercise is revocable, the trusts are not exhaustive in the sense that some of the property could again become subject to the original trusts and where the trustees of the original settlement have continuing duties in relation to the settled property.

10.4.4   Drafting the trustees' powers

Powers given to trustees should be drafted as separate clauses in such a way as to make it abundantly clear whether they are wider form or narrower form powers. Trustees, having considered the effect of the exercise of their powers fully (including the CGT consequences) can then specifically exercise by deed a narrower or a wider form power. By so doing, difficulty of construction and effect of the deed of appointment should be avoided.

10.4.5   The CGT consequences of a separate settlement

If a separate settlement is created by the appointment, the new trustees become absolutely entitled against the old (whether they are the same people or not) so that there is a deemed disposal for CGT. The calculation of the gain (or loss) follows normal principles (including the deductions for the indexation allowance and the trustees' annual exemption of £3,250). The trustees pay any tax due from the settled property.

If cash is appointed no liability to CGT will arise. Hold-over relief may be available to the old trustees under TCGA 1992, s 165 or s 260 depending on the circumstances.

10.4.6   The documentation

In addition to a deed of appointment drafted in the manner discussed earlier, the trustees of the old settlement will need to sign stock transfer forms to transfer the settled stocks and shares to the new trustees. If they are the same people, stock transfer forms will still be required but it may be sensible specifically to designate the transferees as trustees of the newly created settlement so as to avoid confusing the share certificates in their own names for the investments in the new settlement with those belonging to them as trustees of the original settlement.

Chapter 11

WILL TRUSTS

11.1 DISTRIBUTION OF PROPERTY ON DEATH

Apart from the formal aspects and the administrative powers given to executors and trustees, the main contents of a will are the dispositive provisions, ie the clauses which actually leave property to the beneficiaries.

A family will is normally straightforward in its terms. Legacies may be given, within the nil rate band, to the children and residue to the spouse or the children should the spouse predecease the testator. The gift to the spouse may be conditional on surviving the testator by 28 days, ie a survivorship clause may be included in the will, but otherwise the gift to the spouse will usually be vested so that it takes effect in possession on the death of the testator. It is unusual to provide the surviving spouse with a life (a limited) interest although this could be done where the testator is particularly concerned to control by his will the ultimate devolution of the residue of his estate. A life interest for the spouse may be appropriate for use where there is a second marriage; the residue passing at the end of the life interest to the children of the first marriage.

Gifts by will to adult children, whether in the form of a legacy or of residue (or part of residue), will normally be drafted to vest in possession on the death of the testator. However, such gifts to minor children of the testator will involve a trust either because of the minority (the child being unable to receive the property from the personal representatives) even though the gift is otherwise unconditional or because the gift is subject to a contingency which has not yet been satisfied.

In all of these cases the testator has selected the beneficiaries to inherit his estate following his death. The same is true even where property is left for division among a class of beneficiaries rather than named individuals, for example, property in a residuary estate is left to be divided between 'such of my children as survive me and attain the age of 18 years'.

11.2 FLEXIBLE PROVISION BY WILL

If the testator is uncertain about the precise nature of the beneficial gifts, he may wish to draft his will in a form which, in effect, delays the decision as to who shall benefit on death until a later date. Often this can be achieved by authorising the trustees, or others, to determine the matter after death. To achieve this position the will should be drafted in flexible form containing trusts.

There are a number of possibilities for the testator to consider when planning a will which delay the ultimate choice of beneficiary until after his death. A trust is usually involved and in each case the succession and taxation implications must be balanced carefully. This chapter discusses each of these matters as well as the drafting considerations which arise.

11.3   PRECATORY TRUSTS

11.3.1   Misnomer

To create a binding trust there must be certainty of words, ie words of an imperative nature such as 'on trust', of subject matter and of objects, ie the beneficiaries. No binding trust is intended by the testator where he uses 'precatory words' in his will. The testator will intend an absolute gift of property, often of jewellery or other personal chattels, to a beneficiary but will couple this with an expression of wish that the property be distributed by the beneficiary in a given way. The absence of imperative words sufficient to create a trust combined with the precatory words, show that the phrase 'precatory trust' is a contradiction in terms.

11.3.2   Using the clause

Precatory trusts are normally used by testators when disposing of personal chattels, and in particular their jewellery. They are useful where the testator is undecided who should benefit from what on his death, especially in respect of property which may change in extent between the date of the will and the subsequent death. The clause introduces a degree of flexibility giving the testator the opportunity to change his mind as to his wishes but without needing to change the will by codicil or, possibly, by executing a new will.

11.3.3   Drafting the clause

Sample clause

> **I GIVE AND BEQUEATH all my personal chattels as defined by section 55(1)(x) of the Administration of Estates Act 1925 to [my wife] for [her] own absolute use and benefit and I express the wish (but without imposing any legal obligation on [her]) that [she] should distribute such assets in accordance with any instructions I communicate to [her] whether orally or in writing at any time and from time to time.**

Definition of personal chattels
Although it is convenient to adopt the definition used in the Administration of Estates Act 1925 (AEA 1925) for personal chattels, thought should be given as to whether it is appropriate. For example, if a testatrix wishes to make a gift of jewellery only, the clause should be modified by inserting an appropriate description of the gift in place of the words 'personal chattels as defined by s 55(1)(x) of the Administration of Estates Act 1925'.

The nature of the gifts
There is an absolute gift to the testator's wife. She could retain all the personal chattels but the testator hopes that through the use of the precatory words she will retain only certain chattels and will distribute the rest. Flexibility is achieved since the instruction to the testator's wife can be changed as often as the testator pleases by giving further non-testamentary instruction.

11.3.4 Taxation implications of the precatory trust

IHT (IHTA 1984, s 143)

The gift takes effect as an absolute gift to the beneficiary named in the clause. IHT is initially calculated on this basis. Thus, as in the sample clause, no IHT will become payable because of the spouse exemption. If no exemption is available, IHT may be payable immediately on the testator's death.

Section 143 provides that where the named beneficiary transfers property in compliance with the testator's wish within 2 years after the death of the testator 'this Act shall have effect as if the property transferred had been bequeathed by the will to the transferee'. Section 17(b) supports this by stating 'the transfer (by the named beneficiary) shall not be a transfer of value'. The benefit of s 143 is given automatically and does not need to be specifically claimed. Thus the distribution of the property by the named beneficiary in accordance with the 'precatory words' is not a PET by the beneficiary and so will not attract IHT if the named beneficiary dies within 7 years of the distribution.

> *Example*
>
> Martha by will leaves her jewellery to her daughter Emma coupled with the wish that Emma shall distribute it to persons named in a letter handed to her before Martha's death. Emma distributes half of the jewellery to members of the family named in the letter and keeps the remainder.
>
> No IHT exemption is available so that on Martha's death tax is payable on the value of the jewellery. No adjustment of the position will be needed when Emma distributes one half of the jewellery. Whether the property passes to Emma or, following the distribution, to others the IHT position is unchanged. Emma makes no transfer of value provided she re-distributes the jewellery within 2 years of her mother's death.

CGT

There are no CGT provisions equivalent to s 143 of the IHTA 1984. The named beneficiary will make a disposal of assets each time property is transferred in accordance with the precatory trust. However, CGT will only be payable if there is a gain on disposal (after allowing for indexation) which is beyond any available exemption or relief. In view of the time scale between the death and the later transfer of the property, it is unlikely that any taxable gain will arise.

11.4 WILLS CONTAINING DISCRETIONARY TRUSTS

11.4.1 Using the discretionary will

Being unable to anticipate accurately the circumstances prevailing at his death, whether in relation to the extent of his property or his family, the testator may decide his will should be drafted in 'flexible' form. This can be achieved by giving a legacy or the residue (or part of residue) to the executors and trustees on discretionary trusts together with wide powers of appointment over the capital and income. If the powers of appointment are not exercised by the trustees, the property will pass 'in default of appointment' to beneficiaries chosen by the testator and named in the will.

A will of this type enables the trustees to take into account the circumstances prevailing at the death of the testator and use the trust property as best suits those circumstances. For example, a testator's spouse may be financially well provided for and so not require the provision under the testator's will. If so, the trustees could exercise their powers over the income and capital in favour of the testator's children. If the circumstances were different and the spouse was in need of the testator's estate, the whole of it could be made available by exercise of the trustee's power of appointment in favour of the spouse.

11.4.2   Planning the discretionary will

Instructions will be required from the testator on various matters before the will can be drafted.

Legacy or residue on discretionary trusts?
A 'settled legacy', ie a legacy of property to be held on discretionary trusts, is often incorporated into a will which then leaves the residuary estate to other beneficiaries absolutely.

Sample clause: settled legacy

> **(1) I GIVE to my Trustees free of all taxes the sum of [ ] thousand pounds (which said sum and all investments and property for the time being representing the same is hereinafter referred to as 'the Settled Legacy') UPON the TRUSTS and with and subject to the powers discretions and provisions contained in the succeeding paragraphs of this Clause**

> **(2) For so long during the period of eighty years from my death (the perpetuity period applicable hereto) as any of the persons hereinafter mentioned is living my Trustees shall have power at any time and from time to time if and whenever they shall in their absolute discretion think fit to pay or apply the whole or any part or parts of the income or of the capital or of the income and the capital of the Settled Legacy to or for the benefit of all or any one or more exclusively of the others or other of the following persons that is to say my [spouse and issue] and with power during the period of twenty-one years after my death to accumulate any income of the Settled Legacy not so paid or applied and to add any such accumulations to the capital thereof**

> **(3) Subject to the foregoing provisions of this Clause and to any and every exercise of the powers and discretions hereinbefore conferred upon them my Trustees shall hold the Settled Legacy UPON TRUST for such of my [children and grandchildren] . . .**

If there is no settled legacy, the will may provide absolute legacies, for example, to the testator's children and then leave the residuary estate on discretionary trusts for a class of beneficiaries possibly including the testator's spouse and issue (see **11.5**).

If a will creates a discretionary trust, it is generally inadvisable for the will to create another trust. Section 62 of the IHTA 1984 provides that if two settlements are created on the same day by the same person, they are 'related settlements'. An exception to this rule is contained in IHTA 1984, s 80, which provides that a life interest to the testator's spouse will not be a related settlement. The implications of s 62 are that the IHT benefits which are hoped for through the use of discretionary wills may be lost if combined with another trust other than a life interest to the testator's spouse.

Duration of the discretionary trust

The discretionary trust, whether as a settled legacy or of residue, may be drafted so as to be capable of lasting for a full perpetuity period. Even if it is drafted in this way, it is unlikely that it will in fact last so long. Trustees will normally exercise their powers of appointment over capital far earlier.

It is more common to limit the duration of a discretionary trust of residue to a maximum period of 2 years. A 2-year discretionary trust takes advantage of the IHT reliefs afforded by the IHTA 1984, s 144 (see **11.4.3**).

Extent of the property within the discretionary trust

Where the discretionary trust is a settled legacy, it may be limited to property to the value of the available nil rate band for IHT at the testator's death. Such 'nil rate band discretionary trusts' have the advantage that no IHT is payable from them when the trustees exercise their discretionary powers (see further **11.4.3**). If the testator does not wish to restrict the discretionary trust to the nil rate band or instead prefers to impose such a trust over his residuary estate, there is no limit otherwise restricting the extent of the property which may become subject to the trusts.

11.4.3   Taxation implications of discretionary trusts in wills

IHT

SECTION 144 RELIEF

Whether or not a discretionary trust of the residue is drafted as a 2-year discretionary trust, consideration must be given to the relief provided by s 144 of the IHTA 1984. This section is specifically designed to permit distribution of property from a discretionary trust within 2 years of the testator's death, without liability to IHT. Relief is available even if the settled property exceeds the amount of the nil rate band available at the testator's death, ie the trust is not a 'nil rate band discretionary trust'.

The section applies where property is settled by a will if two conditions are satisfied:

(1)   no interest in possession subsists in the settled property, ie the property is held by the trustees on discretionary trusts; and

(2)   an event occurs in relation to the settled property within the period of 2 years after the death of the testator, for example, the distribution of trust property by the trustees to a beneficiary.

If the conditions are met there are two consequences:

(1)   the discretionary will trust is taken outside the normal charging regime for discretionary trusts (see further **10.2**). Thus, the charge to IHT which would normally arise where property ceases to be comprised in a settlement will not apply to the distribution by the trustees; and

(2)   the event, ie the distribution by the trustees, is taxed as if the will had provided that on the testator's death property should be held as it is held after the distribution. A 'writing back' effect is, therefore, achieved in a manner similar to a post-death variation when an election is made.

Example

Mary by her will creates a discretionary trust of her estate of £465,000. The beneficiaries are her husband Henry and their children and grandchildren. She dies in April 1997, having made no lifetime transfers.

Death of Mary: £100,000 IHT is payable (£465,000 – £215,000 = £250,000 @ 40%). The spouse exemption is not available.

Distribution by Mary's trustees in October 1997 (within 2 years of Mary's death but after 3 months (see below)) as follows:

£250,000 to Henry absolutely: spouse exemption

£215,000 to trustees on accumulation and maintenance trusts for the grandchildren: nil rate band.

No IHT is now payable on Mary's death as the trustees' distributions are 'read back' into Mary's will. This writing back effect is automatic; no election is required. The IHT paid by the personal representatives to obtain the grant of probate will be repaid (with interest) by the Inland Revenue. It is not possible to overcome this cash flow disadvantage by exercise of the power of appointment before applying for the grant of probate. This is unfortunate since the PRs will need to fund the IHT payment only to have it repaid to them later.

Section 144 only works to provide the writing back effect where a charge to IHT would otherwise have arisen on the distribution by the discretionary trustees. No exit charge arises within the first 3 months of any discretionary settlement; there must be at least one complete quarter (see **10.2.3**). Any appointment within 3 months of Mary's death would not be read back into her will and taxed accordingly as in the previous example. Spouse relief would not be available and £100,000 IHT would remain payable (see further *Frankland v IRC* [1996] STC 735).

DISTRIBUTIONS AFTER 2 YEARS FROM DEATH

If the discretionary trust of the residuary estate is not limited to the 2-year period following the testator's death, s 144 relief may only be claimed for distributions made within the 2-year period. Later distributions will be taxable in accordance with normal principles which apply to trusts where there is no interest in possession (see **10.2**).

Accordingly, generally no liability will arise on distributions made before the first 10-year anniversary where the settled funds on death did not exceed the testator's available nil rate band. It will not matter that the settled funds have become worth more than the nil rate band when the distribution is made.

If the settled funds are not distributed by the first 10-year anniversary, a charge may then arise based on the value of the property in the settlement at that time. However, if the settled funds are substantial, it is normally prudent for the trustees to distribute them before the first 10-year anniversary specifically to avoid the charge.

NIL RATE BAND DISCRETIONARY TRUSTS

Nil rate band discretionary trusts (a settled legacy, see **11.4.2**) are designed to provide flexibility of testamentary provision while at the same time using the testator's nil rate band for IHT, or as much of it as is available on death. However, to be fully effective it is important that in addition: (i) the residuary estate is given by the will to an exempt beneficiary, for example the testator's spouse (or, less usually, a charity); and (ii) the will does not contain any related settlement (see **11.4.2**).

Nil rate band discretionary trusts rely on the usual discretionary trust charging regime for their effectiveness (see **10.2.4**). The advantage is that distributions made by the trustees before the first 10-year anniversary will not attract IHT liability.

Example
Raymond by will creates a nil rate band discretionary trust of £165,000 and leaves the residue of his estate to his wife Wendy. The beneficiaries of the trust are Wendy, his children and grandchildren. He had made PETs of £50,000 which became chargeable on his death last year.

Step 1: Calculate the IHT on Raymond's death

No IHT is payable because:

(1) the nil rate band discretionary trust is taxed at 0% because the balance of the nil rate band is available;
(2) the residuary estate has the benefit of the spouse exemption.

Step 2: Distribution by the trustees

One year after Raymond's death, Wendy tells the trustees that she can manage without relying on the nil rate band discretionary trust fund and she asks if they will distribute it to the children. The trustees agree to do so. No adjustment to the IHT position in Raymond's estate is needed and no IHT is payable by the trustees from the discretionary trust. The settlement rate will be nil.

CGT

No special rules exist for CGT where distributions are made from discretionary trusts created by a will. In particular, there is no writing back effect for CGT. Thus, ordinary principles must be applied to calculate any liability (see further **10.2.7**). However, in outline the following is the position.

When a beneficiary becomes 'absolutely entitled' to trust property as against the trustees, the trustees are 'deemed to dispose' of the property at its market value and to re-acquire it at the same value as bare trustees, ie it remains in the names of the former trustees but is now the absolute property of the beneficiary.

Example: nil rate band discretionary trust
A testator's will creates a nil rate band discretionary trust. The trustees appoint the trust property to the testator's spouse who thereby becomes absolutely entitled to it. Although the property will remain in the trustees' names (until it is actually transferred to the spouse), they now hold it as 'bare trustees' for the testator's spouse. Hold-over relief is available whenever property leaves the discretionary trust so that no CGT liability will actually arise for the trustees provided the appropriate election is made by the trustees and beneficiary. (IHTA 1984, s 260 – see **4.4.5**).

Example: 2-year discretionary trust
A testator's will creates a 2-year discretionary trust. The trustees exercise the power of appointment which is read back into the testator's will. As there is no chargeable transfer by the trustees, ie IHTA 1984, s 144 applies, hold over relief will not be available under TCGA 1992, s 260. If the trust property is 'business assets' hold over relief under TCGA 1992, s 165 may be available.

Income tax

Distributions by trustees from discretionary trusts created by a will do not fall within the income tax anti-avoidance provisions discussed at **6.2.10**. Thus, consideration of the type necessary in relation to post-death variations (see **12.4.2**) is not relevant to appointments from the trust by the trustees.

> *Example*
>
> David appoints his wife, Sheena, as his executor and trustee. His will bequeaths her a substantial legacy and leaves his residuary estate on a 2-year discretionary trust for Sheena and their children. David dies leaving two young children.
>
> Within 2 years of David's death, Sheena distributes the residuary estate onto new A & M trusts for their infant children. Even though the children's trust was created by appointment by their mother, the trust is not a 'settlement' by a parent on her child within the income tax anti-avoidance provisions. Sheena creates the new settlement in her capacity as trustee of David's will, not as a parent.

Once the discretionary trust is set up following the death, the income from the settled property received by the trustees will attract tax at the rate of 34 per cent. This, and the position of the beneficiaries, is considered in Chapter 13.

11.5 DRAFTING DISCRETIONARY TRUSTS OF RESIDUE

The clauses which follow should be inserted into the will after the clauses establishing the trusts of the residuary estate, directing the payment of the testator's debts, legacies, funeral and testamentary expenses hence establishing the residuary fund to be 'the Trust Fund'. Many of the provisions used to create a discretionary trust by will are similar to those used to establish a discretionary trust by inter vivos settlements. The comments on the clauses which follow are confined to those relevant to will trusts.

11.5.1 Trust definitions

Sample clause

IN my Will where the context so admits

(a) **'the Trust Fund' shall mean**

    (i) **my Estate after the payment of my debts funeral and testamentary expenses and legacies and**

    (ii) **all money investments or other property accepted by the Trustees as additions and**

    (iii) **all accumulations (if any) of income directed to be held as an accretion to capital and**

    (iv) **the money investments and property from time to time representing the above**

(b) **'the Trustees' shall mean my Executors or other of the trustees for the time being of the Trust Fund**

(c) **'the Trust Period' shall mean the period ending on the earlier of**

(i) the last day of the period of eighty years from the date of my death which period (and no other) shall be the applicable perpetuity period or

(ii) such date as the Trustees shall by deed at any time or times specify (not being a date earlier than the date of execution of any such deed or later than a date previously specified)

(d) 'the Discretionary Beneficiaries' shall mean

(i) [my wife] [my husband]

(ii) my children and remoter issue (whether living at my death or born thereafter)

(iii) the husbands wives widowers and widows of my children and remoter issue

(iv) any company trust or other body regarded as charitable under the law of England and Wales

(e) 'the Discretionary Period' shall mean [the period of two years (less one day) from the date of my death] [the Trust Period]

(f) 'the Accumulation Period' shall mean the period of twenty-one years from the date of my death which shall be the applicable accumulation period for all purposes

Clause (e) contains alternatives. If the period of 'two years (less one day) from the date of death' is selected the trust will comply with the provisions of s 144 of the IHTA 1984, ie a 2-year discretionary trust will have been established. By limiting the trustees to a period of 2 years less one day, it is intended to remove uncertainty as to whether the distributions in fact occurred within 2 years of the testator's death. Difficulties can arise if an exact period of 2 years is used instead.

Nil rate band discretionary trust

The clauses set out above may be used to establish a discretionary trust which is not limited to the nil rate band available at the testator's death. If a nil rate band discretionary trust is to be created, these clauses can be used but the definition of the trust fund must be altered to limit its extent.

Sample clause

'the Trust Fund' shall mean

(a) the greatest value (if any) which such Trust Fund can have within the nil rate band of inheritance tax applicable at the date of my death which does not cause inheritance tax to be charged (other than at the said nil rate) in respect of my estate as a consequence of my death

(b) (i)–(iv) [as for (a) in the previous clause]

11.5.2 Residuary gift: discretionary trusts

Sample clause

(a) The Trustees shall hold the capital and income of the Trust Fund upon such trusts in favour or for the benefit of all or such one or more of the Discretionary Beneficiaries exclusive of the other or others of them in such shares or proportions if more than one and

with and subject to such powers and provisions for their respective maintenance education or other benefit or for the accumulation of income for any period expiring before the end of the Accumulation Period (including administrative powers and provisions and discretionary trusts and powers to be executed or exercised by any person or persons whether or not being or including the Trustees or any of them) and so that the exercise of this power of appointment may be delegated to any extent and in such manner generally as the Trustees (subject to the application (if any) of the rule against perpetuities) by any deed or deeds revocable during the Discretionary Period or irrevocable and executed during the Discretionary Period shall appoint provided always that no exercise of this power shall invalidate any prior payment or application of all or any part or parts of the capital or income of the Trust Fund made under any other power or powers conferred by my Will or by law and provided further that this power may be exercised whether or not the administration of my Estate has been completed and whether or not a transfer of the Trust Fund has been effected by my Executors under Clause [   ]

All powers and provisions established by the clause are exercisable by the trustees. It is arguable that these powers are not exercisable until the end of the administration period, ie when the trust is fully established by the executors transferring the assets remaining in the estate to the trustees. In addition, it is sometimes argued that the powers cannot be exercised by the trustees before the grant of probate has been obtained. The proviso at the end of this clause is designed to overcome these arguments by expressly authorising the trustees to exercise the powers in the way set out in the clause.

Sample clause (continued)

    (b) Until and subject to and in default of any appointment under sub-clause (a) the following provisions of this sub-clause shall apply to the Trust Fund during the Discretionary Period

        (i) the Trustees shall pay or apply the income of the Trust Fund to or for the benefit of all or such one or more of the Discretionary Beneficiaries exclusive of the other or others of them as shall for the time being be in existence and in such shares if more than one and in such manner generally as the Trustees shall in their absolute discretion from time to time think fit

        (ii) notwithstanding the provisions of sub-clause (b)(i) the Trustees may in their absolute discretion instead of applying all or any part or parts of the income accumulate the same in the way of compound interest by investing or otherwise applying it and its resulting income from time to time in any applications or investments authorised by my Will or by law and subject to sub-clause (b)(iii) below shall hold such accumulations as an accretion to capital

        (iii) the Trustees may apply the whole or any part or parts of the income accumulated under sub-clause (b)(ii) as if it were income arising in the then current year

   (iv) **notwithstanding the trusts powers and provisions declared
        and contained in this sub-clause the Trustees may**

       (aa) **at any time or times pay or apply the whole or any part
            or parts of the capital of the Trust Fund to or for the
            benefit of all or such one or more of the Discretionary
            Beneficiaries exclusive of the other or others of them in
            such shares if more than one and in such manner
            generally as the Trustees shall in their absolute
            discretion think fit**
       (bb) **(subject to the application (if any) of the rules against
            perpetuities) pay or transfer any income or capital of
            the Trust Fund to the trustees of any other trust
            wherever established or existing under which all or any
            one or more of the Discretionary Beneficiaries is or are
            interested (whether or not all or such one or more of
            the Discretionary Beneficiaries is or are the only
            objects or persons interested or capable of benefiting
            under such other trust) if the Trustees shall in their
            absolute discretion consider such payment or transfer
            to be for the benefit of all or such one or more of the
            Discretionary Beneficiaries**

   (c) **At the end of the Discretionary Period and subject to and in
       default of any appointment under sub-clause (a) the Trustees
       shall hold the Trust Fund upon trust for . . .**

If this clause is used to create a nil rate band settled legacy, the ultimate default
trusts in clause (c) would generally provide that the property in the settled legacy
should pass to the residuary beneficiary under the will of the testator.

11.6   GIFTS BY WILL FOR THE TESTATOR'S MINOR CHILDREN

A testator has a choice, on which instructions will be needed by the draftsman,
when considering gifts for his minor children. The choice is between vested and contingent gifts for the testator's children as minor beneficiaries. This calls for a consideration of the succession and taxation consequences of each.

11.6.1   Vested gifts

Succession

A vested gift by will to an adult beneficiary takes effect in possession on the testator's death. This is the usual situation where the will leaves a beneficiary a legacy or
an interest in the residuary estate. If the beneficiary is the minor child of the
testator, a vested gift cannot take effect in possession because the beneficiary is
unable to hold the property and give the executor a receipt for it. An infant receipt
clause in the will may permit the infant if aged (say) 16 years to give a valid receipt.
In such cases the property may be transferred to the beneficiary by the executors.

Apart from the cases just mentioned, the property will be held by the executors for
the beneficiary until his majority is reached unless use is made of s 42 of the AEA
1925 to transfer the property from the executors to trustees to hold for the bene-

ficiary. However, in either of these cases a trust is inevitable, the trustees holding the property for the beneficiary until he can receive it.

The nature of a vested entitlement is such that the ownership of the property belongs to the minor beneficiary, even though he cannot actually enjoy it until he is 18 years old because of his inability to provide a receipt for it to the trustees. However, the death of the minor beneficiary, which will inevitably be intestate, will cause the property to pass under the intestacy law to his surviving parent or remoter relative. If this is considered undesirable, the gift to the minor beneficiary should be made contingent on attaining a given age.

Taxation

Vested gifts are not treated as gifts into a settlement for any of the three principal taxes. The tax position is the same as in the case of any other property owned absolutely by a taxpayer.

IHT

On the death of the minor beneficiary, his 'estate' includes the vested gift. IHT will be payable on its value to the extent the nil rate band on death is exceeded. In view of the age of the beneficiary, and his probable financial circumstances, it is unlikely that a liability will arise.

CGT

Disposals of the property during the minor beneficiary's lifetime will occur if the trustees holding the property sell it, for example, shares into which the gift has been invested are sold following advice of stockbrokers. Gains (or losses) are determined on normal principles working on the basis that the property belongs to the minor beneficiary. Thus, after the indexation allowance, reliefs and exemptions available to the minor beneficiary may be claimed. The higher £6,500 annual exemption will be available; not the trustees' lower £3,250 exemption. Any gain will be taxed at rates equivalent to the minor beneficiary's income tax rates.

INCOME TAX

Income produced by the property will be taxed as part of the beneficiary's income at his marginal rates, for example, dividends on shares bequeathed to the minor beneficiary. Often in these circumstances the minor beneficiary has a gross income which is less than his personal allowance and so he may reclaim the 20 per cent tax paid at source by the company paying the dividend. If the minor beneficiary is liable at the higher rate (40 per cent) of income tax on the dividend, he must account for an extra 20 per cent on the gross dividend.

11.6.2　Contingent gifts

Succession

A gift which vests at a particular age or other future event requires trustees to hold the property until then. If the beneficiary dies after the testator but before the contingency is satisfied, the property will not pass under the beneficiary's intestacy. Instead, it will devolve on the beneficiary next entitled under the original trusts. Such beneficiary may either be named expressly as being entitled 'in default', ie the person to inherit if the contingent gift fails; or, alternatively, he may be the beneficiary who inherits the residuary estate under the testator's will, ie the gift is declared on failure of the principal trusts to 'fall into and form part of my residuary estate'.

A testator may prefer to leave property, particularly a gift of his residuary estate, to trustees upon express trust for minor beneficiaries with provision that the gift vests in possession when the beneficiary attains a stated age, for example, when the beneficiary is 21 or 25 years old. In such cases the testator establishes a class gift for 'such of my children as shall attain the age of 21 or 25 years' and will provide for gifts over for his grandchildren. A gift of this type permits the testator to achieve a certain degree of flexibility in the terms of the trusts and in particular through the powers given to the trustees.

Taxation

Contingent gifts are gifts into settlement for each of the three principal taxes. It is, therefore, necessary to consider the taxation position of the trustees and of the minor beneficiary separately. It is also advisable to contrast the taxation position of contingent gifts generally with the position relating to vested gifts. A particularly unfavourable taxation position might significantly influence a testator in his choice of gift. However, as always, the taxation position needs careful balancing against the succession consequences.

IHT

On the death of a minor beneficiary before the contingency is satisfied, the gift fails. The property is not in the minor beneficiary's 'estate', ie he does not have an interest in possession in it, so that IHT will not be payable on the value of the property.

If the beneficiary dies after attaining the age of 18 but before the contingency is satisfied, for example, he becomes entitled to the property at 21, IHT may be payable. In these circumstances s 31 of the TA 1925 gives the beneficiary a right to the income produced by the property held in trust for him once he reaches 18, ie the beneficiary now has an interest in possession in the settled property. If a beneficiary with an interest in possession dies, IHT is payable on the value of the settled property as part of his 'estate' for IHT, even if he dies before the contingency has occurred.

> *Example*
> Simon by will leaves his residuary estate on trust for his only child Cathy at 21. Cathy is 15 when her father dies. Section 31 of the TA 1925 applies to Simon's will.
>
> (1) Cathy dies aged 17. No IHT is payable on Simon's will trust as a result of Cathy's death as it does not form part of her estate.
> (2) Cathy dies aged 19. She obtained an interest in possession in the income of Simon's will trust at 18. IHT is payable by the trustees of the trust fund (calculated by adding the value of the trust fund to Cathy's free estate and apportioning the IHT between it and the trust fund).

A contingent gift by will to a minor beneficiary will normally qualify as an A & M settlement as discussed in Chapter 8. As a consequence, the settlement will benefit from the favourable provisions introduced by s 71 of the IHTA 1984 to exclude A & M settlements from the main charging provisions applying to settlements with no interest in possession (IHTA 1984, s 71(4) – see **10.3.2**). The ability to rely on these provisions makes the contingent gift by will to minor beneficiaries particularly attractive to testators, although the capital gains tax and income tax position should not be overlooked. For IHT, there are two advantages in using an A & M settlement. There is no liability to tax when the beneficiary attains an interest in possession, normally on his 18th birthday (unless s 31 of the TA 1925 is modified); nor is there liability when the trustees vest the property in the beneficiary when he satisfies the contingency. However, liability may arise if the beneficiary dies after attaining an interest in possession but before satisfying the contingency as indicated in the previous example.

Example

Samantha by will settles her residuary estate on trust for her only child Charles at 25. Charles is 16 when Samantha dies. Section 31 of the TA 1925 applies to Samantha's will.

(1) Charles becomes 18. No IHT is payable on Charles attaining an interest in possession (under the TA 1925, s 31).
(2) Charles becomes 25. No IHT is payable when the contingency occurs and the trustees transfer the property to him (he is deemed 'beneficially entitled' to the entire settled property).

CGT

Any sales of the trust property by the trustees before the beneficiary satisfies the contingency will be a disposal by the trustees for CGT. The trustees' liability will be determined by applying normal principles. If a gain is made (after allowing for indexation) the trustees deduct their exemptions and reliefs, for example, the annual exemption of £3,250 (not the higher exemption available to individuals). Any tax, calculated by charging the gain at 34 per cent, will be paid by the trustees from the settled property.

If the beneficiary has a right to income, ie an interest in possession throughout the whole tax year, the trustees pay CGT at the lower rate of 23 per cent.

Example

Property is held by the trustees of a will trust for Angela at 25, and s 31 of the TA 1925 applies. She is 10 when the testator dies but is 16 when the trustees sell an investment for £20,000.

Disposal consideration	£20,000
Less: acquisition cost (probate value at the testator's death)	£5,000
	£15,000
indexation allowance (say)	£2,750
	£12,250
Annual exemption	£3,250
Chargeable gain	£9,000

Tax @ 34%   £3,060

If Angela had been 19, the trustees' CGT rate would be reduced to 23%.

When the beneficiary satisfies the contingency, he becomes absolutely entitled to the settled property as against the trustees. They are 'deemed' to dispose (see **10.2.7**) of each item of the settled property at its market value at the time and to re-acquire it at the same value as bare trustees, ie it is now the property of the beneficiary although it remains in the names of the bare trustees until they transfer it to the beneficiary.

Example

The facts are the same as in the previous example. Angela attains 25 and becomes entitled to the settled property.

Disposal consideration (market value of the asset		
at Angela's 25th birthday)		£50,000
Less: acquisition cost		£20,000
		£30,000
indexation allowance (say)		£9,750
		£20,250
Annual exemption		£3,250
Chargeable gain		£17,000
Tax @ 23%	£3,910	

The rate of tax is 23% as Angela had an interest in possession for the whole of the tax year (she acquired her interest at 18).

The gain on the deemed disposal by the trustees when the property leaves the settlement on Angela's 25th birthday will only attract hold-over relief if the assets are relevant business assets under the TCGA 1992, s 165 (see further **10.3.2**). However, the relief will be available automatically if the settlement qualifies as an A & M settlement when the contingency is satisfied. This will be achieved only if the absolute entitlement occurs at the same time as the interest in possession arises. The nature of the assets within the settlement will not affect this position.

Examples
(1) A will leaves property for Alec at 18. Section 31 of the TA 1925 applies. Hold-over relief will be available when Alec reaches 18 and becomes entitled to the settled property.
(2) A will leaves property for Brenda at 21. Section 31 of the TA 1925 applies. Hold-over relief will not be available. The settlement lost A & M status when Brenda became 18. (This is Angela's position in the previous example.)
(3) A will leaves property for Carol at 21. Section 31 of the TA 1925 is varied so that an interest in possession arises at the age of 21. Hold-over relief will be available when Carol reaches 21 and becomes entitled to the settled property.

If the settlement fails to qualify for hold-over relief based on its A & M status, hold-over relief will only be available if the settled property is 'business assets'.

INCOME TAX

Income produced by the settled property will initially be taxed as income of the trustees. The rate of tax depends on the nature of the beneficial interests in the trust (see further Chapter 13). If no beneficiary has a vested interest in the income, ie there is no interest in possession, the trustees pay at 34 per cent. Section 31 of the

TA 1925 will normally ensure the beneficiary attains a vested interest in income at the age of 18. Thereafter, the trustees pay at 23 per cent (20 per cent on dividends or other savings income).

Example

Roy by will leaves his residuary estate on trust for Sulima at 25. Section 31 of the TA 1925 applies. Sulima is aged 16 when Roy dies.

(1) Until Sulima becomes 18: trustees pay income tax at 34%.
(2) After Sulima's 18th birthday: trustees pay income tax at 23% (20% on dividends and other savings income) (s 31 of the TA 1925 gave Sulima a vested entitlement to the income).

The income tax position of the beneficiary depends also on the nature of his interest in the income of the settled property.

Example

The facts are as in the previous example.

(1) Until Sulima becomes 18 she is liable to pay income tax only on the income applied by the trustees for her maintenance, education or benefit under TA 1925, s 31. If her own rate of income tax is less than the 34% paid by the trustees she may reclaim the balance from the Inland Revenue.

Assume trust income of £1,000 – £340 (34%) = £660 net. The trustees apply all the net income in payment of Sulima's school fees. She has no other income and so is not a taxpayer. She will be entitled to a repayment of £340 from the Inland Revenue since her gross income (£1,000) is less than her personal allowance of £4,045. Any income retained by the trustees, ie income not used for Sulima's benefit, is accumulated after tax at 34% has been paid. As this tax is lost to the Inland Revenue once it has been accumulated the trustees should consider applying the income where possible.

(2) After Sulima's 18th birthday. As Sulima now has a vested entitlement to the settlement income, she is liable to pay tax on all income at her marginal rate.

Assume trust dividend income of £1,000 – £200 (20%) = £800 net. The trustees will pay the net income to Sulima as she has entitlement to it. If she pays tax at 40% she must account for the extra tax of £200 to the Inland Revenue (£1,000 × 40% = £400 – £200 (paid by the trustees) = £200). If she has no other income she will be entitled to a repayment of £200 from the Inland Revenue since her gross income (£1,000) is less than her personal allowance.

11.7 WILLS CONTAINING A TERMINABLE LIFE INTEREST

11.7.1 Form of the will

Many testators wish to provide adequately for their surviving spouse and yet wish to incorporate into their wills flexibility whereby other members of the family may benefit should the surviving spouse not require the provision when the testator dies. Although a will containing discretionary trusts (see **11.4**) may be used to achieve the testator's wishes, the testator may prefer a will which gives his surviving spouse a direct benefit in the form of a life interest (coupled with powers of advancement in her favour over the capital) with flexibility provided by 'an overriding power of appointment'. This power, exercisable by the trustees after the testator's death, would enable the trustees to divest the surviving spouse of entitlement should this course of action prove desirable and to 'redirect' the property among a class of beneficiaries identified by the will.

11.7.2 Drafting life interest trusts subject to an overriding power of appointment

After the usual provisions dealing with payment of debts, legacies, testamentary expenses etc and after the residuary fund defined as 'my Trust Fund' has been established, the clauses creating the beneficial trusts should be set out. Extracts of the principal clauses are set out below in the order they usually appear, ie the life interest for the surviving spouse follows the overriding power for the trustees.

Sample clause

> **My Trustees shall hold the capital and income of the Trust Fund upon such trusts in favour or for the benefit of all or such one or more of the Beneficiaries exclusive of the other or others of them in such shares or proportions if more than one and with and subject to such powers and provisions for their respective maintenance education or other benefit or for the accumulation of income . . . as my Trustees (subject to the application (if any) of the rule against perpetuities) by any deed or deeds . . . shall appoint . . .**

This clause subjects the whole of the trust fund to a wide power of appointment. It may be exercised by the trustees to create absolute interests or interests under trusts in favour of the beneficiaries who will have been identified earlier in the will in a clause setting out various definitions (see **6.2.5**). Normally, the beneficiaries would include the testator's spouse, children and remoter issue and their respective spouses. The testator's intention would be that the trustees exercise this power only after consulting the surviving spouse (although there is no express provision requiring the consent of the spouse) and after they have taken into account all the circumstances existing at the testator's death. In such circumstances it would not be unusual for the testator to appoint the surviving spouse as a trustee. The effect of exercising the power is to bring to an end the surviving spouse's life interest (see the following clause) in the whole or part of the trust fund although if included in the class of beneficiaries, the trustees may appoint capital to the former life tenant.

Sample clause

> **UNTIL and subject to and in default of an appointment under clause [ ]**
>
> (a) **My Trustees shall pay the income of the Trust Fund to the Life Tenant for life [or until remarriage] [if the Life Tenant shall survive me by [ ] days]**
>
> (b) (i) **My Trustees may at any time or times during the Trust Period as to the whole or any part of the Trust Fund in which the Life Tenant has for the time being an interest in possession transfer or raise and pay the same to or for the**

> **absolute use or benefit of the Life Tenant or raise and pay or apply the same for the advancement or otherwise for the benefit of the Life Tenant in such manner as my Trustees shall in their absolute discretion think fit**
>
> **(ii) In this clause 'interest in possession' shall have the same meaning it has for the purpose of the Inheritance Tax Act 1984 and any statutory modification or re-enactment of such Act**

(c) ...

(d) ...

This clause gives the trustees express power to advance capital to the life tenant (who would also be identified in the definition clause in the will) should his circumstances so require. Sub-clauses (c) and (d) would set out the further trusts in the event of the trustees not exercising their overriding power of appointment.

11.7.3 Taxation implications of an overriding power

IHT

DEATH OF THE TESTATOR

No IHT is payable on the death of the testator since the spouse exemption is available as a result of the interest in possession given to the surviving spouse. Thus, a grant of probate can be obtained without the need to negotiate a loan to pay any IHT. This is an advantage which is not available where the will contains a discretionary trust (see **11.4.3**).

EXERCISE OF THE OVERRIDING POWER

If the trustees contemplate exercising the power, they should first consider the taxation consequences. Any appointment of capital by the trustees will bring about the 'ending of an interest in possession', ie the life interest will be wholly or partly terminated. Insofar as capital is advanced to the life tenant, no IHT will arise. If the power is exercised in favour of the other beneficiaries, the ending of the interest in possession is a transfer of value which may be a PET (depending on who benefits from the appointment and on what terms) by the life tenant so that IHT is only payable if death occurs within 7 years (IHTA 1984, s 52). Thus, in both cases the IHT position is similar to that discussed at **10.1.4** in relation to partitioning trust funds.

CGT

If the exercise of the power results in someone becoming 'absolutely entitled' to the settled property against the trustees, there is a deemed disposal by the trustees. Absolute entitlement can occur where property leaves the trust following an outright appointment in favour of a beneficiary or where the trustees appoint property to trustees to hold on new trusts (see further **10.4**). Either of these methods is possible under the power of appointment set out at **11.7.2**.

The calculation of the trustees liability, the exemptions, reliefs and rates of tax is also similar to that for inter vivos trusts (see **10.1.4**).

11.7.4 Drafting the deed of appointment

The drafting of the deed, and its contents, will follow closely the drafting of the deed of appointment discussed at **10.2.8**.

Chapter 12

POST-DEATH ARRANGEMENTS

12.1 TYPES OF ARRANGEMENT

12.1.1 Introduction

There are many reasons why beneficiaries and trustees may wish to rearrange dispositions of property in an estate following a death, whether the deceased died testate or intestate. Although estate planning advice given to a beneficiary will often lie behind the particular decision, it is important that the beneficiaries and trustees should reach their decision carefully balancing the succession and taxation aspects involved. The reasons for rearrangements include:

(1) a beneficiary's wish to redirect benefits to other members of the family who are less well provided for, either as a result of the death or generally; and

(2) the saving of tax, usually IHT, particularly where the disposition of the estate does not fully utilise the deceased's nil rate band.

There are many methods whereby the disposition of an estate can be rearranged. Most methods take advantage of specific statutory provision while others use taxation exemptions and reliefs. The following are among the more usual.

A lifetime gift by the beneficiary of an inheritance under a will or under an intestacy

Such a rearrangement may take the form of an outright gift. If so, it will constitute a PET for IHT and a disposal for CGT by the beneficiary. If instead the rearrangement takes the form of a gift to trustees into trust, it will amount to a PET or lifetime chargeable transfer depending upon which type of trust is selected. For CGT a gift to trustees will be a disposal whichever type of trust is selected. Creation of trusts by lifetime gift is considered in Chapter 5.

'Precatory trusts' and wills creating 2-year discretionary trusts

If a testator has included provisions of this type in his will, he had in mind flexibility of testamentary provision. The exact testamentary effect of the will is, effectively, determined after death by the act of the personal representatives (and in some cases, the beneficiaries), and not by the testator at the time of making the will. Wills containing this type of provision are considered in Chapter 11.

Orders made under the Inheritance (Provisions for Family and Dependants) Act 1975 and the capitalisation of a life interest on an intestacy

Both of these amount to rearrangements of the disposition of an estate on death. In either case the devolution of the estate becomes subject to the terms of the rearrangement. This 'reading back' effect will affect the extent of the liability to IHT on the estate on death. (See further the LPC Resource Book *Wills, Probate and Administration* (Jordans, 1997).)

Post-death variations of the dispositions of the deceased's estate

If the variation is followed by the making of the necessary election by the beneficiary, the effect is to read the provisions of the variation back into the terms of the deceased's will or the intestacy law for tax purposes. The estate on death is then charged to IHT on the basis of the amended provisions but the beneficiary suffers no adverse tax consequences. If no election is made, the writing back effect is not obtained and the beneficiary is left in the position of making inter vivos gifts as discussed above. Variations are discussed further at **12.2**.

Disclaimer of benefit

A disclaimer may not achieve the objectives of the beneficiary wishing to make the post-death rearrangement. Disclaimers amount to a rejection of the benefit of the gift under the will or the intestacy law. They will be appropriate for use only if, following the rejection, the property passes to the person who the original beneficiary intends to benefit. However, despite this limitation on their use, in some cases disclaimers offer advantages not available in the case of variations.

12.1.2   Variation or disclaimer?

These provisions permit the redirection of property after a death by a beneficiary whether the deceased died testate or intestate. They offer estate planning opportunities for the beneficiary who can afford 'not to receive' property for whatever reason.

Post-death variations and disclaimers are normally used to redistribute property among members of the family following a death, but variations offer wider possibilities. A variation permits the beneficiary positively to redirect the devolution of the property whereas a disclaimer is merely 'negative' in its operation, ie the beneficiary rejects the gift. As the variation permits redirection by the original beneficiary, it is possible to introduce 'new beneficiaries' into the terms of the deceased's will or the provisions of the intestacy law. If not used to redirect the property among the family, a variation will often be used to provide charitable payments by will attracting the IHT exemption.

Each method of redistribution should be considered on every occasion. Control over the devolution of the property is retained by the original beneficiary only where a variation is used. Thus, if the disclaimed property would pass to the 'wrong beneficiary', a variation will be required to redirect its devolution as appropriate. Although a variation will enable the desired rearrangement to be achieved, the lack of 'writing back' provisions for income tax can cause difficulties where the variation is made in favour of 'new beneficiaries' who are the minor children of the original beneficiary. These difficulties relate to the taxation of the income derived from the property following the variation and are considered at **12.4.2**. The advantage of redirecting property by disclaimer is that there is no equivalent income tax disadvantage. Thus, where possible, a disclaimer by a parent is the favourable method of effecting a post-death rearrangement in favour of minor children.

12.2   POST-DEATH VARIATIONS

12.2.1   The conditions (IHTA 1984, s 142; TCGA 1992, s 62)

IHT

To achieve the desired writing back effect, the beneficiary must enter into the variation, in writing, within 2 years of the deceased's death. In addition, he must give written notice of election to the Inland Revenue within 6 months of the instrument of variation (or such longer period as the Inland Revenue may allow). For the beneficiary, compliance with these conditions will mean that the variation does not amount to a transfer of value by him and so no IHT will be payable (IHTA, s 17(a)).

CGT

The conditions for the beneficiary to satisfy are the same as for IHT, including the need for written notice of election. No CGT is payable on the deceased's death in any event so that the substitution of new beneficiaries will not affect the CGT position on the death. For the beneficiary, no disposal will take place so that no liability to CGT will arise.

12.2.2 Planning the elections

The choice of whether to elect or not lies with the original beneficiary. However, the writing back effect for capital tax purposes will only occur if an election is made and notice is given to the Inland Revenue.

If no IHT election is made, the original beneficiary will make a PET. If he outlives this by 7 years, the PET will never become a chargeable transfer. However, by giving notice of an election and thereby achieving the writing back effect, the beneficiary achieves the certainty of a gift to new beneficiaries without any liability to IHT (other than in the deceased's estate).

If no CGT election is made, the original beneficiary will make a disposal for CGT. If no gain occurs, or if any gain which does arise falls within his annual exemption or is covered by available losses, the omission to make the election will not matter. If he does make the election with notice to the Inland Revenue, certainty is achieved, in that no CGT is payable.

12.2.3 Capacity to make a variation

An original beneficiary under a will or an intestacy can make a variation in relation to his interest provided he has attained 18 years of age and has mental capacity. The beneficiary with an absolute interest may settle it on trusts for the benefit of others or make an outright gift.

> *Example*
> David by will leaves £300,000 to John, who wishes to provide for his own child Carol now aged 19 years. By post-death variation, David's will is varied leaving £100,000 in trust for Carol contingently on her attaining 25 and the residue of £200,000 for John.

Consent of the court

In some cases the consent of the court will be needed before a variation can be made. Under the Variation of Trusts Act 1958 (VTA 1958) the court has power to consent on behalf of beneficiaries who are (inter alia) minors or mentally handicapped. The court's powers are wide enough to permit the variation of beneficial interests whether they are vested, contingent or discretionary but it will only exercise the powers where the proposed arrangement is for the benefit of the beneficiary.

However, VTA 1958 applications to the court are expensive and time-consuming so that, to be justified, the tax saving to be achieved by estate planning should be substantial.

Problems of lack of capacity to consent generally do not arise in the context of 'flexible' wills containing discretionary trusts or an overriding power of appointment. In these cases, any rearrangement of the deceased's estate after death occurs as a result of the decision of the trustees acting under the terms of the will. The lack of ability of a beneficiary to consent is not crucial to the proposed arrangement. This feature of flexible wills tends to make them attractive in practice (see **11.4**).

Can the estate of a deceased beneficiary be varied?

Example

Veronica dies leaving the whole of her estate valued at £250,000 to her husband Arthur. He dies soon after his wife leaving his estate of £500,000 (including the £250,000 inherited from Veronica) to their child, Damon. Arthur's personal representatives can make a variation to redirect Veronica's estate to Damon to use up her nil rate band.

Step 1: IHT on Veronica's death
£250,000 subject to spouse exemption = Nil

Step 2: IHT on Arthur's death
£215,000 @ 0% = Nil
£285,000 @ 40% = £114,000
Damon receives £386,000 as a result of his parents' deaths.

Step 3: PRs make a variation of Veronica's estate in favour of Damon.

    (a) Recalculate IHT on Veronica's estate
£215,000 @ 0% = Nil
£35,000 @ 40% = £14,000

    (b) Recalculate IHT on Arthur's estate
£215,000 @ 0% = Nil
£35,000 @ 40% = £14,000

As a result of the variation, Damon's total entitlement from his parents' estates is £472,000.

The Inland Revenue accept that a variation of the type contemplated by the personal representatives in the example (or any other variation by the personal representatives of the deceased beneficiary) is within the IHT provisions. Provided the personal representatives make the election within 6 months of the variation it will be read back into the will of the first testator to die for IHT purposes.

12.3   THE SCOPE OF THE STATUTORY PROVISIONS FOR VARIATIONS AND DISCLAIMERS

It is possible to vary or disclaim 'any of the dispositions (whether effected by will, under the law relating to intestacy or otherwise) of the property comprised in the estate immediately before his death . . .' (IHTA 1984, s 142).

In the application of this provision the following points should be noted.

12.3.1   Interests in joint property

An interest in property held as joint tenants is an asset of the 'estate' of a deceased person for IHT. Although an interest in property held in joint tenancy passes on death by survivorship to the surviving joint tenant, it is nevertheless within the IHT (and CGT) provisions permitting variations and disclaimers following a death. This is because these provisions apply where a disposition on death is effected 'or otherwise', ie by survivorship.

Example

Alice and Bill inherited Rose Cottage as joint tenants many years ago. Since then they and their respective families have used the cottage for holidays.

Alice has just died leaving her estate by will to her only child, Clara, but her share of the cottage passes to Bill by survivorship. Bill feels Clara should have inherited her mother's interest in the cottage.

Bill can effect a variation so that Alice's estate is taxed as if her will had left her half of the cottage to Clara. This will be effective for tax purposes provided Bill makes the elections. To complete the gift Bill must convey the legal estate to himself and Clara by a separate deed.

12.3.2   Interests in property not capable of variation

The 'estate' of a deceased person includes (inter alia):

(1)   the property in which the deceased had an interest in possession immediately before death, for example, a life tenant under an existing will trust; and

(2)   the property to which the deceased is treated as entitled by application of the 'reservation of benefit' rules (FA 1986, s 102 and see **4.7.5**).

Although both of these interests may attract IHT on death as part of the deceased's estate, it is not possible for either to be the subject of a variation (or disclaimer) for taxation purposes. This is because the definition of 'estate' within the meaning of s 142 of the IHTA 1984 specifically excludes each of these interests. Any estate planning following the death must, therefore, proceed on the basis of excluding these interests from any calculations.

12.3.3   Do the reservation of benefit rules apply to variations?

Do the reservation of benefit rules apply if a beneficiary (the donor) makes a post-death variation but still continues to enjoy the property? If so, any advantage intended through the post-death variation would be lost.

The IHTA 1984 applies 'as if the variation had been effected by the deceased or, as the case may be, the disclaimed benefit never conferred'.

Thus, the effect for IHT purposes of making a valid election after a variation is that the deceased is to be taken as making the variation and, therefore, is the donor of the gift. The original beneficiary under the will or the intestacy is not the donor. As a consequence, any benefit which is reserved by the variation to the beneficiary who made it cannot come within these provisions.

Example 1

Ellen died leaving a will containing a gift of her house to Rex. Rex occupies the house but subsequently redirects this gift by post-death variation to his only child Paula. An election is made and Rex remains in occupation. This will not result in a reservation of benefit to him since the gift of the house is taken to be by Ellen for IHT purposes. Rex's estate on death will be taxed on this basis.

Example 2

Roger dies leaving a substantial cash legacy to Julian absolutely. Julian redirects this property into a discretionary trust by means of variation followed by an election. Julian is named as one of the beneficiaries of the discretionary trust. No reservation of benefit for IHT will result as the discretionary trust is taken to be made by Roger. However, there may be income tax consequences as there are no writing back provisions for income tax equivalent to those for IHT and CGT. Julian, not Roger, will be treated as the settlor making the discretionary settlement for the purposes of the income tax avoidance rules (see **6.2.10**).

12.3.4 More than one variation?

In some instances a number of variations in relation to the same will or intestacy may be contemplated. No difficulty will arise provided each variation deals with a separate part of the estate. Clearly, property given by a legacy in a will and the property in the residuary gift are separate parts each capable of being the subject of a variation. It is also accepted that two or more variations, each relating to property in residue, can be effective. For example, a residuary beneficiary can validly redirect by variation one half of the residuary property to new beneficiary A and the other half to new beneficiary B and in each case achieve the writing back effect for IHT purposes (provided two elections are made).

However, the Inland Revenue has stated (inter alia) that in broad terms their view is that 'an instrument will not fall within s 142 of the IHTA 1984 if it further redirects any item or any part of an item that has already been redirected under an earlier instrument'. A second variation in relation to the same property will, therefore, not be effective for tax purposes.

12.3.5 Beneficiaries other than members of the family

Normally, the rearrangement will involve redistribution of the deceased's property among members of the family. However, there is no restriction in the legislation, whether for IHT or CGT, which restricts the introduction of a new beneficiary who is not a member of the family. This opens up the possibility of introducing as a beneficiary:

(1) A claimant under the Inheritance (Provision for Family and Dependants) Act 1975. For example, a claim by a person 'maintained by the deceased' under s 1(1)(e) of the Act for reasonable financial provision may be compromised within 2 years of the death. If the conditions are satisfied, this may take the form of a variation which, provided an election is made within 6 months of the compromise, will achieve the writing back effect of any other post-death variation and will be effective for both IHT and CGT.

(2) A charity. A charitable donation, within the IHT exemption, can be made from the deceased's estate by introducing a charity as a legatee. If the conditions are satisfied, the terms of the will or of the intestacy law will then be read as if the deceased had made the donation himself to the named charity.

12.4 INCOME TAX AND POST-DEATH ARRANGEMENTS

12.4.1 Income before a variation or disclaimer is made

There are no specific income tax provisions equivalent to the IHT and CGT provisions where a variation or disclaimer has been made. Thus, income received before the variation or disclaimer from the property concerned will be taxed as the income of the original beneficiary. This will apply even if the beneficiary has specifically given up all income from the property since the date of death. For example, if the original beneficiary by variation redirects a specific legacy of shares, he remains liable to pay any income tax on dividends paid before the variation.

12.4.2 Income after a variation or disclaimer is made

Does the original beneficiary continue to pay income tax after the variation or disclaimer on any income produced by the property given away? The intention is that once the rearrangement has been made, the original beneficiary ceases to be liable to pay income tax on this income. In most cases, this result will be achieved. If it is, the new beneficiary will become liable for income tax on income produced by the property concerned. However, the position will be different where the new beneficiary is the minor child of the original beneficiary. In such cases the parent will remain liable for income tax on the income even though he does not enjoy it or own the property which produces it. The reason is the income tax anti-avoidance provisions discussed at **4.7.4**. These are of general application and are not confined to post-death arrangements but they are particularly relevant when advising following the death of a client.

How do the income tax avoidance rules apply to variations?

If the variation creates a 'settlement' for income tax purposes from which the original beneficiary may continue to benefit, he will still be liable to pay income tax on all the settlement income (see **6.2.10**). However, among the beneficiary's reasons for making the variation will be his wish to avoid income tax on the income produced by the property the subject of the variation. Thus, the variation must be drafted so as to exclude him and his spouse from all enjoyment from the property which has been redirected, and from its income.

However, the original beneficiary may nevertheless be caught by the anti-avoidance rules and so still be liable to income tax on the income of the property subject to the variation. This will be the case if his minor unmarried children are constituted the new beneficiaries as a result of the variation and the income is paid for the benefit of those beneficiaries and not accumulated. The same result will occur whether the variation gives the children absolute interests or an interest in new trusts which are created by the variation.

If the anti-avoidance provisions apply, they will cease to do so once the children have reached their majority or have married; from then onwards their parents will no longer be taxed on the settlement income.

> *Example 1*
> A variation by Hannah (to use up the nil rate band of her recently deceased husband) redirects £215,000 absolutely to her adult children. The children will pay income tax on the income of the property.

> *Example 2*
> A similar post-death variation is made by Ania but her children (the new bene-ficiaries) are minors. Even though the children have an absolute (vested) entitlement to the £215,000, the income of the property is deemed to be Ania's for tax purposes, insofar as it is not accumulated.

Disclaimers distinguished

A variation is the positive redirection of benefit by the original beneficiary whereas a disclaimer is merely the rejection of a benefit. The Inland Revenue does not consider a disclaimer to be a 'settlement' and so to come within the income tax anti-avoidance provisions. The consequence is that income of property which is disclaimed by a parent is not taxed as though it is still his, even if his minor un-married child inherits the property as a result of the disclaimer. Parents who are considering post-death rearrangements for the benefit of their children should, where possible, use a disclaimer instead of a variation which might fall within the provisions.

12.5 DRAFTING A POST-DEATH VARIATION AND THE ELECTION

12.5.1 Is a deed required?

Both the IHTA 1984, s 142 and the TCGA 1992, s 62 require only an instrument in writing, but as a post-death variation is a gratuitous promise to transfer property, it should be by deed to be enforceable. Further, unless it is by deed the deceased's personal representatives may not be prepared to act in accordance with its terms.

12.5.2 The date and opening words

Sample clause

> **THIS DEED OF VARIATION is made the [   ] day of [   ]**
> **One thousand nine hundred and . . .**

12.5.3 Parties

Sections 142 and 62 require only 'the persons who benefit or would benefit under the disposition . . . to make the written instrument'. However, often there will be three parties:

(1) the original beneficiaries (who give up the benefit);
(2) the new beneficiaries (who receive the property and thus will include trustees if the variation creates a trust); and
(3) the personal representatives of the deceased's estate (who must also join in any election to the Inland Revenue if additional IHT is payable as a result of the variation).

Sample clause

> **BETWEEN**
>
> **(1) [name] ('the Original Beneficiary')**
> **(2) [name] ('the New Beneficiary')**
> **(3) [name] ('the Executors')**

PRs should be made parties for their own protection when they distribute property in accordance with the post-death variation rather than the will in its original form. It is not essential to join the new beneficiaries in receipt of property as parties but many practitioners prefer to do so.

12.5.4 Supplemental to the will or intestacy

The deed of variation is made to relate expressly to the deceased's death.

Sample clause

> **SUPPLEMENTAL to the will [with . . . codicil(s)] ('the Will') of [name] ('the Deceased') and to the other documents and events specified in the Schedule**

The Schedule will contain details of the will, date of death, grant of probate etc.

12.5.5 Recitals

Recitals will always be used in the deed to explain the circumstances giving rise to the variation. Usually the recitals are restricted to statements relating to:

(1) the entitlement of the original beneficiary under the will or the intestacy of the deceased; and

(2) the wish of the original beneficiary to vary the provisions of the will or the intestacy in the manner stated in the operative part of the variation.

Sample clause

> **WHEREAS**
>
> **(A) Under the Will the Original Beneficiary was given [   ] interest ('the Interest') in [all of the] [x per cent of the] residuary estate of the Deceased**
>
> **(B) The Original Beneficiary wishes to vary the dispositions effected by the Will in relation to the Interest in the following manner**

The interest will be an 'absolute' interest or a 'life interest' and the clause should be completed accordingly, showing whether it relates to the whole or part of the residuary estate.

12.5.6 The operative part

It is often convenient when drafting the operative part of a post-death variation to consider how the will, or a codicil to it, might have been drafted for the testator before his death. This can often give valuable guidance on drafting the post-death variation. For example, in the context of a variation to create a nil rate band legacy for a child, only a short provision is required.

Sample clause

> **'NOW THIS DEED IRREVOCABLY WITNESSES as follows:**
>
> **By way of variation of the disposition made by the Will the Original Beneficiary declares that the Will shall have effect as if it contained a pecuniary legacy to the New Beneficiary of an amount on which no IHT is chargeable other than at the nil rate on the death of the Deceased such legacy to be discharged from the Interest.**

If a legacy is being introduced into the will by the post-death variation, it should be considered whether it is to be a legacy 'subject to' or 'free of' IHT. In the former case, any IHT which does become payable is paid by the legatee. The payment of the legacy will be directed to be made from a particular part of the estate which normally will be the residue.

If trusts, rather than outright gifts, are to be created by the variation, these may either be set out in a schedule to the deed or it may refer to trusts created by a separate instrument. For example, the original beneficiary may wish to direct that his interest be transferred to the trustees of an A & M settlement created by the deceased during his lifetime for his grandchildren.

12.5.7 The elections

To be effective as a variation it is necessary that the election be given to the Inland Revenue within 6 months of the instrument or such longer period as the Inland Revenue may allow (see **12.2.1**). In practice, notice should be given to the Capital Taxes Office (for IHT) and to an Inspector of Taxes (for CGT).

The election may be made within the written variation or by a separate instrument. Most precedents include the election in the operative part of the instrument so that notice is given by sending the variation or a copy of it to the Inland Revenue.

If the variation causes additional IHT to become payable, for example, where a spouse gives up a benefit and the spouse exemption is lost, the personal representatives must join in the election to the Inland Revenue. This is easily achieved if, as a matter of course, the election appears in the written variation to which the personal representatives are made party. If the election is contained in a separate instrument, provision must be made for their signatures. Only if the personal representatives have no funds available to them for payment of any extra IHT, may they refuse to sign the election. This protects personal representatives who have already distributed the estate before they become liable to pay the extra IHT resulting from the written variation.

To be effective as an election the Inland Revenue require specific reference to the relevant statutory provision under which the election is made.

Sample clause

> **THE Parties hereto hereby elect pursuant to section 142(2) of the Inheritance Tax Act 1984 and section 62(7) of the Taxation of Chargeable Gains Act 1992 that section 142(1) of the Inheritance Tax Act 1984 and section 62(6) of the Taxation of Chargeable Gains Act 1992 shall apply to the variation made by this deed**

12.5.8 Stamp duty

Instruments dated on or after 1 May 1987 are exempt from stamp duty if appropriately certified under the Stamp Duty (Exempt Instruments) Regulations 1987. The Regulations list categories for exemptions and post-death variations usually qualify as voluntary dispositions (category M).

Sample clause

> **It is hereby certified that this instrument falls within category M in the Schedule to the Stamp Duty (Exempt Instruments) Regulations 1987**

Chapter 13

TRUST ADMINISTRATION

13.1 INTRODUCTION

Many aspects of trust administration have been considered in the earlier chapters in this book. Most of these matters have related to the dispositive provisions of the trust instrument, ie the provisions dealing with the beneficiaries and beneficial entitlement and include the following:

(1) the TA 1925, ss 31 and 32 in Chapters 5 and 10;
(2) advances and appointments by trustees in favour of beneficiaries in Chapters 9 and 10;
(3) capital tax implications of changes in beneficial entitlement arising from (1) and (2).

There are many other matters relevant to the proper administration of a trust of which the more important are discussed in this chapter including:

(1) the management powers of the trustees;
(2) trustee investments;
(3) the appointment of trustees;
(4) vesting trust property in trustees and in beneficiaries;
(5) taxation liability arising during the trust period, including CGT on sales by trustees on rearrangements of the investment portfolio and the income tax liabilities of the trustees and beneficiaries; and
(6) accounting for the trust assets and income.

13.2 MANAGEMENT POWERS OF TRUSTEES

When creating a settlement, particularly a discretionary settlement, the settlor will wish to incorporate wide ranging powers for his trustees covering all aspects of the trust fund and its administration. He must bear in mind the present and future trust property, the wide ranging nature of the trusts, and the wide class of beneficiaries. The fact that the trust may continue for many years will mean very careful thought is needed as to provisions which may be of assistance to the trustees many years ahead. The modern policy is to incorporate these wide powers by inserting them in a schedule to the trust instrument.

The trustees of a trust instrument created by a settlor during his lifetime derive their powers, dispositive and administrative, from sources similar to the executors and trustees of a testator's will. These are discussed in the LPC Resource Book *Wills, Probate and Administration* (Jordans, 1997) where precedent clauses are supplied with commentary.

13.2.1 Implied statutory powers

The principal statutory powers are contained in:

(1) the TA 1925; and
(2) the Trustee Investments Act 1961 (TIA 1961).

13.2.2 Powers granted by the trust instrument

Modification of statutory powers

It is usual for many of the implied powers to be modified by the trust instrument. The more usual modifications are considered, briefly, at **13.2.3**.

Additional powers

In addition to modification of the implied powers, a trust instrument will frequently contain additional powers for the trustees which are otherwise not available to them. Some of the more common of these are also considered below.

13.2.3 Administrative provisions

Investment

The TIA 1961 (as amended by the Trustee Investments (Division of Fund) Order 1996) gives trustees limited powers of investment. It also contains elaborate and complex rules which the trustees must observe. It is, therefore, usual to give trustees a complete discretion in the choice of investment, for example, 'to invest the trust funds as if they were beneficial owners'. In addition, express provision should (where appropriate) permit:

(1) the purchase of foreign investments; and/or
(2) the purchase of property for the personal enjoyment or occupation by a beneficiary; and/or
(3) the purchase of non-income-producing investments such as insurance policies; and/or
(4) the retention of investments originally settled, for example shares in the settlor's family company.

Powers may also be given to permit delegation of decision making to fund managers, or stockbrokers, so that they may take decisions as to sales and purchases of trust investments without reference to the trustees. A power permitting delegation may also authorise the holding of trust investments in the names of the fund manager's nominees instead of in the names of the trustees. The trustees would be in breach of duty if they allowed this to happen without express provision in the trust instrument.

See **13.3** for a further discussion of trustee investments.

Insurance of trust property

Other than for trustees of land (who have the powers of absolute owners under the TLA 1996, s 6), s 19 of the TA 1925 limits the powers of trustees to insure trust property for up to three-quarters of its value against fire risk only. The payment of premiums must be made from income of the trust property. Express provision should extend this power to permit:

(1) insurance against all risks up to the full value of the trust property; and
(2) the payment of premiums from capital or income at the trustee's discretion; and
(3) the application of insurance moneys in the reinstatement of the insured property.

Payment of the trustees

As a matter of general law, a trustee may not profit from his trust unless authorised to do so by express provision. Express provision should be made:

(1) to permit a solicitor trustee or other professional person to charge for services rendered to the trust. Such a clause would be of the type incorporated into a will but modified to refer to the 'trustees' instead of the personal representatives; and

(2) to permit a trust corporation which may be appointed a trustee in the future to charge in accordance with its standard terms and conditions; and

(3) to permit a trustee to retain remuneration he has received for services given as a director of a company in which the trust holds shares.

Other matters relating to the trustees

Apart from the appointment and retirement of the trustees referred to in **13.4**, express provision in relation to the following will normally be made as follows.

SELF-DEALING

The fiduciary position of the trustees prevents them from purchasing the trust property or entering into any other transaction affecting the trust property where the trustees' duties and personal self-interest are in conflict. Express provision may permit self-dealing by the trustees.

LOSSES

To protect an honest trustee, the trust instrument will often contain a general indemnity against loss to the trust fund caused by the trustee or an agent (other than where there is wilful fraud or dishonesty of the trustee).

DELEGATION OF POWERS

Section 23 of the TA 1925 permits trustees to employ and pay agents to do any executive functions (but not to exercise discretions) in relation to the trust property. Section 25 of the TA 1925 (as amended by the Powers of Attorney Act 1971, s 9) permits the trustees to delegate by power of attorney any of their powers and discretions for up to 12 months. These powers may be extended by express provision permitting general delegation of all powers and provisions conferred on the trustees even though the powers are fiduciary in nature. In addition, s 9 of the TLA 1996 permits trustees of land to delegate by power of attorney their functions in relation to the land, for example their power of sale, to beneficiaries of full age who are beneficially entitled to an interest in possession in the land.

Receipts clause

An express provision should be included to allow the trustees to accept the receipt of the parent or guardian of a minor, or of the minor himself if aged 16 or more, for capital advanced or income applied on the minor's behalf. In the absence of such a clause, trustees have powers to accept receipts in relation to income paid for the beneficiary's maintenance education or benefit under s 31 of the TA 1925 or capital paid for a minor's benefit under s 32 of the TA 1925 to his parent or guardian.

Appropriation of assets

Section 41 of the AEA 1925 does not apply to trustees. An express provision, equivalent to s 41, will permit the trustees to appropriate trust property towards beneficial interests arising under the trust, whether absolute interests or interests in trust, without the prior consent of the beneficiary.

Exclusion of apportionments

As in the case of wills where trusts are created, an express provision excluding the statutory and equitable rules of apportionment is usually included in the trust instrument. This will avoid the complication and expense involved in making the apportionment calculations. Such a clause should be drafted widely so as to exclude apportionment (inter alia) on the death of a life tenant in an interest in possession settlement.

13.3   TRUSTEE INVESTMENTS

13.3.1   Retention of the original trust fund

For a settlement to be effective it needs property to be subject to the trusts. When a settlement is created the initial trust fund may consist of cash, or assets (eg shares or land), or a combination of cash and assets. The trustees must decide whether they are permitted to keep the initial trust fund as it is and, if so, whether in fact they should do so.

Trustees of a settlement which arises by virtue of the intestacy rules on a death intestate are in a different position. The AEA 1925 imposes a statutory trust and all assets not authorised by the TIA 1961 must be sold and the proceeds reinvested in investments authorised by that statute.

Most inter vivos settlements and will trusts are drafted by professionals who will ensure that the settlement gives the trustees the widest possible powers of investment and enables them to keep any assets transferred to them by the settlor or from the estate.

13.3.2   Suitable investments

In deciding whether to retain permitted assets the trustees must consider the suitability of the assets for the aims of the settlement. This is also a governing factor when deciding how to invest any cash that may have been settled.

> *Example 1*
> A settlement is created for Donna for life with remainder to Nigel. The trustees are faced with competing needs: Donna requires an income from the trust fund whilst Nigel needs the real value of the capital to improve. As a general rule, assets producing a good income return, for example, a building society account, offer little or no capital growth, and vice versa.
>
> The trustees need to invest the trust fund in a range of investments which provide overall income and capital growth; perhaps gilts and a National Savings Income Bond for income and quoted shares or unit trusts for growth.

> *Example 2*
> An A & M settlement is created for Adam and Belinda, 6-year-old twins contingent as to both capital and income on their attaining 25 years of age. They are unlikely to need any income for at least the first 5 years of the settlement and any income accumulated in the settlement will suffer 34% income tax (see **13.5.2**).
>
> As there is no need for income, the trustees can concentrate on improving the capital value of the trust fund, perhaps by investing in quoted shares.

13.3.3 Subsequent changes to the trust fund

Although with an express power of investment the bulk of the fund is likely to be invested in land and/or securities, most trustees should consider retaining a degree of liquidity by holding a small amount of cash in an interest-bearing instant access bank or building society account. This will provide the trustees with cash to meet expenses, such as solicitors' or accountants' fees, and their own out-of-pocket expenses. It will also provide them with the ability to make a new purchase for the trust fund if an opportunity suddenly arises. On occasion they may also use such an account to retain the proceeds of sale of an investment where there is not to be an immediate reinvestment of the realised fund.

Once a settlement has been created, trustees need to review the trust fund regularly. Trustees can make many of the investments which an individual concerned with his personal estate planning might make (see Appendix 2). How often trustees review their investments depends on a number of factors but should not be less than once a year and may be more frequently. This is to ensure that the fund continues to provide for the aims of the settlement; to minimise the liability to CGT; and to protect the fund against economic forces.

Changes to reflect the aims of the settlement

Settlements are designed to last for many years. An investment strategy that was appropriate at the outset may not be appropriate 10 years later; in particular, the beneficiaries needs may have changed or there may be about to be a change in the beneficial interests in the settlement. Trustees may need to alter the investments in the trust fund to reflect these changes.

Example

Twelve years ago, Damien settled £100,000 cash on discretionary trusts for his three grandchildren then aged 5, 4 and 2 years. The children had no immediate need for income and as all income accumulated within the trust suffers income tax at a non-recoverable 34%, the trustees invested the majority of the trust fund in low income, high growth shares and unit trusts. The trust fund is now worth £180,000 and produces £2,000 per annum income. The eldest beneficiary intends to start medical school in 3 months' time and the trustees have decided to exercise their discretion and pay her £5,000 per annum income from the trust fund.

The trustees must, therefore, sell some of their investments and reinvest the proceeds to increase the income generated by the trust fund. As a known amount of income is required, the trustees might consider achieving this by investing in gilts or a guaranteed rate building society account.

Minimising CGT

A large proportion of a trust fund is likely to be invested in assets such as quoted shares which attract a charge to CGT on their disposal. As trustees only have an annual exemption of £3,250 and gains are charged at 34 per cent in all settlements without an immediate interest in possession, it is sensible (where possible) to manage the fund to minimise the liability. For example, trustees may invest in land to be occupied by a beneficiary under a trust as his residence qualifies for the principal private residence exemption. If such investment and occupation occur under the terms of a discretionary trust, this (at least in the view of the Inland Revenue) may amount to giving the beneficiary an interest in possession in the part of the settled property represented by the private residence (see **4.7.4**).

A charge to CGT will arise on two occasions: on a deemed disposal when a beneficiary becomes absolutely entitled to trust property; and on an actual disposal when trust property is sold as a result of investment changes (see **13.5**). Trustees should always aim to utilise their annual exemption as it cannot be carried forward to future tax years or transferred to beneficiaries.

In a year in which a deemed disposal will occur, trustees should consider carefully whether any investment changes need to be made or whether they can leave the changes to the next tax year so keeping their annual exemption available to set against the charge on the deemed disposal.

Where neither changes to the portfolio nor deemed disposals are envisaged in any year, trustees might consider 'bed and breakfasting' to utilise their annual exemption (see further **4.6.3**).

General reviews

Most investors who invest in the stock market, whether through the direct purchase of shares or via unit trusts, do so to make money rather than as a desire to be part of a particular company. The stock market is divided into sectors with companies predominantly involved in particular activities being grouped together, for example, both WH Smith plc and Marks & Spencer plc are in the 'Retailers General' sector whilst Whitbread plc and Bass plc are both 'Breweries'. Trustees, like most individual investors, are looking for a spread of investments, investing in companies from a number of sectors rather than concentrating on companies in one sector. This is because sectors of the economy perform differently depending on different economic factors and, if one sector is suffering, the value of the shares in the majority of companies in that sector is likely to fall. It is unusual, however, for all sectors to be depressed at the same time and the theory of investing in a number of sectors is that the gains and losses should be evened out.

Trustees may be advised to sell their shares in companies in a particular sector and invest the proceeds in a different sector for a while, or to change companies within a sector.

> *Example*
> The trustees of an A & M settlement have invested a quarter of the trust fund in gilts and the remainder equally between A plc (an insurance company), B plc (a food manufacturer) and C plc (an oil company). Their stockbrokers advise that the insurance market is depressed and that the value of their shareholding is falling but that companies in the 'Water' sector look set to make large profits. The trustees decide to sell their shares in A plc and use the proceeds to buy shares in D plc, a water company.

13.4 APPOINTMENT OF TRUSTEES

13.4.1 The original trustees

Choice of trustees

The choice of the original trustees of the settlement is made by the settlor at the time he makes a settlement. Their appointment as trustees takes effect immediately the trust instrument is executed. Once appointed, they are in a fiduciary position and so must act with good faith. Their duty is to administer the trust for the benefit of its beneficiaries.

Number of trustees

Although every trust must have at least one trustee, it is usual for the settlor to appoint between two and four individuals to act as trustees of his settlement. A maximum of four trustees can be appointed for trusts of land but at least two trustees (or a trust corporation) are required to give a buyer a valid receipt for the proceeds of sale of land held in a settlement. There is no limit to the number of trustees who can be appointed for trusts of personalty but the appointment of more than four can cause the trust administration to be unnecessarily cumbersome.

Selection of trustees

Considerable care should be taken by the settlor in choosing the original trustees. It is possible to appoint a trust corporation to act as trustee but most settlors prefer to appoint individuals because of the personal involvement this will bring to the administration of the trusts. In selecting individuals the settlor should consider the following.

A PROFESSIONAL TRUSTEE

It is of advantage if a solicitor or other professional person is appointed to be a trustee often together with member(s) of the settlor's own family. Where a professional is appointed initially, or in case such a person may be appointed as a trustee in the future, a charging clause should be included among the administrative powers of the trust (see **13.2.3**).

THE SETTLOR AS TRUSTEE

The settlor may appoint himself to be the sole trustee or one of several trustees of his settlement. He may wish to be a trustee since this allows him to retain an involvement in the settlement and have some influence over how it is administered, for example, he will have a say in whether the trustees should exercise their discretion in favour of a particular beneficiary under a discretionary settlement. If he is appointed a trustee, the settlor must not allow his personal wishes to overshadow his duties as trustee.

Instead of being appointed a trustee, the settlor may prefer to exercise some influence over the trustees through the use of a 'letter of wishes' (or a side letter) addressed to the trustees. Clearly, such a letter will have no binding effect on the trustees but, by setting out how he hopes the settlement will be administered in the future, the settlor hopes the trustees will have some regard to his intentions.

A BENEFICIARY AS TRUSTEE

The settlor may appoint one or more of the beneficiaries to be a trustee of the settlement but this may cause difficulty, for example, a conflict of interest may arise between the individual's position as trustee on the one hand and as beneficiary on the other. In view of this, a beneficiary should not be a sole trustee. Two or more trustees provide safeguards in that they must supervise one another, must be unanimous in the exercise of their powers (an important protection for the beneficiaries) and their appointment will ensure a continuing trustee if one were to die or to retire from the trusts.

13.4.2 Subsequent trustees

Appointment by the settlor

Once the original trustees have been appointed the settlor has no further power to appoint trustees. If a settlor (who is not also a trustee) wishes to control the selection of trustees during his lifetime, he can only do so if the trust instrument gives him the express power to appoint new trustees.

Sample clause

> **During the lifetime of the Settlor the power of appointing new trustees shall be vested in the Settlor.**

The statutory power of appointing new or additional trustees

If there is no person nominated in the trust instrument (eg the settlor), s 36 of the TA 1925 provides wide statutory powers for the appointment of new trustees.

REPLACEMENT TRUSTEES (TA 1925, s 36(1))

The appointment of a new trustee must be made in writing (but will normally be by deed, see **13.4.4**) by:

(1) the surviving or continuing trustees, including any retiring or disclaiming trustee if he wishes to join in the appointment; or
(2) the personal representatives of the last surviving trustee.

A new trustee can be appointed under s 36(1) to replace (inter alia) a trustee who has died, is incapable of acting, or who retires.

ADDITIONAL TRUSTEES (TA 1925, s 36(6))

The appointment of additional trustees must be made in writing by the continuing trustee(s). The number of trustees after the new appointment is made must not exceed four.

DIRECTIONS AS TO TRUSTEES (TLA 1996, s 19)

If there is no person still alive nominated in the trust instrument to appoint new trustees, the beneficiaries of full age and capacity who together are entitled to the trust property can give written directions to the trustees for the retirement and appointment of a trustee. This provision applies to interest in possession settlements only (whatever the nature of the settled property) since beneficiaries of discretionary settlements are not 'together entitled to the trust property'. As it is possible for the trust instrument to exclude s 19, settlors should be invited to consider whether they prefer future control over the appointment and retirement of trustees to remain with the existing trustees or to pass instead to the beneficiaries.

13.4.3 Vesting the trust property in the trustees

On creation of the settlement

Once the original trustees have been appointed, the settlor must transfer to them the 'settled property', ie the assets mentioned in the trust instrument as being subject to the trusts of the settlement. It is a duty of the trustees to bring all the trust property under their control.

The settled property will be transferred to the trustees by using whatever means of transfer is appropriate to that property. For example, stock transfer forms will be used to transfer shares; a deed will be used to transfer the legal estate in land.

On the appointment of replacement or additional trustees

Following a change in the trustees, the trust property must be vested in the new trustee(s). If the appointment of the new trustee(s) is by deed, s 40(1) of the TA 1925 provides that the vesting of the trust property will occur automatically. There are, however, circumstances where s 40(1) does not apply so that formal transfer of the trust property to the new trustee(s) will be required. In particular, there is no automatic vesting of stocks and shares. In these cases a stock transfer form transferring the shares into the names of all the trustees must be signed by the 'old trustees' and registered with the company. Although the shares are held by the trustees as trust property, there is no reference to this on the company's membership register. Shares are shown as registered in the individual names of the trustees without reference to their capacity as trustees.

13.4.4 Drafting a deed of appointment of new trustees

Heading and date

Sample clause

> **DEED OF APPOINTMENT AND RETIREMENT**
>
> **DATE: [   ]**

Parties

Who the parties are will depend on the circumstances giving rise to the appointment of new trustees. The person(s) with the power to appoint will always be parties; so too will the new trustee(s) and any retiring trustee.

Sample clause

> **BETWEEN**
> **(1) [name] ('the Continuing Trustees')**
> **(2) [name] ('the New Trustee')**
> **(3) [name] ('the Retiring Trustee')**

Recitals

Normally, there will be three or four separate provisions detailing the circumstances giving rise to the change of the trustees.

Sample clause

> **RECITALS**
>
> **(A)** **This Deed is supplemental to the settlement (the 'Settlement') [and to the other documents and events] specified in the [First] Schedule.**
>
> **(B)** **The statutory power of appointment applies to the Settlement and is exercisable by the Continuing Trustees and the Retiring Trustee.**
>
> **(C)** **The Continuing Trustees and the Retiring Trustee are the present trustees of the Settlement.**
>
> **(D)** **The Continuing Trustees and the Retiring Trustee wish to appoint the New Trustee to act as a trustee of the Settlement in place of the Retiring Trustee.**
>
> **(E)** **It is intended that the property now in the Settlement [, details of which are set out in the Second Schedule,] shall be transferred**

> **to, or under the control of, the Continuing Trustees and the New Trustee**

Such clauses allow for the retirement of the trustee. If no trustee is retiring, all references to 'the Retiring Trustee' should be deleted from the clauses as well as from 'the parties'.

Clause (E) is intended to enable the trust property to be detailed in the schedule to the deed of appointment. It is not an express declaration vesting property in the new trustee.

The operative part

By this clause, those with the power to do so make the appointment of the new trustee. If power to appoint new trustees has been retained by the settlor (see **13.2**), the settlor, defined as 'the Appointor', would be added as a 'party' and would make the appointment in the operative part. If the present trustees are to exercise the statutory power to appoint the new trustees, they will do so in this part of the deed.

Sample clause

> **Appointment of New Trustee in place of Retiring Trustee**
>
> **In exercise of the power of appointment conferred by the Trustee Act 1925 and of all other powers (if any), the Continuing Trustees and the Retiring Trustee hereby appoint the New Trustee as a trustee of the Settlement to act jointly with the Continuing Trustees in place of the Retiring Trustee who hereby retires and is discharged from the trusts of the Settlement.**

Again, if no trustee is to retire, the references to 'the Retiring Trustee' should be deleted. The appointment is then made by 'the Continuing Trustees', ie they do so in exercise of the statutory power.

Schedules

It is usual to include in the Schedules particulars of the settlement to which the deed of appointment is supplemental as well as details of the trust property currently held by the trustees. This list of trust property is useful for the new trustee who must now exercise his duties as trustee in relation to it.

13.5　TAXATION DURING THE ADMINISTRATION OF A SETTLEMENT

The settlor's liability to IHT and CGT on the creation of the settlement is considered in Chapter 5 and liability to the same taxes which arises on trust advances and appointments is considered in Chapter 10. Broadly, these earlier chapters covered the capital tax position on creation and termination of the settlement. The liability to CGT and income tax arising on the trust capital and its income during the administration of a settlement are considered in this section; any relevant IHT liabilities during the trust's existence are considered in the chapters referred to above.

13.5.1 Actual disposals: CGT

If the trustees of the settlement are advised by stockbrokers to rearrange their portfolio of investments, CGT liability may arise on any sales. If so, the trustees are liable to pay the tax and will do so from the settled funds. Sales by the trustees are 'actual disposals' giving rise to CGT liability in a manner similar to disposals by an individual.

Example

Trustees are holding 5,000 XYZ plc shares as part of a trust fund. These shares are sold for £30,000 having been worth only £5,000 when the settlement was created. The RPI has increased by 20% during the period the trustees held the shares.

Disposal consideration		£30,000
Less:		
(1) acquisition cost, ie the value of the shares when the settlement was created	£5,000	
		£25,000
(2) indexation allowance, ie the increase in the RPI since the settlement was created 20% × £5,000	£1,000	
Chargeable gain		£24,000

The calculation is the same as any CGT calculation. It is based on the trustee's disposal consideration and their acquisition cost, ie the value of the shares when transferred to them by the settlor at the time the settlement was created. The indexation allowance is calculated in the normal way.

Reliefs, exemption and rates of tax

The rate at which the trustees pay CGT depends on the particular type of settlement. Normally, the CGT rate is the same as the income tax rate and is governed by the existence or absence of an interest in possession in the settled property.

RATES OF CGT

(1) Discretionary settlement: 34 per cent.
(2) Accumulation and maintenance settlement: 34 per cent.
(3) Interest in possession settlement: 23 per cent.

The 34 per cent rate applies where all or any part of the trust income is taxed at 34 per cent (see **13.5.2**). Thus, if the trust is a 'mixed trust', ie the trusts are partly interest in possession trusts and partly not (discretionary or A & M trusts), the higher 34 per cent rate applies to all the trustees' gains. This situation most often occurs in an A & M trust where one of the beneficiaries has an interest in possession.

Example

Property is held on A & M trusts for Fred (20) and Joyce (17) contingently on them attaining 25 years. Trustee Act 1925, s 31 applies. Fred (having attained 18) has an interest in possession but Joyce has not. As this is a mixed trust, all trustees' gains will be taxed at 34% (even though only Joyce's share of the income would suffer income tax at 34%).

If the settlor has 'an interest in his settlement', for example, he is a beneficiary of a discretionary settlement which he created, the CGT position is different. The anti-avoidance provisions (TCGA 1992, ss 77 and 78) discussed at **6.2.10** prevent the settlor who would otherwise pay CGT at 40 per cent from using the settlement to realise his gains and pay tax at a relatively lower rate. Where the provisions apply, all gains are deemed made by the settlor and not by the trustees. The settlor, and not the trustees, must therefore pay tax on the settlement gains at the rate appropriate to the settlor, ie 20 per cent, 23 per cent or 40 per cent depending on his income tax position. The exclusion of the settlor from benefiting from his own settlement is also discussed at **6.2.10**.

EXEMPTIONS

Trustees of any settlement are entitled to an annual exemption of £3,250, ie one half of the exemption for individuals. If the settlor has created a number of settlements the exemption is divided between them with a minimum of £650 in each case.

RELIEFS

As hold-over relief is not available to the trustees (it is available only on deemed disposals by trustees), they must pay tax, after claiming the annual exemption, at the rate appropriate to the settlement.

Assuming the trustees reinvest the proceeds of sale after paying any tax, the purchase price of the new investments is their acquisition cost for CGT purposes, ie on any future sale this price will be deducted when calculating any gain (or loss).

Losses

Example

Trustees of an A & M settlement are advised by their stockbrokers to sell the trust's holding of shares in A plc which are now worth £10,000 having been purchased 3 years ago for £25,000. The indexation allowance for the period is £5,000 but this cannot be used when calculating the trustees' loss.

Disposal consideration	£10,000
Less: acquisition cost	£25,000
	Loss (£15,000)

As this loss is incurred by the trustees they are entitled to claim loss relief. They do so by setting the loss against gains they make on other sales in the same tax year. If there are none, or if there are insufficient gains to absorb the loss, the trustees may carry the loss forward to set against gains made in future years. If the settlement ends at a time when the trustees have unabsorbed capital losses, they may 'hand these' to the beneficiary for his use to set against his own gains.

13.5.2   Income tax

It is necessary to distinguish the liability of the settlement trustees from the beneficiary's liability.

Trustees' liability

The trustees must pay tax on all income produced by the trust assets. In many cases, the trustees will receive the income after tax has been paid to the Inland Revenue, ie tax is paid at source. For example, the trustees will receive dividends and other savings income after tax at 20 per cent has been paid; in other cases, tax at 23 per cent will have been paid. In either case the trustees have a 'net' income. Whether the trustees have any further income tax liability depends on the type of settlement since the nature of the beneficial interests in the settlement governs the rate of tax for which the trustees are liable. Generally, the existence or not of an interest in possession in settled property will determine the appropriate tax rate.

Where there is no interest in possession the rate of income tax will be 34 per cent. This 'rate applicable to trusts' (ICTA 1988, s 686(1A)) is the sum of basic rate (23 per cent) and the additional rate (11 per cent (ibid, s 832)) and results in a charge on the trustees of 14 per cent on dividends and savings income (20 per cent + 14 per cent = 34 per cent) and 11 per cent on any other income (23 per cent + 11 per cent = 34 per cent).

In interest in possession trusts the rate of income tax is 23 per cent or 20 per cent on dividends and savings income. As in the majority of cases the trustees will receive net income (with credit for the tax deducted at source) no further liability to income tax will arise.

If any trustees receive gross income, ie income with no credit for tax already paid, they will be charged to tax at full rates of either 34 per cent or 23 per cent depending on the beneficial interests in the trust.

RATE(S) OF TAX

(1) Discretionary settlement: 34 per cent.
(2) Accumulation and maintenance settlement: 34 per cent.
(3) Interest in possession settlement: 23 per cent (20 per cent savings income).

Example 1

Trustees of a discretionary settlement have invested the entire trust fund in stocks and shares. They receive dividends of £800 from various companies. Their gross income is £1,000 – £200 (dividends are paid net of 20% tax only) = £800 net. The trustees' liability has, therefore, only been satisfied at 20%. As trustees of a settlement without an interest in possession their liability is 34% and the additional tax (14%) calculated as follows, remains to be paid.

Gross income	£1,000
Less: gross expenses (say)	£ 100
	£ 900
Additional tax (14%)	= £126

Trustees may deduct their expenses 'properly' chargeable to income (ICTA 1988, s 686(2)(d)) when calculating their additional 14% liability.

Example 2

If trustees of an interest in possession settlement receive dividends of £800 (ie £1,000 gross) they have no further tax to pay. Their entire liability is satisfied by the payment of £200 tax to the Inland Revenue by the companies when paying the dividends.

The beneficiary's liability

It is convenient to distinguish the position of a beneficiary who has a right to the income of the settled property, ie the beneficiary with an interest in possession, from other beneficiaries, for example, beneficiaries of a discretionary settlement.

INTEREST IN POSSESSION

The beneficiary with a vested entitlement to the settlement income will receive dividend and savings income from the trustees after tax at 20 per cent has been paid on it. The beneficiary is liable to tax on this income in the same way as he pays tax on any other income he may have. As the trustees have paid tax at 20 per cent, the beneficiary's liability (if any) is confined to tax at the higher rate. To justify their payment of tax, the trustees provide the beneficiary with a tax deduction certificate in Form R185 which he will pass on to the Inland Revenue.

> *Example 1*
> Trustees are holding a trust fund for 'Tony for life, with remainder to June'. Tony, the life tenant, has an interest in possession. The trustee's gross income is £1,000. They pay £800 to Tony to whom they give Form R185 justifying the payment of £200 tax. Tony's gross income from the trust is £1,000, ie £800 + £200.
>
> Tony's tax position depends on the amount of his other income:
>
> (1) If he is a higher rate tax payer
> | | |
> |---|---:|
> | gross trust income £1,000 × 40% = | £400 |
> | *less* tax paid by the trustees | £200 |
> | tax due | £200 |
>
> (2) If he is not a tax payer (ie he has no other income)
> | | |
> |---|---:|
> | net income | £800 |
> | tax paid by the trustees (refunded by the Inland Revenue) | £200 |
> | gross income | £1,000 |

In the latter case, Tony uses the R185 to support a claim to the Inland Revenue to refund the tax paid by the trustees.

> *Example 2*
> Trustees held property on A & M trusts for Eva on attaining the age of 25. Eva is now aged 21. The TA 1925, s 31 gave Eva the right to the income of the trust property from the age of 18, ie she now has an interest in possession. The trustees receive a dividend of £800 which they pay to Eva, together with Form R185. Eva's position is the same as Tony's position in the previous example.

NO INTEREST IN POSSESSION

Where no beneficiary has the right to receive the income of the trust property, the trustees may exercise their discretion to pay it to a beneficiary or they may accumulate the income. If they do pay out income to a beneficiary, the amount of tax deducted will be evidenced by Form R185 which the trustees will give to the beneficiary to pass on to the Inland Revenue.

Example 1

The trustees of a discretionary settlement receive a dividend of £800. They pay additional rate tax of £140 on their gross income, ie £1,000 @ 14%. They have no expenses. None of the income is paid to beneficiaries. The trustees accumulate the remaining £660 by adding it to the capital of the trust. The £340 tax paid on the gross income of £1,000, ie £200 plus the £140 additional rate tax cannot be recovered from the Inland Revenue.

Example 2

The facts are the same as in the previous example but the trustees pay £660 to a discretionary beneficiary Abdul with an R185 certificate justifying payment of £340 tax to the Inland Revenue.

Abdul's tax position depends on the amount of his other income:

(1) If he is a higher rate tax payer

gross trust income £1,000 × 40% =	£400
less tax paid by the trustees	£340
tax due	£60

(2) If he is not a tax payer (ie he has no other income)

net income	£660
tax paid by the trustees (refunded by the Inland Revenue)	£340
gross income	£1,000

Where possible, the trustees should exercise their discretion over the income, for example, under s 31 of the TA 1925 and pay it for the maintenance, education or benefit of a beneficiary since the tax paid by the trustees can in appropriate circumstances be repaid to the beneficiary (see Example 2). If the income is accumulated, the tax cannot be reclaimed.

13.6 DISTRIBUTING THE TRUST FUNDS

13.6.1 Accounting to the beneficiaries

It will generally be necessary for the trustees to prepare capital and income accounts when changes in the beneficial interests under the settlement occur. The most likely occasions of this happening are:

(1) when a beneficiary becomes entitled to receive settled property from the trustees, for example, following the exercise of a power of advancement under s 32 of the TA 1925; or

(2) when the trustees exercise a power of appointment, for example, when they appoint property to or for a beneficiary.

The accounts will show the investments and any cash in the trust fund together with any income which the trustees hold in their income account. From these accounts the beneficiary can ascertain precisely what his entitlement amounts to. The task of producing these accounts will be considerably eased if the trustees have kept full and accurate records of all transactions affecting the trust during the period of its administration. These will include records of sales and purchases of investments, advances made to the beneficiaries and any tax liabilities discharged.

13.6.2 Form and content of accounts

There is no prescribed form for trust accounts. The aim is to present clear and concise accounts which can easily be understood by the beneficiaries. Normally, trust accounts are produced in a vertical format showing the trust fund, payments made from it, for example, IHT and solicitors' costs and a balance for the beneficiary. A separate income account will reveal the income available for distribution, less any expenses payable from it, for example, any income tax due to the Inland Revenue. The form of trust account shown in Appendix 6 adopts this more usual vertical format.

13.6.3 Vesting the trust property in beneficiaries

Once the trustees have paid any tax liabilities and have prepared their accounts, the trust fund (or the appropriate part of it) must be transferred to the beneficiary. The means of vesting property in the beneficiary will depend on the nature of the property. The legal estate in land can be vested in the beneficiary by means of a deed; a stock transfer form will be required to transfer shares. Chattels (if any) pass to the beneficiary by delivery and any remaining cash will be transferred by cheque drawn on the trustee's bank account.

Chapter 14

THE OVERSEAS DIMENSION

14.1 THE FOREIGN ELEMENT

The previous chapters in this book assume that private clients are UK resident and are domiciled in the UK. It has also been assumed that the property owned by these private clients is situated in the UK. However, the affairs of many private clients have an overseas dimension, for example:

(1) a UK resident and domiciled client may be leaving the UK to work abroad, or may be leaving the UK to emigrate; or

(2) an individual, while remaining a UK resident, is buying property overseas; or

(3) a foreign national is proposing to come to the UK on a temporary or long term basis, or intends to invest in the UK.

14.1.1 The issues involved

There are many practical and legal issues where a client's affairs take on an overseas dimension.

Practical issues

The solicitor in the private client department tends not to be involved with the many practical issues when a client intends to leave or come to the UK. These matters include visa applications, work permits and accommodation. Clearly, in these areas there are legal issues involved about which the solicitor may be asked to advise but generally the client will be able to handle practical matters for himself.

Legal issues

The solicitor should be asked to advise and become involved as early as possible where legal issues arise. Two particular aspects may call for early consideration.

OWNERSHIP AND DEVOLUTION OF PROPERTY

The UK client may need advice in relation to a property he is proposing to buy in a foreign country. If, for example, he is purchasing a holiday cottage in France he will need advice as to French succession law and the extent to which he can leave that property by a will made in England or in France.

This advice should be given by a lawyer from, or specialising in the law of, the jurisdiction in which the property is situated. Not only may the laws of the foreign country differ from those of the UK, but the law may vary from state to state within that country.

TAXATION, AND IN PARTICULAR THE CONCEPTS OF RESIDENCE, ORDINARY RESIDENCE AND DOMICILE

These concepts affect such matters as the basis of assessment, territorial scope and reliefs in relation to UK taxes. The private client will need to know the extent to which he becomes or remains liable to income tax, CGT and IHT following immigration to or emigration from the UK.

14.1.2   Scope of this chapter

Where a foreign element is involved, there are always many complex issues to be considered. Essentially, a solicitor is required to plan the client's affairs in relation to the international dimension to achieve the most favourable tax position for his client. There is often a considerable degree of urgency so that appropriate advice must be given quickly before the client changes his residential or domiciliary status. The remainder of this chapter is limited to introducing some basic tax concepts as a basis for further study.

14.2   RESIDENCE AND DOMICILE

Whether a client is an immigrant or an emigrant or whether he intends to invest in the UK or overseas, the rules of income tax, CGT and IHT can apply to him but frequently in a modified form depending on his particular circumstances. The keys to an understanding of a client's tax position are the concepts of residence and domicile.

14.2.1   Residence

In view of the importance of residence within the UK tax system, it is surprising there is no statutory definition. There are three statutory provisions in the ICTA 1988, Part VII, Chapter V entitled 'Residence of Individuals'. These provisions merely adapt the concepts of residence and ordinary residence as developed by the courts in a series of cases over many years. The decisions have developed the criteria against which residence is assessed. In order to give practical guidance, the Inland Revenue has produced a set of rules in its booklet IR20 (1996) 'Residents and non-residents – liability to tax in the UK'. Although without statutory authority, and therefore capable of challenge, this booklet is generally accepted by practitioners as a basis from which to provide advice to immigrant and emigrant clients.

Residence as a concept is concerned with physical presence in the UK. If an individual is physically present in the UK at some time in a tax year, it is a question of fact whether he is resident for tax purposes for that year. The fact that an individual is in the UK involuntarily is not generally relevant to this question. Basically, an individual will be considered resident in the UK if, for the time he is in the UK, it can be said to be his 'home'. It is not necessary that he owns a property in the UK; he may be resident even if he is living in hotel accommodation.

Either of the following tests may determine whether an individual will be treated as resident in the UK.

183 days in the UK: temporary residence
An individual will generally be treated as resident if he is present there for, in aggregate, 6 months or more in the year of assessment. Six months is taken as 183 days but days of arrival and departure are ignored. In the Inland Revenue's view 'there are no exceptions to this (rule)' (IR20 (1996) para 1.2), even in cases of hardship, for example where an individual's presence continues through ill health.

Visits to the UK for some temporary purpose only (eg a holiday), and which are for less than 6 months, will not usually give rise to tax. In determining whether the visit is for a 'temporary purpose', any available accommodation in the UK is disregarded.

Regular visits (IR20 (1996) para 3.3)

An individual will be treated as UK resident if he makes 'habitual and substantial' visits to the UK. The Inland Revenue regards visits averaging 3 months per annum over 4 years as both 'habitual' and 'substantial'. If the average is met, he is treated as resident for tax purposes from the 5th year. Generally, days spent in the UK because of exceptional circumstances beyond the individual's control are ignored, for example an extended stay in the UK because of ill health.

Available accommodation in the UK

Until 5 April 1993, one of the most important factors in determining whether an individual was UK resident was the availability of accommodation in the UK for his use. The Inland Revenue's view was that if he had available accommodation any visit, however short, would cause the individual to be treated as UK resident. Property could be available even if not owned by the individual, for example if it was owned by the individual's employer or a relative who kept it for the individual's use. In certain circumstances UK accommodation was ignored, for example property which an individual owned but which was let on lease while the owner was abroad.

However, since 5 April 1993, available accommodation in the UK is no longer a factor when determining whether a 'person is in the UK for some temporary purpose only and not with the intention of establishing his residence there' (ICTA 1988, s 336(3)).

14.2.2 Ordinary residence

The phrase 'ordinary residence' is often used in the legislation, particularly in relation to CGT, but nowhere is it defined. The concept of ordinary residence is used to prevent an individual from avoiding liability to tax simply by ceasing to be resident in the UK.

The courts have considered the phrase on a number of occasions. It is best described in the following extract from the judgment in *IRC v Lysaght* [1928] AC 234:

> 'ordinarily means . . . established custom or practice or a matter of regular practice or occurrence . . . to be contrasted with casual or occasional.'

The Inland Revenue has given its view as to the meaning of ordinary residence in the booklet IR20 (1996) para 1.3 as follows:

> 'If you are resident in the UK year after year, you are treated as **ordinarily resident** here. You may be resident but not ordinarily resident in the UK for the tax year if, for example, you normally live outside the UK but are in this country for 183 days or more in the year [see **14.2.1**]. Or you may be ordinarily resident but not resident for a tax year if, for example, you usually live in the UK but have gone abroad for a long holiday and do not set foot in the UK during that year.'

14.2.3 Domicile

Unlike residence and ordinary residence, an individual's domicile is not confined to determining liability to taxation. It is relevant to many other matters, for example when determining in private international law which system of law governs succession to property owned in a foreign jurisdiction. Like residence and ordinary residence, domicile is not defined in statute but its meaning has been established by the courts in a number of decisions. An individual can only be domiciled in a country which has its own system of law, for example England and Wales. The Inland Revenue in its booklet IR20 (1996) at para 5.2 states:

> 'Broadly speaking you are domiciled in the country where you have your permanent home. Domicile is distinct from nationality or residence. You can only have one domicile at any given time.'

An individual is usually domiciled in the country which he considers as 'home'. Thus, an individual who emigrates to the USA where he lives for 20 or 30 years will not necessarily cease to be domiciled in some part of the UK.

Domicile of origin

Every individual must have a domicile. Normally, a domicile of origin will be determined at birth, ie a child acquires as his domicile of origin his father's domicile at the date of his birth. This may not be the country in which the child is actually born; nor need it be a country which the child has visited.

Domicile of dependency

A minor child who derived his domicile of origin from his father will acquire a new domicile, ie a domicile of dependency in place of his domicile of origin if his father acquires a new domicile (see below).

Domicile of choice

Domicile can change where an individual voluntarily acquires a new domicile, ie a domicile of choice. There is a heavy burden of proof before an individual can show that a domicile of choice has been acquired. Domicile is a matter of intent but a mere intention to change domicile is insufficient. Many factors are relevant including abandoning an existing domicile. Unless all connections with the previous domicile are broken, it may be difficult (if not impossible) to show the acquisition of a domicile of choice.

A client who, at the time of emigrating from the UK, is considering acquiring a new domicile of choice should compile all available evidence of intention. Inter alia the following should be considered:

(1) he should take up residence in the country involved, preferably acquiring property in that country and selling all property in the UK; and

(2) he must have a permanent intention to remain indefinitely in the new country in order to show a change in domicile. This requirement as to intention is often the most difficult obstacle for a client to overcome when endeavouring to change domicile. Ideally, he should make a written statement, or statutory declaration, before leaving the UK, setting out all personal circumstances giving rise to the decision to change domicile. Such a statement is not conclusive but will always be of assistance when attempting to convince third parties, particularly the Inland Revenue, of the change of domicile; and

(3) in addition to purchasing the residence in the new country, he should forge as many associations with that country as possible while at the same time ending associations with the old country. He should consider a new business or employment, make a will valid under local law, open a new bank account, sell investments and reinvest in the new country etc.

14.2.4   United Kingdom

The UK consists of England and Wales, Scotland and Northern Ireland. It does not include the Channel Islands or the Isle of Man which, because of their relatively lower tax rates, are often termed 'tax havens'.

It is incorrect to link the concept of domicile with the UK. An individual has a domicile in a territory or a state which has its own legal system. Thus, an individual may be domiciled in Scotland or in England and Wales.

14.3 TAXATION OF THE INDIVIDUAL AND THE FOREIGN ELEMENT

The effect of the rules as to residence and domicile on an individual's liability to tax depends upon the tax involved. Spouses are independent persons for tax purposes. Their residence and ordinary residence status, and their domicile, are determined by reference to their individual circumstances and so may not coincide with the status of their spouse.

Transfers of property between spouses both of whom are domiciled in the UK are free of IHT by virtue of the spouse exemption. However, transfers by a UK domiciled spouse to a non-UK domiciled spouse are exempt up to a cumulative limit of £55,000 (IHTA 1984, s 18(2)).

14.3.1 Income tax and CGT

An individual who is UK resident is liable to income tax on his worldwide income, ie he must pay income tax on all income whether its source is within the UK or elsewhere.

A non-UK resident is only liable to income tax on income arising from a source within the UK. The rules to determine whether a person is resident in the UK are considered at **14.2**.

Whether a source of income is within the UK depends on the type of income. For example, income from employment within the UK, rent from land within the UK and dividends from companies whose membership register is kept within the UK are all sources of income within the UK. If the duties of the employment, the situs of the land or the membership register are outside the UK, the income will have a non-UK source.

CGT
An individual who is UK resident is liable to pay CGT on gains made on disposals of assets wherever they are situated. A non-resident individual will not necessarily avoid liability to CGT since liability is extended to cover gains made by someone who is 'ordinarily resident' in the UK, for example a person whose residence is within the UK but who is temporarily overseas.

If an individual is neither resident nor ordinarily resident in the UK, he is not normally liable to CGT whether the gains arise on disposals of assets in the UK or elsewhere.

14.3.2 Effect of ceasing to be resident and ordinarily resident for income tax and CGT

If an individual is resident in the UK for part of a tax year and absent for the remainder of it, the general rule is that income tax and CGT is charged for the whole tax year. By concession (ESC A11), the Inland Revenue may split the tax year so that an individual is treated as resident in the UK for only part of the year. For example, where an individual leaves to live permanently outside the UK, the Inland Revenue treats him as non-resident from the date of departure (IR20 (1996), para 1.5).

Tax planning by emigrating from the UK is perhaps the ultimate form of tax avoidance. To be successful, the individual will need to convince the Inland Revenue that he is no longer resident or ordinarily resident in the UK on the date on which the liability to tax arose.

The operative date will depend on the tax in question. For CGT purposes, liability arises on the date of disposal of the asset in question. This is generally the date on which a binding contract is made (and not the date of later completion). If an individual is still a UK resident when the terms of the contract were substantially agreed, the Inland Revenue may argue that this should be taken as the date of disposal, even though a formal contract had not yet been made. For effective tax planning, therefore, a client may be best advised to become non-resident well before negotiations are concluded.

If emigration is for a relatively short period, even though technically it may meet the non-residence test, the Inland Revenue may argue that absence from the UK was always intended as temporary and, therefore, the individual was never truly non-resident. Although there is nothing to stop an emigrant from subsequently returning to the UK and resuming resident status, it is usually advisable for the period of emigration to be for at least one tax year if non-residency is to be achieved.

Employment overseas

Although an employee going overseas to work full time on a contract of employment may not consider he is emigrating, he is effectively doing so for income tax and CGT purposes. The employee will be treated as non-resident and not ordinarily resident from the day after leaving the UK to the day before returning if all the following conditions are satisfied (IR 20 (1996), para 2.2):

> 'If you leave the UK to work full time abroad under a contract of employment, you are treated as not resident and not ordinarily resident if you meet all the following conditions:
>
> [i]   your absence from the UK and your employment abroad both last for at least a whole tax year; and
> [ii] during your absence any visits you make to the UK:
>
>> [1]   total less than 183 days in any tax year; and
>> [2]   average less than 91 days a tax year (the average is taken over the period of absence up to a maximum of 4 years; any days spent in the UK because of exceptional circumstances beyond your control, for example, the illness of yourself or a member of your immediate family, are not normally counted for this purpose).'

Once in the overseas employment, the employee can dispose of assets within the UK without liability to CGT on gains realised. To achieve this, he should be advised to enter into contracts disposing of assets likely to realise substantial gains only after he has gone overseas and achieved non-resident status (see above).

Any income which the employee may have from sources within the UK remains subject to income tax.

Longer-term emigrants

Emigrants in circumstances where an overseas employment is not intended will need to convince the Inland Revenue of change in their residential status. Normally, this would entail selling a UK house before departure and purchasing a house in the new country. Return visits should be avoided in the tax year of departure and limited in the immediately following years. The individual may be treated as UK resident subsequently, if he falls foul of the tests set out at **14.2.1**.

Emigration of itself does not give rise to a disposal of assets for CGT purposes so that assets showing large in-built gains should be sold after the individual is no longer ordinarily resident in the UK.

EMIGRATION WITHIN 6 YEARS OF A GIFT

Hold-over relief on the disposal of assets by way of gift has been discussed in Chapter 4. The relief is only available if an election is made by the donor and donee and if the donee was resident or ordinarily resident in the UK at the time. If the donee emigrates within 6 years of the gift, an emigration charge arises whereby the held-over gain becomes immediately chargeable. Tax is payable by the donee but the Inland Revenue can recover it from the donor if it remains unpaid 12 months after the due date. The charge does not apply if the donee is an employee who leaves to work abroad under a full time contract of employment.

Example

In 1992, Dana gave her son her shareholding in ABC Ltd. The gain of £10,000 was held over. In 1995, her son emigrated from the UK and took up residence in France. The £10,000 is immediately chargeable, ie at the rates of tax relevant in 1995. The actual value of the shareholding in 1995 is irrelevant.

Long-term immigrants

Foreign nationals who retain their original domicile but who work in or are based in the UK for a certain length of time may, under the rules considered above, become 'resident' or 'ordinarily resident'. They will thus, in principle, become liable to UK taxation on all their income and gains, wherever arising. However, if such individuals still retain their foreign domicile, the rules are relaxed. Broadly, their foreign income suffers UK tax only to the extent that it is remitted to the UK (under Schs IV and V of the ICTA 1988 for income from foreign securities, shares and other property and Schedule E, Case III for employments performed and remunerated wholly abroad). Furthermore, their overseas gains only become chargeable if remitted (in any form) to the UK.

14.3.3 Double taxation treaties

An individual may be liable to tax in the UK and in a foreign country at the same time. The client may be 'dual resident' because the residence criteria in the two countries where he has lived treat him as resident in each country. If there is a double taxation agreement between the countries, this will provide relief from double taxation of income and gains. If no double taxation agreement exists, unilateral relief may be granted by one of the countries. There are no special EC tax rules and the rules of individual Member States have not yet been harmonised, but there are various double taxation provisions and reliefs between EC countries.

14.3.4 IHT

Residence (or ordinary residence) is not relevant as a concept to determine liability to IHT. Instead, an individual's domicile governs liability to IHT.

An individual who is domiciled in (some part of) the UK is liable to IHT on a transfer of value of assets whether the assets are in the UK or elsewhere. If an individual is not domiciled in the UK, liability arises only on the transfer of value of property situated in the UK, although there are some exceptions to this rule, for example, exempt gilts (government stock).

Deemed domicile for IHT (IHTA 1984, s 267)

Section 267 of the IHTA 1984 contains provisions extending the meaning of domicile. An individual not domiciled in the UK under the principles discussed at **14.2.3** may nevertheless be deemed to be domiciled in the UK for IHT. This can happen in one of two circumstances.

THE DOMICILE TEST

An individual actually domiciled in the UK within the 3 years immediately preceding a transfer of value will be deemed domiciled there at the time of the transfer. The aim of this provision is to stop an individual transferring his property from the UK and then emigrating in the hope of avoiding IHT on future transfers of his property.

> *Example*
>
> Alexis acquired a domicile of choice in California in January 1993 when she emigrated there from England. She died 2 years later. As Alexis had given up her UK domicile within 3 years of her death (the transfer of value), her entire estate is chargeable to IHT.

THE RESIDENCE TEST

An individual who was resident in the UK for income tax purposes in not less than 17 of the 20 years of assessment ending with the year in which the transfer of value occurs is deemed to be domiciled in the UK. In determining whether an individual is resident in any year, the income tax tests discussed at **14.2** are used (ignoring from 6 April 1993 onwards any available accommodation in the UK).

This provision is intended to bring long-term residents who have not become UK domiciliaries into the charge to IHT.

> *Example*
>
> Alexandra's employment in the UK since July 1970 has just ended following the failure of her employer's business. As a result, she plans to return home to Greece as soon as possible. Last year, she gave some land she owned outside Athens to her daughter. In view of Alexandra's residence in the UK for over 20 years, she will be deemed domiciled in the UK so that her death within 7 years of the gift of the land would cause the gift to become subject to IHT.

Death of a UK domiciliary with foreign property

SUCCESSION

If the testator left two wills, one dealing with his foreign property, and an English will dealing with his other assets, a foreign lawyer should be instructed to prove the foreign will and to administer the foreign property in accordance with its terms.

If the testator left only an English will, this should be proved in the usual way and then a foreign lawyer instructed either to reseal the English grant in the foreign jurisdiction or to extract the appropriate grant in that jurisdiction using sealed and certified copies of the English grant and will. As a grant obtained in the UK contains a 'notation of domicile', ie the deceased's domicile at death is noted on the grant, the grant will be recognised in other parts of the UK without further formality (AEA 1971). Thus, the English executors of a deceased client can prove title to property in Scotland or Northern Ireland without resealing their grant in either jurisdiction (and vice versa).

Devolution of foreign property, particularly land, is often subject to local succession taxes (or equivalent) and to local laws of entitlement which may override (to a given extent) the terms of an English will. For example, in Scotland, Spain and France a stated proportion of the testator's estate passes automatically (and not by will) to certain relatives; in the USA and Scandinavian countries there is 'community of property' provision for spouses. In view of these local succession laws, it is usually appropriate for the clients to be advised to make a will in the particular jurisdiction taking local law into account; any English will should in terms exclude the property in the foreign jurisdiction.

IHT

Worldwide assets are part of the estate of a client domiciled in the UK for IHT purposes (under either of the tests discussed above) and should be disclosed in Inland Revenue Account IHT 200. Subject to any relief under a double taxation agreement or convention, the English personal representatives are liable to pay any IHT which is due although their liability is limited to the extent of assets received or which might have been received but for their neglect or default (IHTA 1984, s 204). Unless the testator's will provides otherwise, the beneficiaries of the foreign property bear the burden of the IHT which that property attracts (IHTA 1984, s 211). Thus, the UK personal representatives, having paid the IHT to the Inland Revenue will need to recover an equivalent amount from the beneficiary of the property.

Death of a non-UK domiciliary with UK property

SUCCESSION

Foreign personal representatives may obtain title to the property in the UK by resealing their foreign grant in the appropriate court in the UK. Except in Scotland (where local laws apply), succession to the property is generally in accordance with the terms of the deceased's will.

IHT

Certain government stock and other property is exempt from IHT, even though situated in the UK, if owned by an individual who is neither domiciled nor ordinarily resident in the UK. Otherwise, property physically situated in the UK is subject to IHT. All such property should be disclosed in Inland Revenue Account IHT 201.

14.4 TRUSTEES AND THE FOREIGN ELEMENT

The residence and ordinary residence of trustees is generally determined separately from the status of the settlor or the beneficiaries and without regard to the location of the trust assets.

14.4.1 Income tax

For income tax purposes, the residence of trustees is governed by FA 1989, s 110. If there is one trustee who is a UK resident and others who are not, all the trustees will be regarded by the Inland Revenue as UK resident. This means that the trustees are subject to UK income tax on all trust income, whether from a UK or an overseas source. All tax (including on the overseas source income) can be assessed on the UK resident trustee.

Overseas settlors

The rule mentioned above does not apply if the settlor was neither domiciled, resident nor ordinarily resident in the UK when he created the settlement. If all the trustees of such a settlement are non-UK residents, the trust is only liable to UK tax on UK source income. For this purpose, if at least one of the trustees is resident in the UK and the others are not, the UK trustee(s) will be regarded by the Inland Revenue as resident outside the UK. If, however, all of the trustees become UK resident, then all trust income, whatever the source, is subject to UK tax.

Non-resident trustees are not liable to UK income tax other than on income arising in the UK (see above). In such cases, basic or lower rate tax (23 or 20 per cent) is generally deducted at source so that the trustees receive income net of tax. Trustees of accumulation and maintenance settlements and discretionary settlements are liable to tax at the 'rate applicable to the trust', ie to an extra 11 or 14 per cent (see **13.5.2**); in practice, the Inland Revenue often cannot collect this extra tax from the non-resident trustees because there is no means of withholding it at source nor can they enforce the liability in the overseas jurisdiction.

14.4.2   Capital gains tax

Trustees are treated as 'a single continuing body of persons distinct from the persons who may from time to time be the trustees' (TCGA 1992, s 69). Thus, normally, if one trustee is replaced by another there is no disposal for CGT purposes.

The general rule is that trustees are not treated as UK resident and ordinarily resident if the general administration of the trust is carried on outside the UK and the trustees (or a majority of them) are not resident or ordinarily resident in the UK. If these conditions are satisfied, the trustees are treated as non-resident and are, therefore, outside the UK CGT net so that disposals by them do not attract CGT. It is this exemption from CGT which has in the past made non-resident settlements attractive to UK taxpayers (see below).

14.5   NON-RESIDENT SETTLEMENTS

14.5.1   What is a non-resident settlement?

Because the trustees of a settlement are treated as a single and continuing body of persons, a settlement is a separate entity for CGT purposes no matter what type of settlement it may be, and whether or not it is resident in the UK. The only exceptions to this general rule are where the trustees are either nominees or bare trustees when the trust property is treated as belonging to the beneficiary (as discussed at **4.6.4**). If such property is sold, any gain (subject to any relevant relief or exemption) is taxed as the beneficiary's gain.

A settlement, and its trustees, is treated as being non-UK resident if:

(1)   all or a majority of its trustees are neither resident nor ordinarily resident in the UK; and

(2)   the general administration of the trust is ordinarily carried on outside the UK. This includes such matters as trust administration, investment management

decisions and trust banking and accounting. Although not entirely free from doubt, trustees decisions, for example as to the exercise of a fiduciary power can probably be made within the UK without denying the trust its non-resident status.

A trustee resident in the UK is nonetheless treated as non-resident if:

(1) his business includes trust management;
(2) he is acting in the trust in the course of his business; and
(3) the settlement was created by an individual who was at the time not resident, ordinarily resident or domiciled in the UK.

This rule permits professional trust companies in the UK to carry on the administration of a non-resident trust without prejudicing its non-resident status. Some solicitors' firms have their own trust company (a company whose objects include trust administration and whose shares are owned by partners) to run and manage non-resident trusts in this way.

Sheltering trustees' gains

Non-resident settlements have been popular with clients and estate planners as providing a ready method of sheltering the trust's gains from CGT. Non-resident trustees are in the same position as individuals who are not resident in the UK. Thus they are not liable to pay CGT on their chargeable gains on disposal of trust assets, provided the settlement is a non-resident settlement for the entire tax year in question. If the trustees become non-resident part way through the year, the Inland Revenue will not split the year for assessment purposes so allowing avoidance of CGT for the period when the trust is non-resident. Ideally a client should be advised to set up his non-resident trust, or export his existing trust (see below), well before 6 April in the relevant year.

14.5.2 Anti-avoidance legislation

Ever since the introduction of CGT in 1965, estate planners have advised clients to use non-resident settlements (normally discretionary settlements) to shelter the trustees' gains from CGT. Over the same period, various legislative attempts have been made to counter loss of revenue through use of these settlements but only recently has the large-scale use of non-resident settlements been substantially halted. Even now some opportunities remain for use of such settlements.

On the whole, clients were less concerned with avoidance of inheritance tax (or its predecessor capital transfer tax) or income tax in relation to their non-resident settlement, although sometimes this was the result even if not the overriding intention. Often clients wished some continuing enjoyment from the settled property or its income. The real objective, therefore, was sheltering the non-resident gains from CGT while, so far as the legislation permitted, continuing to enjoy the property.

Anti-avoidance legislation is always complex even if the objective is reasonably certain. Whether the objective is achieved, is, of course, another matter. Apart from in 1965 (with the introduction of CGT) there have been two principal occasions when anti-avoidance legislation has been introduced: the first by FA 1981, s 80, and the second 10 years later by FA 1991, Sch 16. Neither of these was entirely successful in that estate planners continued to find ways round the provisions and so defeat the intention of the legislation. Each of these provisions has been retained, and strengthened, and appear now as ss 86 and 87 of the TCGA 1992. A further provision, TCGA 1992 s 80, has introduced an export charge. Each of these provisions is discussed below.

14.5.3   Anti-avoidance legislation – the position now

The current position in relation to anti-avoidance legislation is set out below.

Migrant settlements – export charge (TCGA 1992, s 80(2))
Consider the following example.

> *Example*
> Derek Godfrey formed his electrical engineering company. He settled the shares on UK resident trustees to hold on family discretionary trusts. He continued to draw director's fees. Expecting imminent growth in value of the shares due to the success of the company, the UK trustees retired in favour of non-resident trustees. The company prospered. The non-resident trustees sold the shares realising a substantial capital profit.
>
> Derek Godfrey's tax position:
>
> (1)   Deemed disposal on transfer of shares to the UK trustees: no significant capital gains realised and so covered by the indexation allowance and the annual exemption.
> (2)   Appointment of non-resident trustees: no disposal, the trustees are a single continuing body of persons (TCGA 1992, s 69, see **14.4.2**).

The consequence of these transactions (before 1981) was that any increase in value of the shares by the time the appointment of the new trustees was not charged to capital gains tax. The gain (not always small as in the example) was free of CGT. To counter this, an 'export charge' was introduced to tax gains which had accrued but which had not been realised to the date of the appointment of the non-resident trustees by FA 1981, s 83 (now TCGA 1992, s 80).

Advice to clients contemplating the 'export' of their settlement covers two main aspects; legal and taxation issues.

LEGAL ISSUES
What is at issue is the export of a UK trust to avoid CGT. Export of the trust is simply achieved by appointing persons who are resident abroad as trustees and ensuring that the administration of the trust is carried on outside the UK (see **14.5.1**). But what considerations should the present trustees have in mind when faced with a proposal that the trust be exported? First, there is no absolute bar in English law preventing the appointment of non-resident trustees of a UK trust and, secondly, such an appointment should only be made in 'appropriate circumstances' because the result is to remove the trust from control by the English courts. The following extract is from the judgment of Pennycuick V-C in *Re Whitehead's Will Trusts* [1971] 1 WLR 833:

> '. . . The law has been quite well established for upwards of a century that there is no absolute bar to the appointment of persons resident abroad as trustees of an English trust. I say 'no absolute bar', in the sense that such an appointment would be prohibited by law and would consequently be invalid. On the other hand, apart from exceptional circumstances, it is not proper to make such an appointment, that is to say, the court would not apart from exceptional circumstances, make such an appointment; nor would it be right for the donees of the power to make such an appointment out of court. If they did, presumably the court would be likely to interfere at the instance of the beneficiaries. There do, however, exist exceptional circumstances in which such an appointment can properly be made. The most obvious exceptional circumstances are those in which the beneficiaries have settled

permanently in some country outside the United Kingdom and what is proposed to be done is to appoint new trustees in that country.'

Clearly, if the court would appoint non-resident trustees, it will be proper for the trustees themselves to do so, for example where all the beneficiaries are resident in the country where the trust is to become resident following the appointment. If the trustees made an appointment where the court might not, there is unlikely to be any real concern if all the beneficiaries have approved the non-resident appointment. This will require all beneficiaries to be ascertained and to be sui juris. If the trustees are in doubt about a proposed appointment it would be sensible to apply to the court first (as in *Re Whitehead*).

In many cases there will be appropriate express provision in the trust instrument for the trustees to retire in favour of non-resident trustees. Such a power can be exercised without further consideration by the trustees, provided its exercise is in the best interests of the beneficiaries.

The choice of overseas jurisdiction requires some thought by the trustees. It is prudent to appoint the non-resident trustees in a jurisdiction which will, if necessary, enforce the trustees' duties; the concept of a trust and the division of legal and beneficial ownership is not known in many civil law jurisdictions. Care should also be taken to choose a country where tax laws are less stringent than the UK since, otherwise, the trustees may be taxed as heavily, if not more so, than in the UK. It is also sensible to choose a jurisdiction which is likely to be stable – the Channel Islands or the Isle of Man – and to select reputable trustees, for example a well known trust company or a firm of lawyers practising within the jurisdiction.

TAXATION ISSUES

The export charge is levied under s 80 in a manner familiar to the CGT legislation. When the trustees become neither resident nor ordinarily resident in the UK, they are deemed to have disposed of the trust assets at market value and to have re-acquired them at the same value. The retiring trustees are primarily responsible for the tax due on the chargeable gain; if it is not paid by them within 6 months of the due date, the Inland Revenue can recover the tax from any person who was a trustee in the 12 months before the export of the trust (unless, broadly, when he ceased to be a trustee there was then no proposal to export the trust). Because of their personal liability for the tax, the retiring trustees should retain sufficient assets under their control so that they can pay it.

Tax is charged at the rate appropriate to the trustees. As the settlement is likely to be a discretionary settlement, the rate will in most cases be 34 per cent. If the settlor has 'an interest in his (UK) settlement', for example the settlor or his spouse can benefit from the settled property or its income, the gains deemed made by the trustees will be assessable on the settlor (TCGA 1992, ss 77–79).

This export charge may not necessarily deter the use of a non-resident settlement by a settlor, particularly where the growth in the settled assets is expected to occur after the export rather than before it.

The charge is suspended in cases where an 'inadvertent' change in the residence status of the settlement occurs provided the UK resident status is resumed within 6 months. For example, the death of the only UK resident trustee, would cause the settlement to become non-resident. If the trustee is replaced by another UK trustee within 6 months no charge is made under s 80.

Non-resident settlements – attribution of gains to settlors (TCGA 1992, s 86 and Sch 5)

Under this provision, the settlor will be taxed on any gains realised by the non-resident trustees unless he is:

(1) domiciled outside the UK in the relevant tax year, ie the year when the gain is realised; or

(2) neither resident nor ordinarily resident in the UK during any part of the relevant tax year.

Thus, the provision only applies where the settlor is domiciled *and* either resident or ordinarily resident in the UK; gains made by the trustees in other years will not be charged on the settlor. Further, the provision only applies to settlements created after 19 March 1991 (although settlements existing on that date will be brought within the provisions if, for example, new property is added to the settlement after that date).

The trustees' annual exemption cannot be taken into account when calculating the gains to be attributed to the settlor. However, the settlor has his own annual exemption which can be set against attributed gains.

To be within the provision there must be a 'defined person' (see below) who benefits from, or will or may become entitled to benefit from, the settled property or its income (directly or indirectly). A person who is within the class of discretionary beneficiaries will clearly come within this wide-ranging definition.

A 'defined person' includes:

(i)   the settlor;
(ii)   the settlor's spouse;
(iii)   any child of the settlor or the settlor's spouse;
(iv)   the spouse of any such child;
(v)–(vi) . . .

This is a particularly wide-ranging list which effectively restricts non-resident trusts to limited classes of beneficiaries, for example the settlor's grandchildren, nephews and nieces.

Referring to the example of Derek Godfrey's discretionary settlement, if created after 1991, it would be caught by both s 80 (export charge) and s 86 (interest of settlor – Derek at least is among the beneficiaries); it is assumed that he remains resident and domiciled within the UK. However, if it is assumed that s 86 does not apply to Derek's settlement (perhaps because he is now domiciled and resident in France following his retirement from the company), the provisions in s 87 – attribution of gains to beneficiaries – must be considered since these instead may be applicable.

Non-resident settlements – attribution of gains to beneficiaries (TCGA 1992, s 87)

These provisions apply to gains of non-resident settlements for the years 1981/82 onwards. They will be relevant where s 86 does not apply. Where they apply, a charge to CGT can arise on any beneficiary who has received 'capital payments' from the non-resident trustees. If the trustees make a capital payment to a beneficiary who is domiciled and resident (or ordinarily resident) in the UK, the Inland Revenue will regard that beneficiary as having received part of the capital gain made by the trustees. Accordingly, the beneficiary will be liable to CGT in respect of such payment.

APPLICATION OF THE PROVISIONS

Gains realised by the non-resident trustees cannot be assessed on the beneficiaries unless the settlor was resident (or ordinarily resident) and domiciled in the UK on either of the following two occasions:

(1) when he made the settlement; or
(2) at any time in the tax year when the gains accrued to the trustees.

Effectively, therefore, if a settlor makes a settlement when non-domiciled or non-resident, (and not ordinarily resident) capital payment to beneficiaries will not be taxed until he becomes a UK domiciliary resident or ordinarily resident in the UK. Even then, only if the beneficiary is UK domiciled and resident (or ordinarily resident) will his capital payment be subject to CGT (s 87(7)). If the settlor was domiciled and resident (or ordinarily resident) in the UK when he made the settlement, the rules will always apply to it.

> *Example*
> When domiciled and resident in Hong Kong, Davina settled her shares in the Hong Kong and Shanghai bank on discretionary trusts for the benefit of her family. At the end of her secondment to Hong Kong in 2 years' time, Davina intends to return to the UK to live. By then, it is expected her shares will have trebled in value. Her return to the UK will bring the settlement within s 87. The trustees should therefore realise the gain on the shares before this happens.

CALCULATION OF TRUST GAINS

The following three steps must be followed.

Step 1: The trust gains are the gains on which the trustees would have been chargeable had they been resident in the UK (losses are taken into account, but not the trustees annual exemption as these are not available to non-residents). Trust gains do not include gains attributable to the settlor under s 86 (above).

Step 2: The trust gains are attributed to beneficiaries to the extent that they receive 'capital payments' from the trustees.

Capital payments are not restricted to money payments. They include assets transferred in specie, benefits conferred on the beneficiary and the occasion when a beneficiary becomes absolutely entitled to trust property, for example a trust to A when he attains 25 and the contingency is satisfied. Payments subject to income tax are not capital payments.

Step 3: Capital payments are taxed as chargeable gains of the beneficiaries from which their annual exemption may first be deducted.

> *Example*
> The XYZ discretionary settlement is a non-resident settlement created by A in 1992. He has no interest in the settlement and at all times has been domiciled, resident and ordinarily resident in the UK. There are two beneficiaries, B1 and B2, who are domiciled and resident in the UK.

Assume: £

(1)	trust gains	1992/93		50,000
		1993/94		20,000
		1994/95		100,000

(2)	capital payments to B1 and B2		B1	B2
			£	£
		1992/93	20,000	10,000
		1993/94	50,000	75,000
		1994/95	10,000	5,000

Allocation of trust gains:

1992/93

	£	£	£
capital payments		20,000	10,000
trust gains	50,000		
gains : apportioned	30,000	20,000	10,000
: c/fwd	20,000	–	–

1993/94

	£	£	£
capital payments		50,000	75,000
trust gains	20,000		
:b/fwd	20,000		
	40,000		
gains apportioned	40,000	16,000	24,000
capital payments: c/fwd	–	34,000	51,000

1994/95

		£	£
capital payments		10,000	5,000
		44,000	56,000
trust gains	100,000		
gains : apportioned	100,000	44,000	56,000
: c/fwd	–	–	–

Non-resident settlements – the supplementary charge (TCGA 1992, ss 91–95)

CGT under s 87 can be avoided if the trustees do not make capital payments to the beneficiaries. The intention behind the supplementary charge is to discourage the retention of capital gains within a non-resident trust by imposing an 'interest charge' on whatever amount of CGT is in fact paid by a beneficiary under s 87, ie it only applies if and when s 87 applies. In effect, interest is charged on delayed payments of CGT. If capital payments escape CGT under s 87, so too will the capital payment escape the supplementary charge.

CALCULATION OF THE 'INTEREST CHARGE'

The provisions governing the interest charge are particularly complex. Broadly, they work by matching capital payments made on or after 6 April 1991 with gains realised by the non-resident trustees in each tax year. Earlier gains are matched before later gains.

The rate of interest is 10 per cent per annum (maximum period of 6 years) applied to the CGT paid by the beneficiary under s 87. It is calculated for the period starting on 1 December following the tax year in which the gains are realised by the trustees and ends on 30 November following the tax year when the capital payment was made.

Example

	1993/94	1994/95	1995/96	1996/97	
trust gains realised	£100	£600		£500 (capital payment)	

Assume that s 87 applies and the beneficiary receiving the capital payment is resident and domiciled in the UK. He is a higher rate tax payer.

(1) The CGT liability on the capital payment amounts to £500 × 40% = £200.
(2) The supplementary interest charge is calculated by matching the capital payment first with the 1993/94 gain, then with the 1994/95 gain.

1993/94 (interest period 1/12/94–30/11/97)

$$£200 \times \frac{100}{500} \times 10\% \times 3 \text{ years} \qquad \begin{array}{c} £ \\ 12 \end{array}$$

1994/95 (interest period 1/12/95–30/11/97)

$$£200 \times \frac{400}{500} \times 10\% \times 2 \text{ years} \qquad \underline{32}$$

$$\text{'interest' payable} \qquad \underline{\underline{44}}$$

APPENDICES

Appendix 1

INCOME TAX RATES AND ALLOWANCES

Rates		1997/98		1996/97
Lower rate	20%	£1–£4,100	20%	£1–£3,900
Basic rate	23%	£4,101–£26,100	24%	£3,901–£25,500
Higher rate	40%	over £26,100	40%	over £25,500

Allowance	1997/98	1996/97	Reduction in tax	
			1997/98 15%	1996/97 15%
	£	£	£	£
Personal	4,045	3,765		
Aged 65–74	5,220	4,910		
Aged 75 and over	5,400	5,090		
Married couple	1,830	1,790	274.50	268.50
Aged 65–74	3,185	3,115	477.75	467.25
Aged 74 and over	3,225	3,155	483.75	473.25
Additional single parent	1,830	1,790	274.50	268.50
Widow's bereavement	1,830	1,790	274.50	268.50
Blind person	1,280	1,250		
Income limit for age-related allowances:	15,600	15,200		

Note: (i) The 'Reduction in tax' column shows the amount of tax credit available where relief is restricted to 15%. It is given by reducing the individual's total tax liability by the amount of the credit.

(ii) Age-related allowances (see **2.6.4**):
income limit: £15,600/£15,200.
income below limit: allowance in full.
income exceeds limit: allowance reduced by 50% of the excess.

Appendix 2

INVESTMENT AND FINANCIAL PRODUCTS

The purpose of this Appendix is to provide a brief introduction to some of the more popular types of investment and financial products currently available to individuals and trustees. It is not intended to be a definitive list. Suggestions are made as to the type of client for whom the investment might be suitable but many factors will determine the actual choice of investment for a particular client. The tax rules are those for the client and not for the product. Where appropriate, for each investment there is a brief summary indicating risk and showing income and capital growth potential.

The investments listed are:

(1)   Bank accounts

The two most common accounts are the current account and the deposit account.

Current account

The current account is one where the saver's money is immediately available to him and he may have a cheque book and a cash card to enable him to spend the money in or withdraw the money from the account at any time. Because the money is always available the bank is unlikely to pay interest to the saver on the amount in the account, and where it does, the interest rate will be very low.

Deposit account

A deposit account is an account which pays interest to the saver. The saver can withdraw money from the account on demand but will lose interest equivalent to that which would have been earned during the notice period. The bank will require notice (generally of 7 days) of an intended withdrawal to release funds from the account. Amounts in accounts and transactions are shown by the bank on regular statements which are sent to the saver.

TAX

All interest paid by a bank on these accounts will be paid net of lower rate tax. If the saver is a non-tax payer, he may sign a declaration to this effect and hand it to the bank so enabling it to pay the interest gross. A tax repayment claim by the client can thus be avoided in appropriate cases.

SUITABILITY

The majority of a solicitor's clients both individuals and trustees will have at least a current account in which a sufficient balance is maintained to enable regular expenditure such as utility bills to be met.

However, because of the lack of interest or comparatively poor interest rates it is inadvisable for the majority of a client's savings to remain in such an account.

Banks and building societies encourage people to place their savings with them by offering interest on the money deposited. The bank or building society then uses this money to fund loans and mortgages to borrowers. The borrowers pay back not only the amount borrowed but also interest on the loan. This rate of interest is higher than that paid to the people saving with the bank or society. The difference covers the institution's running costs and provides a profit for the bank or society.

Example

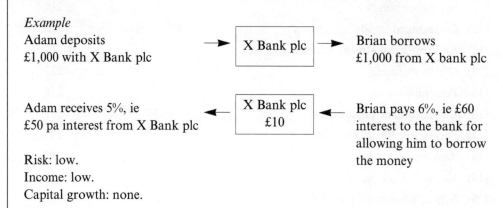

Adam deposits £1,000 with X Bank plc → X Bank plc → Brian borrows £1,000 from X bank plc

Adam receives 5%, ie £50 pa interest from X Bank plc ← X Bank plc £10 ← Brian pays 6%, ie £60 interest to the bank for allowing him to borrow the money

Risk: low.
Income: low.
Capital growth: none.

(2) Building society accounts

Building societies offer deposit accounts and an array of share accounts. Ownership of an account is evidenced by a passbook held by the account holder in which the building society records all payments to and withdrawals from the account. Interest rates vary from time to time.

Deposit accounts

Money is repayable on demand and interest calculated on a daily basis is paid on the amount in the account. In the event of the building society ceasing to exist, deposit account holders will receive back their money in priority to all other savers. Hence, this is the safest type of building society account and, therefore, pays a lower rate of interest than a share account.

Share accounts

There are a wide variety of accounts offered by the various societies. For small sums or as an alternative to a current bank account, an ordinary share account offers a higher rate of interest than a deposit account and access to all money in the account on demand. Where immediate access is not required, higher rates of interest are paid on 'notice' accounts, for example, 28-day access account. The saver has to give the society a specified length of notice of his intention to withdraw his money. The longer the notice period, the higher the rate of interest paid on the account.

These accounts often also have a tiered interest system so that interest is paid at different rates on the amount in the account.

> *Example*
> Charly has £30,000 in a 60-day notice account. She is paid interest on:
>
> (1) the first £10,000 @ x% pa;
> (2) the next £15,000 @ $x + \frac{1}{2}$% pa;
> (3) the balance @ $x + \frac{3}{4}$% pa.

TAX

The tax treatment of building society accounts is exactly the same as for bank accounts.

SUITABILITY

Building societies offer a relatively safe investment with a reasonably good rate of return. Most clients concerned with financial planning should consider holding at least one share account as they offer liquidity and interest. However, if the interest is required to supplement income, the underlying value of the capital will be eroded by inflation.

Trustees with wide express investment powers can invest in all types of building society account. Where the TIA 1961 applies, deposit accounts are narrower-range investments requiring advice whilst share accounts are wider-range investments.

Risk: low.
Income: low.
Capital growth: none.

(3) TESSAs

Since their introduction by the government in January 1991, Tax Exempt Special Savings Accounts (TESSAs) are now offered by most banks and building societies enabling savers to receive tax-free income on investments up to £9,000. A TESSA must run for at least 5 years. Single capital payments are made into the account each year. In the first year the maximum amount is £3,000 with a maximum of £1,800 pa over the next few years (subject to the overall £9,000 maximum).

'Follow up' TESSAs

The first TESSAs matured in January 1996 and the interest earned on the account thereafter is taxable. However, investors who held their first TESSA for the full 5 years and have invested £3,000 or more can reinvest the capital (not the interest) up to £9,000 in the first year of a new TESSA – a follow up TESSA.

If capital of more than £3,000 but less than £9,000 is reinvested in the follow up TESSA, investment up to the overall maximum of £9,000 can then be made subject to the maximum of £1,800 per annum and the usual 5 year period.

An individual may only own one TESSA.

TAX

Interest is credited to the account annually. That interest, after deduction of lower rate tax, can be withdrawn by the saver. Instead it can be left in the account and reinvested.

If the capital remains in the account for the full 5 years, the tax payer receives a refund of the lower rate tax deducted from the interest and after 5 years can withdraw the capital and interest tax free.

It is possible for the capital to be withdrawn within the 5 years but the saver then loses the right to recover the income tax.

SUITABILITY

TESSAs are popular with small savers who can afford to tie up a small amount of capital for 5 years. Higher rate tax payers should also consider owning a TESSA but for a wealthy individual the £9,000 ceiling means it will only be a small part of his overall financial planning strategy.

Risk: low.
Income: medium.
Capital growth: low.

(4) National Savings

National Savings are schemes offered by the government which guarantee the security of the money invested with it. There are a number of National Savings products and some of the most common are identified below.

National Savings Bank accounts

This bank offers an ordinary and an investment account both of which are operated with a passbook through the saver's local post office.

Interest is paid annually on both accounts, but is higher on the deposit account. The interest rate may change from time to time.

ORDINARY ACCOUNT

The minimum amount for each payment into the account is £10 and the maximum holding in the account is £10,000. The money is usually available on demand although if a large amount (in excess of £250) is required a few days' notice may be required.

TAX

The first £70 pa of interest is tax free. Interest is paid gross.

SUITABILITY

It may be particularly useful for non-tax payers such as children and the elderly providing easy and convenient access and a small amount of tax-free income. By receiving the income gross, non-tax payers do not have to worry about tax reclaims or filing tax returns. The low rate of interest is unlikely to make it an attractive account for others. The once a year interest payment makes it unattractive for those needing a regular income.

Risk, income and capital growth: low.

INVESTMENT ACCOUNT

The minimum investment at any time is £20 and the maximum that can be held in the account is £100,000. The rate of interest is competitive with banks and building societies but one month's notice must be given before any withdrawal can be made.

TAX

All the interest is taxable but is paid gross.

SUITABILITY

The convenience of withdrawing money at the post office and the receipt of gross interest appeal to the elderly. The notice period and annual interest payment can be deterrents for those needing regular income or access to capital.

Income bonds

Income bonds provide a regular monthly income. Ownership is evidenced by a bond or certificate. The minimum purchase is £2,000 and the maximum holding £250,000. Income is paid monthly to the investor. The interest rate may vary from time to time. Three months' notice is required to cash in all or part of the bond.

TAX

All the interest is taxable but paid gross.

SUITABILITY

The bond provides an attractive rate of interest for non-tax payers and a regular income. It is, therefore, particularly suitable for elderly clients with limited savings. The main disadvantages are the need for tax payers to account for income tax on income received each year and the lack of protection of the capital against inflation.

Risk, income and capital growth: low.

National Savings Certificates

Savings Certificates can be purchased from the post office and offer tax-free interest. In return for the purchase of Certificates the interest rate is guaranteed. The rate of interest increases each year the Certificates are held over a 5-year period but averaged over the 5 years is equivalent to the guaranteed annual rate. For example, a guaranteed average rate of 5.75 per cent pa over 5 years will be achieved by paying 4 per cent in year 1 increasing to 7.9 per cent in year 5. The interest is added to the capital each year and only paid out when the Certificates are cashed. To achieve the maximum interest the Certificates must be held for the full 5 years. The minimum purchase is £100 and generally the maximum holding in any issue is £10,000.

Certificates should normally be cashed in after 5 years as thereafter the annual rate of interest paid drops significantly.

Certificates can be repaid early but this is penalised by interest being calculated at a lower rate for the period of ownership.

TAX
There is no income tax or CGT to pay.

SUITABILITY
Because of their favourable tax treatment, National Savings Certificates offer an attractive investment to higher rate tax payers. They are also suitable for parents or trustees wishing to invest money for minor children.

Because the interest is compounded and only paid out when the Certificates are redeemed, this is not a suitable investment for anybody requiring a regular income.

Risk and income: low.
Capital growth: medium (interest is added to the capital).

Pensioners Guaranteed Income Bonds

In 1994, Pensioners Guaranteed Income Bonds ('granny bonds') were introduced for people aged 65 (reduced to 60 for 1996/97) or over. The minimum investment is £500; the maximum investment is £50,000 (doubled for joint holdings). Income rates are guaranteed for 5 years. Income is taxable but is paid gross. After 5 years the money may be withdrawn without any penalty. These bonds are suitable for elderly people with modest amounts of cash to invest. There is little risk and no capital growth. Income rates should be compared to rates available from an equivalent investment elsewhere, for example in a building society.

Premium bonds

Premium bonds are purchased from the post office. Bond holders are automatically entered for regular prize draws. Bonds are divided into £1 units and each unit has a separate chance in the draws, ie a £100-bond has 100 chances of winning a prize in every draw. Prizes range from £50 to £1,000,000. Bond holders can reclaim their money from the bonds at any time. The minimum holding is £100; the maximum holding is £20,000.

TAX
All prizes are totally tax free.

SUITABILITY
Statistics suggest that holders of bonds to the maximum limit should receive an acceptable level of prizes each year to make it a worthwhile purchase for wealthy higher rate tax payers. For others, there is no income and no capital growth, merely the gamble that a bond will win one of the larger prizes.

Trustees whose investment powers come from the TIA 1961 cannot purchase premium bonds and they are unlikely to be suitable for most trusts.

Risk, income and capital growth: low.

(5)   Local authority bonds

These bonds are a way of investing in local authorities. When a local authority needs to raise money, it may encourage investors to deposit money with them in return for a competitive rate of interest. The minimum investment is usually £1,000 with no maximum. The bond will last for between one and 4 years and must be held to maturity. The local authority guarantees the rate of interest to be paid throughout the period.

TAX

There is no CGT on these bonds. The interest is paid net of lower rate tax.

SUITABILITY

The guaranteed interest rate may be attractive at a time of falling interest rates and is usually competitive when compared to other forms of interest-only savings. The safety of the money invested depends upon the standing of the local authority. Because it is a fixed-term investment, these bonds are not suitable for people needing immediate access to their capital. The bonds may be suitable investments for some trustees, and are authorised narrower-range investments requiring advice under the TIA 1961.

Risk, income and capital growth: low.

(6)   Gilts

'Gilts' is the popular name for government stocks otherwise known as 'gilt-edged' securities. They are issued by the UK government as a way of raising money and are a secure form of investment as interest and repayment are guaranteed by the government.

The majority of gilts pay a fixed rate of interest ('the coupon') over the life of the stock and guarantee repayment of the nominal value of the stock (known as par value) on a given date (known as the redemption date). Interest is usually paid half yearly in two equal amounts.

> *Example*
> John purchases £100 nominal of 10 per cent Treasury Stock 1998. He will receive an annual guaranteed income of £10 (10 per cent) gross until 1998 when he will be paid £100.

Normally, when the government issues the gilt, it does so at a discount to its par value.

> *Example*
> Assume that in 1990 the government issued 10 per cent Treasury Stock 1998 at 94p. This means that for every 94p invested with it in 1990, the government guarantees to pay £1 on redemption in 1996.
>
> So when John purchased £100 nominal in 1990, it actually cost him £94. If he holds the stock until the government redeems it at par, he will receive £100, ie a profit of £6.

Once a person has purchased a gilt, he does not have to continue holding it until its redemption date. He can sell his holding to another investor via the stock market. The stock market determines how much a stock is worth on any given day prior to its redemption date. The seller pays commission to the stockbroker or NSSR (see below) for arranging the sale.

Example

Having bought £100 nominal 10 per cent Treasury Stock 1998 in 1990, John needed some money to pay for his 1993 holiday. He therefore decided to sell his stock. The market price on the day of sale is 96p. John will receive £96 less commission.

TAX

The profit made from selling or redeeming a gilt is exempt from CGT.

All interest payments are liable to income tax.

Gilts can either be bought and sold through the National Savings Stocks Register (NSSR) or through a stockbroker. Where an investor has used the NSSR the interest will be paid to him gross. This is very useful for non-tax payers but means tax payers have to remember to pay income tax on their interest payments. Interest on all other gilts is paid net of lower rate tax meaning that non taxpayers have to reclaim the tax deducted.

SUITABILITY

Higher rate tax payers appreciate the CGT exemption but capital gains tend to be moderate and sales (as opposed to redemption) are subject to commission charges. A fixed rate of interest can be advantageous at times of falling interest rates but, conversely, unattractive if interest rates rise during the period of ownership for people on a limited income. A guaranteed rate of return can help budgeting. Gilts are often suitable investments for trustees where a beneficiary requires income and are authorised investments (narrower-range requiring advice) under the TIA 1961.

Risk: low.
Income: medium/high.
Capital growth: if held to redemption, depends on whether bought for a premium or at a discount; otherwise prices vary according to the coupon and prevailing interest rates.

(7)   Quoted shares

An investor may wish to invest money in a company listed (quoted) on The Stock Exchange. The aim is to receive an income and also real (net of inflation) capital growth from the investment. Income is received in the form of dividends paid by the company. The size of a dividend is decided by the company and is normally paid in two, not necessarily equal, instalments. The dividend can vary from year to year.

The capital value of the shares is determined by the market and is based on a number of factors including past and projected profits and takeover rumours.

Shares are, therefore, a speculative investment which may increase or decrease (sometimes spectacularly) in value, and whose value can change daily.

Example 1

In 1994, Taj bought 1,000 shares in A plc at £1 each (cost £1,000). In 1995 he received a dividend of £70 and in 1996 a dividend of £83 as the company made good profits, had good industrial relations and a secure market for its products. Early in 1997, shares were listed as being worth £1.20 each. Taj sold his 1,000 shares for £1,200 less commission.

Example 2

In 1995, Victor bought 1,000 shares in B plc for £1 each (cost £1,000 plus commission and stamp duty). Soon afterwards the company suffered a strike by its workforce and introduced a new product which incorporated a faulty design and had to be withdrawn and compensation paid to people who had already bought the product. In 1996 the company borrowed money to enable it to pay shareholders a dividend. Victor received £50. Shortly afterwards the company went into liquidation. Victor's 1,000 shares are now worth £20.

TAX

All profits on the disposal of shares are liable to CGT. Any losses made on disposal can be set against gains in the same tax year and any excess carried forward to set against gains in future years.

Dividends are paid net of 20 per cent income tax. This tax can be recovered by non-tax payers but higher rate tax payers will have additional tax to pay.

SUITABILITY

Because of the financial risks, shares should only be purchased by those who can afford to lose the money invested. In return for that risk, shares offer both income and capital gains opportunities but fairly substantial sums need to be invested in a 'portfolio of shares' (ie several shareholdings in different companies) to produce significant gains.

Shares are often purchased by trustees and may form the bulk of trust investments but extra care must be taken where the trustees' investment powers are given by the TIA 1961 as the Act imposes restrictions on the type of quoted shares that may be held and limits the amount of investment.

Risk: medium/high.
Income: low/medium.
Capital growth: medium/high.

(8) Investment trusts

Investment trusts are quoted companies whose assets consist solely of shares in other companies. The investment trust company may specialise in acquiring shares in companies in one particular sector of the market or it may own shares in a wide variety of companies. The advantage for the investor holding shares in the investment trust is that he can have an indirect interest in a number of companies with the investment management handled by professional managers: the investment trust.

The investment trust pays dividends and the value of investment trust is determined by the stock market.

TAX

Dividends are paid by the investment trust net of income tax at 20 per cent which can be reclaimed by non-tax payers.

When an investor disposes of his shares in an investment trust a liability to CGT can arise.

SUITABILITY

Investment trusts are suitable for anybody, including trustees, who might reasonably consider investing in quoted shares and also smaller investors who lack the expertise to manage their own portfolio or for whom transaction costs on shares are high compared to their amount of investment. The risk of loss as compared with investment in individual companies may be reduced due to the spread of investment by the trust but an investment trust may have to be held for several years to realise much capital growth.

Risk: medium.
Income: medium.
Capital growth: medium/high.

(9)   Unit trusts

Unit trusts provide a method of investing on the stock market for anybody who wishes to invest in a range of companies but lacks the time or expertise to manage his own share portfolio.

Unit trusts are offered by a number of banks and other institutions who employ investment managers. The managers charge an annual management fee for their expertise and there is also an initial 'setting-up' charge. The investor hands his investment money to the investment manager in return for a number of units. The value of the units is determined by the value of the shares in the companies in which the managers invest. The investment manager then uses the investor's money to buy additional shares. Different unit trusts invest in different types of company, for example UK Gilt Unit Trust only invests in UK government securities; M&G Far Eastern Unit Trust only invests in companies quoted on stock exchanges of countries in the Far East (eg Japan and Hong Kong).

An investor can sell his units back to the unit trust managers at any time. If the unit trust has performed well, the sale price should be greater than the price at which the investor purchased his units. Unit trusts have two prices: the bid price which is what an investor will receive if he sells his units, and the offer price which is the price at which the units can be purchased.

> *Example*
> Daisy decides to invest £1,100 in the Magic Unit Trust which invests in UK companies. On the day of her investment the bid price is £1 and the offer price £1.10. She receives 1,000 units.
>
> Daisy must wait until the bid price of units in Magic Unit Trust increases to at least £1.10 before she sells in order to get back her full investment. The bid price must increase further for her to make a capital gain on her investment.
>
> Unit trusts also pay dividends to investors.

TAX
Interest paid to unit holders is paid net of 20 per cent income tax which can be reclaimed by non-tax payers.

Any profit made by an investor on the sale of his units is liable to CGT.

SUITABILITY
Anybody including trustees wishing to invest in UK or overseas companies but without the time or expertise to manage their own portfolio should consider unit trusts. However, the initial costs mean that unit trusts are not suitable for short-term investment.

Risk: medium.
Income: low/medium.
Capital growth: medium/high.

(10) PEPs

A personal equity plan (PEP) is a way of making a tax-free investment in shares. The scheme was introduced by the government in 1987 as a way of encouraging investment in UK companies. Because it is tax free there is a limit on the amount which can be invested in PEPs each year. The current amount is £6,000 per annum per tax payer. In addition, a further £3,000 per annum may be invested in a single company PEP, ie the entire investment in the PEP is in the shares of one company only.

A wide variety of PEPs is offered by a large number of institutions.

Clients with an existing portfolio of shares can transfer an appropriate portion of the portfolio to a PEP. Clients investing for the first time may invest in unit or investment trust PEPs or PEPs investing directly in companies.

The investor hands his money to an investment manager who then selects and invests that money in what he considers to be appropriate unit trusts or shares in selected companies.

The investment manager then manages that new portfolio, or the existing shares where they have been transferred, by buying and selling investments with the aim of increasing the value of the initial investment. Sale proceeds may be reinvested without affecting the £6,000 annual allowance.

The investment manager charges an annual fee for managing the portfolio.

TAX
To obtain any tax benefit from a PEP, the investment must be maintained for a minimum of one year plus one day.

Income tax
The shares and unit trusts within the PEP will pay dividends in the usual way. Lower-rate income tax deducted at source by the companies can be reclaimed by the PEP owner, and the dividends will not be subject to basic or higher rates of tax. For this reason, high income shares (instead of capital growth) should be put into a PEP.

CGT
Any profits made on sales by the investment managers within the PEP will not be subject to CGT. When an investor withdraws his money from a PEP any increase in value over the original investment is also free of CGT.

SUITABILITY
A PEP is suitable for anyone who is considering diversifying their investments by investing in the stock market and clients with existing share portfolios. Because of the tax advantages, PEPs are particularly attractive to higher rate income tax payers.

However, PEPs must be seen as a medium to long-term investment. They have to be held for more than one year to obtain the tax breaks. Because setting up fees and annual management charges are high, it may take time to show a net profit. Investors should always check whether these charges outweigh any benefit from the tax savings.

There are a number of restrictions on how money in PEPs can be invested and the plans are only available to those who are resident or ordinarily resident for UK tax purposes.

Risk: medium/high.
Income: medium/high.
Capital growth: medium/high.

(11)   Insurance bonds

Usually known as 'investment bonds' or 'single premium bonds', insurance bonds are single premium (one off capital payment, not the more usual regular insurance premiums) non-qualifying policies (ie not satisfying ICTA 1988, s 267 and so attracting tax at maturity). The bonds are normally 'unit linked' with profit policies so that bonuses are added to the value of the units by the life company.

Income and capital are retained within the bond. Withdrawals up to 5 per cent of the premiums paid can be taken tax free for the first 20 years of the bond.

TAX
No tax is payable by the investor during the life of the bond providing withdrawals do not exceed 5 per cent. Gains arising on maturity of the bond are subject to higher rate tax (as non-qualifying policies) but not to lower or basic rate tax.

SUITABILITY
These bonds are suitable for higher rate tax payers with a lump sum to invest as there is no tax to pay during the life of the bond. The 5 per cent tax free withdrawal represents the income entitlement from the investment. Ideally the bond should be planned to mature when the investor's tax rate has fallen below higher rate (so as to avoid income tax), for example the bond could mature following retirement when income is less.

Risk: medium.
Income: low (max 5%).
Capital growth: medium/high.

(12)   Guaranteed bonds

These are single premium non-qualifying life policies which last for a fixed period. Guaranteed income bonds guarantee income at fixed rates, and guaranteed growth bonds guarantee a fixed return when the bond ends.

TAX
As non-qualifying life policies there is no basic rate liability but higher rate tax may be payable.

SUITABILITY
Both bonds may be suitable for basic rate tax payers (as only higher rate tax may be payable) with capital to invest.

Risk: low/medium.
Income: low/medium (none on guaranteed growth bonds).
Capital growth: medium (income on guaranteed income bonds).

(13)   Enterprise Investment Scheme (EIS Relief)

A scheme introduced by the Finance Act 1994 to replace the existing Business Expansion Scheme. Individuals with capital to invest (maximum £100,000 in any tax year) obtain income tax relief at 20 per cent. Provided the qualifying investments are held for 5 years, capital gains made on disposal are free of CGT. Gains on disposals of any assets can be 'heldover' when the investor subscribes for EIS shares. Meanwhile, dividends are taxed under Schedule F in the usual way.

Qualifying investments are shares in unquoted trading companies carrying on business in the UK; the company must continue to do so for 3 years from the share issue. UK resident tax payers may obtain the relief but they are not eligible if they are connected with the company, for example as an employee or paid director. Further, relief will not be available if more than 30 per cent of the share capital is involved.

Example
£50,000 is invested in EIS shares in January 1996 (1995/96).

(1)   The initial investment – attracts 20% relief, so that the effective cost of the shares is £40,000.
(2)   If shares are sold in January 2100, ie more than 5 years later – any gain is free of CGT.

Because of the generous nature of the relief, and in an attempt to restrict its abuse, there are many detailed conditions in FA 1994, Sch 15.

SUITABILITY
Investors with substantial capital to invest in unquoted trading companies with which they are not connected. Although income tax relief at 20 per cent is available on the investment, dividends received will attract income tax. Generally, it should be remembered the company's articles of association and questions of marketability of the shares may make it difficult to find a buyer for the shares. The danger is getting 'locked into' the investment – or perhaps only being able to sell at a reduced price.

Risk: medium/high.
Income: possibly none, depending on whether the company pays dividends.
Capital growth: medium/high (but marketability may make sale difficult).

(14)   Off-shore funds

These funds are managed by companies registered outside the UK tax and regulatory system under the Financial Services Act 1986 in places such as the Channel Islands and the Isle of Man.

Funds actively marketed in the UK (being approved by the Securities and Investments Board) are either Distributor Funds (ie a fund which pays dividends equivalent to 85 per cent of its income) or Accumulator Funds (where gross income is retained within the fund to increase its value).

TAX
Dividends from Distributor Funds are paid gross but are taxable on receipt into the UK. Income and capital gains of Accumulator Funds are subject to tax on sale of the investment and rates then prevailing.

SUITABILITY

These funds are similar to UK unit and investment trusts and so are suitable for anyone with capital to invest. Distributor Funds (paid gross) may be particularly suited to non-tax payers. Accumulator Funds are more likely to be attractive to higher rate tax payers who can afford to retain their investment off-shore until after retirement when their tax rates are lower.

Risk: medium/high.
Income: medium/high.
Capital growth: medium/high.

(15) Pensions

Pension schemes are a way of saving for old age, so providing an income after retirement.

The main categories of scheme include state pensions, occupational pensions for employees, and personal pension schemes.

The state scheme

The state scheme is funded by the self-employed, employees and employers paying national insurance (NI) contributions. The scheme has two parts: a compulsory contribution and an earnings-related pension (State Earnings-Related Pension Scheme – SERPS) from which employers and employees can 'contract-out' and which is not available to the self-employed.

All employers, employees and the self-employed must contribute to the compulsory part of the scheme. Provided a person has made sufficient contributions during his or her working life, he or she will currently receive the old age pension at 60 (for women) or 65 (for men).

SERPS is an additional pension related to an employee's earnings and paid by the state if employer and employee have paid extra NI contributions. Contributions are based on the employee's annual earnings and there is no income tax relief for the employee's contributions. The pension will currently be paid at 60 for a woman, and 65 for a man. It is possible to 'contract out' of SERPS. In this case, a lower level of NI contributions is payable but only the old age pension will be received after retirement. Because of the costs involved in operating SERPS the government has actively encouraged 'contracting out'.

Occupational pension schemes

These are often called company pension schemes but apply equally to those employed by partnerships and other non-corporate entities. The scheme must be offered by any employer who wishes to contract out of SERPS and may be contributory or non-contributory.

A non-contributory scheme is one where only the employer pays into the scheme to provide his employees with appropriate pension benefits on retirement. Such payments by the employer are not treated as an emolument of the employee for his income tax purposes and are based on a percentage of the employee's earnings.

In a contributory scheme, both the employer and employee contribute. Again, the employer's contributions are based on a percentage of the employee's annual earnings and do not count as emoluments. The employee's contributions are an agreed minimum percentage of earnings. In addition he may pay additional voluntary contributions (AVCs) into the scheme or free standing AVCs (FSAVCs) into a separately run scheme. An employee may only obtain tax relief to the extent that his total contributions do not exceed the prescribed limit. The current limit for contributions is 15 per cent of earnings. However, earnings over £84,000 (1997/98) (the earnings limit) are ignored.

All contributions and AVCs are paid into a fund which is invested by the trustees of the pension scheme with the aim of increasing the value of the fund.

On retirement, an employee will receive either an annual pension based on the amount of his final salary or a cash lump sum and a smaller annual pension. Legislation controls the maximum amount of pension and lump sum that can be received.

Where an employee dies before retirement age a lump sum based on contributions made to the scheme may be payable to the employee's dependants. Having started to receive a pension, all rights to it ceases on the employee's death. However, an employee can elect to receive a smaller pension than he would normally be entitled to with the guarantee that on his death, the pension will continue to be paid to his widow for the remainder of her life.

TAX

If the scheme is 'exempt approved' under ICTA 1988, s 612 (which most occupational pension schemes will be – there are other special rules governing unapproved occupational pension schemes) it enjoys a number of valuable tax concessions:

(1) As stated earlier, the employer's contributions will not be taxed as a benefit in kind as part of the employee's emoluments.

(2) The employer's annual contributions can be deducted before tax is calculated.

(3) The employee can obtain tax relief on his contributions up to 15 per cent of remuneration. For the year 1997/98 the 'earnings limit' for this purpose is £84,000.

Example

An employee earning £100,000 per annum can make contributions, ie ordinary contributions, AVCs and FSAVCs of £15,000 (15% × £84,000) and obtain tax relief at his highest rate by deducting this amount from his emoluments for Schedule E purposes.

(4) On retirement the maximum pension is two-thirds of the earnings limit of £84,000 (1997/98). If pensionable employment is less than 40 years the amount of the pension will be reduced.

Example

If the employee in the previous example is earning £125,000 per annum at retirement and has put in 40 years' service, his maximum pension will be two-thirds of £84,000, ie £56,000 per annum.

(5) Instead of taking a full pension, the employee can commute part of his entitlement for a tax-free cash sum. Conventional wisdom is that the tax-free cash be taken and invested to produce further income in retirement. Again the earnings limit applies. The maximum which can be taken in this way is 1.5 × final salary subject to the earnings limit.

Example

For the employee in the previous example the maximum tax-free lump sum is 1.5 × £84,000 = £126,000. He would also be entitled to a reduced pension (taxable under Schedule E).

(6) Any payment made to the employee's dependants on his death will not be charged to IHT provided the trustees of the pension scheme have the discretion to choose who should benefit.

(7) The pension fund builds up free of tax, ie the trustees do not pay income tax on income received from investment of the contributions; nor do they pay CGT on disposal of investments.

SUITABILITY

An occupational pension scheme is suitable for any employee in paid employment. The ultimate pension benefits are likely to be significantly better than benefits paid by the state. There is, however, no obligation on an employer to set up such a scheme nor can the employer require an employee to become a member of the scheme, ie he can 'opt out' in favour of a personal pension should he prefer.

Self-employed pension schemes

These schemes are available to the self-employed and also employees who either do not wish to join their employer's occupational pension scheme or whose employers do not provide an occupational pension scheme.

An individual taking out a scheme for the first time is now limited to a personal pension but until 1988 pension provision was made through retirement annuity contracts. Although it is no longer possible to buy new retirement annuity contracts, it is still possible for contributions to be made to contracts taken out before 1988 and most people who have existing retirement annuity contracts continue to pay into them in preference to acquiring a new personal pension because the various maximum limits are often more favourable.

Personal pensions

Contributions are paid to the pension fund company – usually one of the life assurance companies – which invests them to provide a cash lump sum and/or an annual income and annuity, for the individual when he reaches retirement age. The pension can start at any time between the ages of 50 and 75 years.

Contributions are limited to a percentage of the individual's 'net relevant earnings' (earned income less certain deductions) in the tax year. Once again the earnings limit of £84,000 (1997/98) applies so that earnings over this amount are ignored. The percentage which can be invested increases with the age of the individual.

Age	Contribution %
Up to 36	17.5
36–45	20.0
46–50	25.0
51–55	30.0
56–60	35.0
61 and over	40.0

Example

An individual aged 50 can pay a maximum contribution attracting tax relief of 25% of £84,000, ie £21,000.

Individuals, especially when first contributing to a personal pension, may not be able to afford the full permitted contribution each year. In such cases, the contributions shortfall can be carried forward as 'unused contributions' for up to 6 tax years.

On retirement, the individual can choose to receive an annuity, ie a pension for life or a reduced annuity plus a tax-free lump sum. This lump sum is calculated as a percentage of the total value of the fund available to the individual.

TAX

Contributions up to the limit attract tax relief at the individual's highest rate. For employed persons, relief at basic rate is obtained by paying the contribution net of basic rate tax. The pension company recovers an equivalent amount from the Inland Revenue. Higher rate relief is obtained through the employee's tax return. The self employed pay contributions in full and obtain relief by making a claim in their tax return after the income tax year in which the contributions were paid.

The lump sum is tax free. The annuity is taxed as income.

If the individual dies before retirement the pension company will pay out a lump sum calculated in accordance with the scheme. To avoid this sum forming part of the individual's estate on death, and so chargeable to IHT, death benefits should be settled during the individual's life on, usually, discretionary trusts for the family and dependants.

SUITABILITY

A personal pension is suitable for all self-employed people and those employees who cannot or do not wish to be part of an occupational scheme.

OCCUPATIONAL AND PERSONAL PENSIONS – SUMMARY

Risk: low/medium (trustees hold the funds but investment may be in gilts and/or equities).
Income: low (depending on investment of contributions).
Capital growth: medium (due to tax-free nature of the funds).

(16) Life assurance (insurance)

There are a number of life assurance products only the most common types of which are explained here.

Whole life assurance (whole of life assurance)

In return for a regular monthly or annual premium an assurance company will contract to pay out an agreed fixed sum on the death of the life assured.

Most assurance companies refuse to insure the life of anybody over the age of 80 years and the older a person when they enter into a contract, the more expensive the premium. For example, a person aged 30 years might insure his life for a given sum for £50 per annum while a person aged 60 years might pay £100 per annum for the same level of life cover.

Whole life policies can be written on single lives and also on joint lives. In the latter case, two lives are insured and the assurance company will either pay out on the first death or on the death of the survivor of the joint lives depending on the policy purchased. It is also possible for a person to insure a second person's life provided that he has an insurable interest in the second life. The fixed sum is paid out to the proposer on the death of the life assured.

If the policy is non-profit only a specified sum is payable on death. If it is with profit or unit linked there is an investment element. The sum assured will be paid with bonuses (with profit) or accumulated units (unit linked).

TAX

Premiums may be paid out of capital or income. No income tax relief is available for premiums paid.

On the death of the life assured, the assured sum forms part of his estate and will be liable to IHT unless the policy has been written in trust or assigned.

SUITABILITY

Whole life assurance is suitable for anyone who wishes to provide a lump sum for his family or dependants on his death.

This may be to provide another asset, or to provide cash with which to meet debts such as an IHT bill or a mortgage or to provide funds to buy a deceased partner's share or the shares of a deceased shareholder/director whose shares might have to be sold to an outsider if the other members cannot afford to buy them.

It is not suitable for anybody wishing to save to provide a benefit for themselves.

Term assurance

In return for the payment of a regular premium the assurance company will pay out an agreed sum if the life assured dies within a fixed period of time from the purchase of the assurance policy. The term assurance provides protection only. There is no investment element.

If the proposer ceases to pay the premiums during the agreed term or the life assured survives the term, the policy comes to an end. It has no surrender value.

TAX

The tax treatment is the same as for whole life assurance.

SUITABILITY

Term assurance is suitable for anyone, including trustees who needs to provide a lump sum with which to pay IHT which would become chargeable on a lifetime transfer if the transferor died within 7 years of the transfer.

It may also be used by an individual to cover a fixed-term commitment such as a mortgage or school fees.

It is not suitable for anyone aiming to provide a benefit for himself.

Endowment assurance

In return for regular premiums the assurance company contracts to pay the sum assured on the earlier of a given date or the death of the life assured. In these cases, there is clearly the possibility of personal enjoyment of the policy proceeds by the life assured.

The policy may be with profits or unit linked. It can be written on single or joint lives. There is an investment element.

Endowment policies provide protection as well as a sum payable on the maturity date for the policy or the earlier death of the life assured. These policies are frequently used in planning for the repayment of mortgages (where they are linked to the date for repayment of the mortgage) or school fees (where they are planned to mature at a time appropriate to payment of the fees).

TAX

Policies are normally for a minimum period of 10 years so that as 'qualifying policies' under ICTA 1988, s 267 the sum payable on maturity is tax free. If the life assured survives to the given date, he will receive the assured lump sum free of all taxes. If the payment is made on death, the sum forms part of the estate of the assured.

SUITABILITY

Endowment assurance is suitable for any tax payer looking to build up a tax-free lump sum over a long period either for his own benefit or to meet commitments such as the repayment of a mortgage or the payment of school fees.

Keyman assurance

Where a person is a 'key' man or woman within an organisation his premature death will affect the profitability of the company or partnership. The company or partnership may, therefore, insure that person's life so that the company or partnership receives a lump sum on the death of the 'key' man. The life assurance may be a whole life, term or endowment policy.

(17) Permanent health insurance

A person who is in employment anticipates receiving a regular wage or salary or share of partnership profits in return for working. If that person becomes disabled and, therefore, unable to continue working, he will lose this source of income. He can, therefore, insure himself by paying an annual premium so that if he is no longer able to work, the insurance policy will provide him with regular sums of money for a stated period or up to a stated age. There is a limit on the annual amount which can be received from permanent health insurance.

Payment may not commence immediately after the disability arises as the policyholder can defer claiming benefit, for example, for 3 months. The longer the agreed period of deferral, the lower the annual premium.

An employer often provides permanent health insurance through group arrangements. Contributions paid are generally deductible as trading expenses.

TAX

An individual does not receive tax relief on the premiums paid.

Once benefits are claimed they are taxable as income.

SUITABILITY

Permanent health insurance is suitable for anyone in work who has dependants but cover may not be available for a person who is already in poor health when he applies to purchase the insurance cover. PHI is particularly suitable for the self-employed for whom replacement of income when permanently disabled will be essential. The effect on the business through absence of the 'owner' may cause it to fold.

(18) Annuities

In return for the investment of a capital lump sum, a life company will guarantee a regular amount of income (annuity) to the investor – purchased life annuity. The annuity can be paid annually, quarterly or monthly as the investor wishes. A good rate of return can be obtained if the annuity is purchased when interest rates are high. But the cost of the annuity depends partly on the age of the annuitant and may not be worthwhile until he reaches 70 years of age. On the death of the annuitant or expiry of the agreed term, usually no capital is returnable.

TAX

The Inland Revenue regards purchased life annuity payments as being partly income and partly a return of the original capital invested (ICTA 1988, s 656). Only the income element is subject to income tax at the annuitant's income tax rates and is received net of lower rate tax. Some or all of this tax can be recovered by non and lower rate tax payers.

No tax is payable on the capital element.

SUITABILITY

Annuities are suitable for anyone who needs a guaranteed income or income for life and who can afford to spend capital. The main disadvantages are that the real value of the income may be eroded by inflation and that once purchased there is no ability to surrender the annuity or recover the initial capital investment. Annuities may be suitable for elderly clients, or younger clients with children wishing to make provision for school fees.

Risk: low.
Income: medium/high (depending on age at purchase).
Capital growth: nil.

(19)   Home income plans

Elderly people are often 'assets rich but income poor'. Home income plans are of various types; they are only available to elderly home owners (aged 65 or more) and are a method of using the capital value of the home to provide an income. Life companies lend a sum of money to the home owner secured by a mortgage over the home. The home owner must use at least 90 per cent of the loan to buy an annuity (an income for life) for himself – a purchased life annuity (see para (18) above). The intention is that the annuity will be sufficient to pay the mortgage interest and leave the home owner with an income.

When the home owner dies the money borrowed is repaid from the proceeds of sale of the home (or other available funds).

TAX

(1) Mortgage interest relief.

Most schemes satisfy the criteria (ICTA 1988, s 365) which allows the home owner tax relief on interest paid on the loan (up to a maximum of £30,000). Relief is at 23 per cent (not 15 per cent as in the case of other mortgage interest). The MIRAS scheme provides the relief by allowing payment of 77 per cent of the mortgage interest leaving the life company (the lender) to recover the remaining 23 per cent from the Inland Revenue.

(2) Purchased life annuity (ICTA 1988, s 656).

Under s 656 annuity payments are regarded as partly a payment of income and partly a return of the capital invested in the purchase of the annuity. Only the income is subject to income tax; the capital element is tax free.

Lower rate income tax is normally deducted from the annuity at source but can be reclaimed in whole or in part by a lower rate or non-tax payer. Arrangements can be made for the annuity to be paid gross (in full) if the home owner prefers.

Example (non taxpayer)

	£	£
Annuity (net)	6,400	
Lower rate tax re-paid	1,600	
		8,000
Mortgage interest	6,000	
less MIRAS (basic rate)	1,380	4,620
Increase in income		3,380

Note that in some cases the increase in income may cause the individual to become a tax payer.

SUITABILITY

Home income plans are suitable for elderly people who own their own home, have exhausted all other sources of capital, and need to increase their income. However, clients should be made aware that: (i) inflation and changes in interest rates can substantially reduce the value of the annuity; (ii) interest rates may rise and the annuity may end up producing less income than the mortgage interest payments; and (iii) less capital is available at death for the home owner's beneficiaries.

(20) School fee plans

There are a number of commercial plans available or parents can create their own provision. Those listed below are intended to give an indication of how some of these plans work. The deciding factor as to the type of plan is often whether the parent can afford a 'one off' lump sum payment out of capital, or whether the cost of the plan has to be met from income.

Funding from income

LIFE ASSURANCE SCHEMES

Certain qualifying with profits or endowment life assurance policies enable the proceeds to be received completely tax free provided that premiums are payable for at least 10 years. The idea is that a series of such policies are purchased each maturing in consecutive years to provide annual funds for annual school fees.

DEFERRED ANNUITIES

Monthly premiums are paid to purchase an annuity equivalent to the level of fees whose payment is deferred until the fees are needed. The premium payments need not commence until shortly before school fees start to become due and continue until the last term for which fees are required.

The income element of the annuity will be subject to income tax at the parent's highest marginal rate.

Funding from capital

COMPOUNDING

Many schools offer their own fee plan. In return for a guaranteed level of fees parents pay a lump sum to the school in advance of the child starting at that school.

This can result in a substantial saving to the parents but care should be taken to check what happens to the lump sum if the child does not subsequently start at that school or leaves before the anticipated year.

There should be no tax consequences.

EDUCATIONAL TRUSTS

There are a number of charitable educational trusts which, in return for an administration fee, invest the parents' lump sum in the purchase of an annuity payable termly to meet the fees. The annuity can start immediately or be deferred. The longer the deferral (eg the plan is established on the birth of a child, to commence when he is 7 years old) the greater the value of the annuity. Any over-provision against the school fees can be paid to the parent.

Any annuity paid to the school is unlikely to be subject to income tax, but any surplus paid to the parent will suffer income tax at his rate(s) on the income element.

GILT-EDGED SECURITIES

A lump sum can be invested in gilts with a range of redemption dates to mature over the school life of the child. If suitable redemption dates are not available, long-dated gifts can be purchased and holdings sold as and when school fees become due.

There is no CGT to pay on any gains made on the redemption or sale of gilts.

(21)   Mortgages

Mortgages cannot be described as investments from the point of view of the borrower. Frequently, but not necessarily, they are linked to insurance policies which are investments. The insurance policy is designed to repay the mortgage debt at the end of the term or on the earlier death of the borrower so that the property on which it is secured can pass free of mortgage to the beneficiary under the borrower's will or intestacy.

There are many types of mortgage. The borrower must be advised to 'shop around' to find the type which best suits his particular circumstances. This is particularly true for the first-time buyer needing a large mortgage (or large as a proportion of the purchase price for the house).

In principle, there are two types of mortgage: the repayment mortgage and the interest only mortgage.

Repayment mortgages

Here, the monthly repayment is partly interest and partly a repayment of the capital sum outstanding. In the early years, the payments are largely of interest but include some capital repayment. As the capital is repaid, the proportion of interest in the monthly repayment reduces and the capital proportion increases.

To cover the possibility of the borrower dying before the capital is repaid at the end of the mortgage term, the lender will require a mortgage protection policy. A decreasing term assurance (with no investment element) is usual. It is decreasing in that the cover provided equates to the reducing capital sum due to the lender.

Tax relief is available (within limits) on the interest paid to the lender in each year, see **2.6.3**. The amount of this interest is certified to the Inland Revenue by the lender for tax relief purposes.

Interest only mortgages

In these cases, the lender does not expect monthly repayment of capital but he will require interest on the amount borrowed. The capital remains due at the end of the mortgage term. Arrangements should be made by the borrower to fund this liability (sometimes the lender will only lend if adequate arrangements have been put in place). There are three main types of interest only mortgages.

(1) THE 'ENDOWMENT MORTGAGE'

This is a misleading phrase for a commonly met arrangement. There are two transactions – the mortgage and the endowment policy. The premiums on the policy attract no tax relief and represent a further outlay by the borrower but he is, at least, acquiring a valuable asset.

The policy is assigned to the lender. At the end of the mortgage the policy will mature. After the mortgage debt is discharged, any balance will be paid to the borrower. If the policy was a 'with profits' policy, there will often be a considerable sum to come to the borrower. In this way, the policy may prove to be a good investment.

Some 'with profit' policies assume that when bonuses are added at the end of the term, the sum assured will then be the equivalent of the sum borrowed. In such cases, the premium payable on the policy may be reduced because the sum assured is reduced. This will be attractive to many borrowers but increases the risk that the policy may not be sufficient to pay off the sum borrowed when it matures.

(2) A 'PENSION MORTGAGE'

This phrase is also misleading. Again there are two transactions – the mortgage and the pension. The assumption is that the repayment of the mortgage at the end of the term is funded from the 'tax free' lump sum payable from a personal pension (see para (15) above).

While superficially very attractive (bearing in mind the favourable tax position of a personal pension), it must be remembered that the real purpose of the pension is to provide an income for retirement (and not a lump sum to repay a mortgage debt).

(3) A 'PEP MORTGAGE'

Again, this is a confusing term. Here the fund is built up in the PEP or a number of PEPs taken out annually over a number of years (with the associated tax advantages – see (10) above). The intention is that the relatively good growth rate achieved by the PEPs (if well managed) should produce a fund sufficient (in part) to repay the mortgage at the end of the term.

Appendix 3

ENDURING POWER OF ATTORNEY

SCHEDULE   Regulations 2 and 3

ENDURING POWER OF ATTORNEY

Part A: About using this form

1. You may choose one attorney or more than one. If you choose one attorney then you must delete everything between the square brackets on the first page of the form. If you choose more than one, you must decide whether they are able to act:
- Jointly (that is, they must all act together and cannot act separately) or
- Jointly and severally (that is, they can all act together but they can also act separately if they wish).

On the first page of the form, show what you have decided by crossing out one of the alternatives.

2. If you give your attorney(s) general power in relation to all your property and affairs, it means that they will be able to deal with your money or property and may be able to sell your house.

3. If you don't want your attorney(s) to have such wide powers, you can include any restrictions you like. For example, you can include a restriction that your attorney(s) must not act on your behalf until they have reason to believe that you are becoming mentally incapable; or a restriction as to what your attorney(s) may do. Any restrictions you choose must be written or typed where indicated on the second page of the form.

4. If you are a trustee (and please remember that co-ownership of a home involves trusteeship), you should seek legal advice if you want your attorney(s) to act as a trustee on your behalf.

5. Unless you put in a restriction preventing it your attorney(s) will be able to use any of your money or property to make any provision which you yourself might be expected to make for their own needs or the needs of other people. Your attorney(s) will also be able to use your money to make gifts, but only for reasonable amounts in relation to the value of your money and property.

6. Your attorney(s) can recover the out-of-pocket expenses of acting as your attorney(s). If your attorney(s) are professional people, for example solicitors or accountants, they may be able to charge for their professional services as well. You may wish to provide expressly for remuneration of your attorney(s) (although if they are trustees they may not be allowed to accept it).

7. If your attorney(s) have reason to believe that you have become or are becoming mentally incapable of managing your affairs, your attorney(s) will have to apply to the Court of Protection for registration of this power.

8. Before applying to the Court of Protection for registration of this power, your attorney(s) must give written notice that that is what they are going to do, to you and your nearest relatives as defined in the Enduring Powers of Attorney Act 1985. You or your relatives will be able to object if you or they disagree with registration.

9. This is a simpified explanation of what the Enduring Powers of Attorney Act 1985 and the Rules and Regulations say. If you need more guidance, you or your advisers will need to look at the Act itself and the Rules and Regulations. The Rules are the Court of Protection (Enduring Powers of Attorney) Rules 1986 (Statutory Instrument 1986 No. 127). The Regulations are the Enduring Powers of Attorney (Prescribed Form) Regulations 1990 (Statutory Instrument 1990 No. 1376).

10. Note to Attorney(s)

After the power has been registered you should notify the Court of Protection if the donor dies or recovers.

11. Note to Donor

Some of these explanatory notes may not apply to the form you are using if it has already been adapted to suit your particular requirements.

YOU CAN CANCEL THIS POWER AT ANY TIME BEFORE IT HAS TO BE REGISTERED

Part B: To be completed by the 'donor' (the person appointing the attorney(s))

Don't sign this form unless you understand what it means

Please read the notes in the margin
which follow and which are part of
the form itself.

Donor's name and address

Donor's date of birth

See note 1 on the front of this form. If
you are appointing only one attorney
you should cross out everything
between the square brackets. If
appointing more than two attorneys
please give the additional name(s) on
an attached sheet.

Cross out the one which does not
apply (see note 1 on the front of this
form).

Cross out the one which does not
apply (see note 2 on the front of this
form). Add any additional powers.

If you don't want the attorney(s) to
have general power, you must give
details here of what authority you are
giving the attorney(s).

Cross out the one which does not
apply.

I _____

of _____

born on _____

appoint _____

of _____

● [and_____

    of _____

● jointly
● jointly and severally]
to be my attorney(s) for the purpose of the Enduring Powers
of Attorney Act 1985

● with general authority to act on my behalf
● with authority to do the following on my behalf:

in relation to
● all my property and affairs:
● the following property and affairs:

Part B: continued

Please read the notes in the margin which follow and which are part of the form itself.

If there are restrictions or conditions, insert them here; if not, cross out these words if you wish (see note 3 on the front of this form).

● subject to the following restrictions and conditions

If this form is being signed at your direction:—
● the person signing must not be an attorney or any witness (to Parts B or C).
● you must add a statement that this form has been signed at your direction.
● a second witness is necessary (please see below).

I intend that this power shall continue even if I become mentally incapable.

I have read or have had read to me the notes in Part A which are part of, and explain, this form.

Your signature (or mark).

Signed by me as a deed _____
and delivered

Date.

on _____

Someone must witness your signature
Signature of witness.

in the presence of _____
Full name of witness _____

Your attorney(s) cannot be your witness. It is not advisable for your husband or wife to be your witness.

Address of witness _____
_____
_____

A second witness is only necessary if this form is not being signed by you personally but at your direction (for example, if a physical disability prevents you from signing).

Signature of second witness.

in the presence of _____
Full name of witness _____

Address of witness _____
_____
_____

Part C: To be completed by the attorney(s)
Note: 1   This form may be adapted to provide for execution by a corporation
          2   If there is more than one attorney additional sheets in the form as shown below must be
             added to this Part C

Please read the notes in the margin
which follow and which are part of
the form itself.

Don't sign this form before the donor
has signed Part B or if, in your
opinion, the donor was already
mentally incapable at the time of
signing Part B.

> I understand that I have a duty to apply to the Court for the registration of this form under the Enduring Powers of Attorney Act 1985 when the donor is becoming or has become mentally incapable.

If this form is being signed at your
direction:—
●   the person signing must not be an
attorney or any witness (to Parts B or
C).
●   you must add a statement that this
form has been signed at your
direction.
●   a second witness is necessary
(please see below).

> I also understand my limited power to use the donor's property to benefit persons other than the donor.
>
> I am not a minor.

Signature (or mark) of attorney.

> Signed by me as a deed _____
> and delivered

Date.

> on _____

Signature of witness.

The attorney must sign the form and
his signature must be witnessed. The
donor may not be the witness and one
attorney may not witness the
signature of the other.

> in the presence of _____
> Full name of witness _____
>
> Address of witness _____
> _____
> _____

_____

A second witness is only necessary if
this form is not being signed by you
personally but at your direction (for
example, if a physical disability
prevents you from signing).

Signature of second witness.

> in the presence of _____
> Full name of witness _____
>
> Address of witness _____
> _____
> _____

Appendix 4

DISCRETIONARY SETTLEMENT

Table of contents

SETTLEMENT

DATE: [   ]

PARTIES:

(1)   [   ] (the **'Settlor'**); and

(2)   [   ] (the **'Trustees'**).

RECITALS

(A)   The Settlor wishes to make this Settlement and has transferred or delivered to the Trustees or otherwise placed under their control the property specified in the Schedule. Further money, investments or other property may be paid or transferred to the Trustees by way of addition.

(B)   It is intended that this Settlement shall be irrevocable.

PART 1—OPERATIVE PROVISIONS

1. Definitions and construction

In this Deed, where the context admits, the following definitions and rules of construction shall apply.

1.1   The **'Trust Fund'** shall mean:

(a)   the property specified in the Schedule;

(b)   all money, investments or other property paid or transferred by any person to, or so as to be under the control of, and, in either case, accepted by the Trustees as additions;

(c) all accumulations (if any) of income added to the Trust Fund; and

(d) the money, investments and property from time to time representing the above.

1.2 The **'Trust Period'** shall mean the period ending on the earlier of:

(a) the last day of the period of 80 years from the date of this Deed, which period, and no other, shall be the applicable perpetuity period; and

(b) such date as the Trustees shall at any time specify by deed, not being a date earlier than the date of execution of such deed or later than a date previously specified.

1.3 The **'Accumulation Period'** shall mean the period of 21 years from the date of this Deed, or the Trust Period if shorter.

1.4 The **'Beneficiaries'** shall mean:

(a) the Settlor's children and remoter issue;

(b) the spouses, widows and widowers (whether or not such widows or widowers have remarried) of the Settlor's children and remoter issue;

(c) [   ];

[(d) Charities;] and

[(e)] such other objects or persons as are added under clause 3.

1.5 **'Charity'** shall mean any trust, foundation, company or other organisation whatever established only for purposes regarded as charitable under the law of England and Wales.

1.6 The expression **'the Trustees'** shall, where the context admits, include the trustees for the time being of this Trust.

1.7 References to the children, grandchildren and issue of any person shall include his children, grandchildren and remoter issue, whether legitimate, legitimated[, illegitimate] or adopted [but shall exclude any illegitimate person and his descendants].

1.8 Words denoting the singular shall include the plural and vice versa.

1.9 Words denoting any gender shall include both the other genders.

1.10 The table of contents and clause headings are included for reference only and shall not affect the interpretation of this Deed.

2. Trust for sale

The Trustees shall hold the Trust Fund upon trust in their discretion either to allow the same or remain in the state in which it is received or held for so long as they shall think fit or to sell or convert the same into money. The Trustees may, in their discretion, invest such money in their names or under their control in any of the investments authorised by this Deed or by law, with power from time to time to vary or transpose any such investments for or into others so authorised.

3. Power to add Beneficiaries

3.1 The Settlor, or such person as the Settlor shall have nominated in writing, may, at any time during the Trust Period, add to the Beneficiaries such objects or persons or classes of objects or persons as the Settlor or such other person shall, subject to the application (if any) of the rule against perpetuities, determine.

3.2 Any such addition shall be made by deed:

(a) naming or describing the objects or persons or classes of objects or persons to be added; and

(b) specifying the date or event, not being earlier than the date of execution of the deed but before the end of the Trust Period, on the happening of which the addition shall take effect.

[3.3 This power shall not be exercised so as to add to the Beneficiaries either the Settlor or any person who shall previously have added property to the Trust Fund or the spouse for the time being of the Settlor or any such person.]

4. Power to receive additional property

The Trustees may, at any time during the Trust Period, accept additional money, investments or other property, of whatever nature and wherever situate, paid or transferred to them by the Settlor or any other person. Such additional money, investments or other property shall, subject to any contrary direction, be held upon the trusts and with and subject to the powers and provisions of this Deed.

5. Discretionary trust of capital and income

5.1 The Trustees shall hold the capital and income of the Trust Fund upon trust for or for the benefit of such of the Beneficiaries, at such ages or times, in such shares, upon such trusts (which may include discretionary or protective powers or trusts) and in such manner generally as the Trustees shall in their discretion appoint. Any such appointment may include such powers and provisions for the maintenance, education or other benefit of the Beneficiaries or for the accumulation of income and such administrative powers and provisions as the Trustees think fit.

5.2 No exercise of the power conferred by sub-clause 5.1 shall invalidate any prior payment or application of all or any part of the capital or income of the Trust Fund under the trusts of this Deed or made under any other power conferred by this Deed or by law.

5.3 Any trusts and powers created by an appointment under sub-clause 5.1 may be delegated to any extent to any person, whether or not including the Trustees or any of them.

[5.4 Notwithstanding clause [   ], the Trustees may not release or restrict this power during the Settlor's lifetime without his written consent.]

5.5 The exercise of the power of appointment conferred by sub-clause 5.1 shall:
(a) be subject to the application, if any, of the rule against perpetuities and the law concerning excessive accumulations of income; [and]
(b) be by deed, revocable during the Trust Period or irrevocable, executed during the Trust Period [; and
(c) be subject to the written consent of the Settlor during his lifetime].

6. Income trusts in default of appointment

The provisions of this clause shall apply during the Trust Period until, subject to and in default of any appointment under sub-clause 5.1.

6.1 The Trustees shall pay or apply the income of the Trust Fund to or for the benefit of such of the Beneficiaries as shall for the time being be in existence, in such shares and in such manner generally as the Trustees shall in their discretion from time to time think fit.

6.2 Notwithstanding the provisions of sub-clause 6.1, the Trustees may at any time during the Accumulation Period in their discretion accumulate the income by investing it in any investments authorised by this Deed or by law and, subject to sub-clause 6.3, shall hold such accumulations as an accretion to capital.

6.3 The Trustees may apply the whole or any part of the income accumulated under sub-clause 6.2 as if it were income arising in the then current year.

7. Power to apply capital for Beneficiaries

The provisions of this clause shall apply during the Trust Period notwithstanding the provisions of clause 6 but subject to any appointment made under sub-clause 5.1.

7.1 The Trustees may pay or apply the whole or any part of the capital of the Trust Fund to or for the benefit of all or such of the Beneficiaries, in such shares and in such manner generally as the Trustees shall in their discretion think fit.

7.2 The Trustees may, subject to the application (if any) of the rule against perpetuities, pay or transfer any income or capital of the Trust Fund to the trustees of any other trust, wherever established or existing, under which any Beneficiary is interested (whether or not such Beneficiary is the only object or person interested or capable of benefiting under such other trust) if the Trustees in their discretion consider such payment or transfer to be for the benefit of such Beneficiary.

8. Trusts in default of appointment

From and after the expiration of the Trust Period, and subject to any appointment made under sub-clause 5.1, the Trustees shall hold the capital and income of the Trust Fund upon trust absolutely for such of [   ] as shall then be living and, if more than one, in equal shares per stirpes, provided that no issue shall take whose parent is alive and so capable of taking.

9. Ultimate default trusts

Subject as above and if and so far as not wholly disposed of for any reason whatever by the above provisions, the capital and income of the Trust Fund shall be held upon trust for [   ] absolutely.

10. Administrative powers

The Trustees shall, in addition and without prejudice to all statutory powers, have the powers and immunities set out in Part 2 of this Deed. No power conferred on the Trustees shall be exercised so as to conflict with the beneficial provisions of this Deed.

11. Extended power of maintenance

The statutory provisions for maintenance and education shall apply but so that the power of maintenance shall be exercisable in the discretion of the Trustees and free from the obligation to apply part only of the income for maintenance where other income is available.

12. Extended power of advancement

The statutory provisions for advancement shall apply but so that the power of advancement shall extend to the whole, rather than one half, of the share or interest of the person for whose benefit the advancement is made.

13. Appointment of new trustees

13.1 During the lifetime of the Settlor the power of appointing new trustees shall be vested in the Settlor.

13.2 A person may not be appointed to be a trustee notwithstanding that such person is not resident in the United Kingdom. Remaining out of the United Kingdom for more than 12 months shall not be a ground for the removal of a trustee.

14. Proper law, forum and place of administration

14.1 The proper law of this Trust shall be that of England and Wales. All rights under this Deed and its construction and effect shall be subject to the jurisdiction of, and construed according to, the laws of England and Wales.

14.2 The courts of England and Wales shall be the forum for the administration of these trusts.

14.3 Notwithstanding the provisions of sub-clauses 14.1 and 14.2:

[(a)] The Trustees shall have power, subject to the application (if any) of the rule against perpetuities, to carry on the general administration of these trusts in any jurisdiction in the world. This power shall be exercisable whether or not the law of such jurisdiction is for the time being the proper law of this Trust or the courts of such jurisdiction are for the time being the forum for the administration of these trusts, and whether or not the Trustees or any of them are for the time being resident or domiciled in, or otherwise connected with, such jurisdiction.

[(b) The Trustees may at any time declare in writing that, from the date of such declaration, the proper law of this Trust shall be that of any specified jurisdiction. No exercise of this power shall be effective unless the law of the jurisdiction specified is one under which this Trust remains irrevocable and all, or substantially all, of the trusts, powers and provisions contained in this Deed remain enforceable and capable of being exercised and so taking effect.

(c) Following any exercise of the power contained in sub-clause 14.3(b), the Trustees shall, by deed, make such consequential alterations or additions to this Deed as they consider necessary or desirable to ensure that, so far as may be possible, the trusts, powers and provisions of this Deed shall be as valid and effective as they were immediately prior to such change.

(d) The Trustees may, at any time, declare in writing that, from the date of such declaration, the forum for the administration of these trusts shall be the courts of any specified jurisdiction.]

15. Exclusion of Settlor and spouse

15.1 No discretion or power conferred on the Trustees or any other person by this Deed or by law shall be exercised, and no provision of this Deed shall operate directly or indirectly, so as to cause or permit any part of the capital or income of the Trust Fund to become in any way payable to or applicable for the benefit of the Settlor or any person who shall previously have added property to the Trust Fund or the spouse for the time being of the Settlor or any such person.

15.2 The provisions of sub-clause 15.1 shall not preclude the Settlor or any such person from exercising any statutory right to claim reimbursement from the

Trustees for any income tax or capital gains tax paid by him in respect of income arising to the Trustees or capital gains realised or deemed or treated as realised by them.

15.3 Subject to sub-clause 15.2, the prohibition in this clause shall apply notwithstanding anything else contained or implied in this Deed.

PART 2—ADMINISTRATIVE PROVISIONS

SCHEDULE

[*The initial Trust Fund*]

Signed as a deed and delivered   )
by [   ])
in the presence of:)

Appendix 5

ACCUMULATION AND MAINTENANCE SETTLEMENT

Table of contents

PART 1—OPERATIVE PROVISIONS

SETTLEMENT

DATE: [   ]

PARTIES:

(1) [   ] (the **'Settlor'**); and

(2) [   ] (the **'Trustees'**).

RECITALS

(A) The Settlor wishes to make this Settlement and has transferred or delivered to the Trustees or otherwise placed under their control the property specified in the Schedule. Further money, investments or other property may be paid or transferred to the Trustees by way of addition.

(B) It is intended that this Settlement shall be irrevocable.

PART 1—OPERATIVE PROVISIONS

1. Definitions and construction

In this Deed, where the context admits, the following definitions and rules of construction shall apply.

1.1 The **'Trust Fund'** shall mean:

    (a) the property specified in the Schedule;

    (b) all money, investments or other property paid or transferred by any person to, or so as to be under the control of, and, in either case, accepted by the Trustees as additions;

(c)   all accumulations (if any) of income added to the Trust Fund; and

(d)   the money, investments and property from time to time representing the above.

1.2   The **'Trust Period'** shall mean the period ending on the earlier of:

(a)   the last day of the period of 80 years from the date of this Deed, which period, and no other, shall be the applicable perpetuity period; and

(b)   such date as the Trustees shall at any time specify by deed, not being a date earlier than the date of execution of such deed or later than a date previously specified.

1.3   **'Primary Beneficiary'** shall mean:

(a)   the existing [grand]children of the Settlor, namely

[   ]   who   was   born   on   [   ];
[   ]   who   was   born   on   [   ];
[   ]   who   was   born   on   [   ];   and
[   ] who was born on [   ]; and

(b)   every other [grand]child of the Settlor born after the date of this Deed and before the Closing Date.

1.4   **'Beneficiary'** shall mean any person actually or prospectively entitled to any share or interest in the capital or income of the Trust Fund.

1.5   The **'Closing Date'** shall mean whichever shall be the earlier of:

(a)   the date on which the first Primary Beneficiary to do so attains the age of 25; and

(b)   the date on which the Trust Period shall determine.

1.6   The **'Accumulation Period'** shall mean the period of 21 years from the date of this Deed, or the Trust Period if shorter.

1.7   **'interest in possession'** shall have the meaning it has for the purposes of s 71 of the Inheritance Tax Act 1984 or any statutory modification or re-enactment of such section.

1.8   The expression **'the Trustees'** shall, where the context admits, include the trustees for the time being of this Trust.

1.9   References to the children, grandchildren and issue of any person shall include his children, grandchildren and remoter issue, whether legitimate, legitimated[, illegitimate] or adopted [, but shall exclude any illegitimate person and his descendants].

1.10 Words denoting the singular shall include the plural and vice versa.

1.11 Words denoting any gender shall include both the other genders.

1.12 The table of contents and clause headings are included for reference only and shall not affect the interpretation of this Deed.

2. Trust for sale

The Trustees shall hold the Trust Fund upon trust in their discretion either to allow the same or remain in the state in which it is received or held for so long as they shall think fit or to sell or convert the same into money. The Trustees may, in their discretion, invest such money in their names or under their control in any of the investments authorised by this Deed or by law, with power from time to time to vary or transpose any such investments for or into others so authorised.

3. Power to receive additional property

The Trustees may, at any time during the Trust Period, accept additional money, investments or other property, of whatever nature and wherever situate, paid or transferred to them by the Settlor or any other person. Such additional money, investment or other property shall, subject to any contrary direction, be held upon the trusts and with and subject to the powers and provisions of this Deed.

4. Principal trusts

4.1 The Trust Fund shall be held upon trust for such of the Primary Beneficiaries as:
(a) attain the age of 25 before the end of the Trust Period; or
(b) are living and under that age at the end of the Trust Period and, if more than one, in equal shares absolutely.

4.2 The provisions of clause 5 shall apply to the share of the Trust Fund to which any of the Primary Beneficiaries is or may become entitled under sub-clause 4.1. In those provisions, such share is called the **'Share'** and that one of the Primary Beneficiaries who is primarily interested in the Share is called the **'Primary Beneficiary'**.

4.3 No Primary Beneficiary shall be entitled to any share of the Trust Fund without bringing any assets or interest advanced to him or paid or applied for his benefit (in exercise of any of the powers conferred by sub-clause 5.2 or clause 10) into account in such manner as the Trustees shall in their discretion determine with a view to achieving an equitable division of the unadvanced part of the Trust Fund.

5. Trusts for Primary Beneficiaries under 25

This clause shall apply, during the Trust Period, in respect of the Share of any Primary Beneficiary who is living and under the age of 25.

5.1 The Trustees may pay or apply any income of the Share to or for the maintenance or education or otherwise for the benefit of the Primary Beneficiary, or any other Primary Beneficiaries who are for the time being living and under the age of 25.

5.2 The Trustees may also pay or apply any capital of the Share to or for the maintenance, education, advancement or otherwise for the benefit of the Primary Beneficiary. No capital may be so applied in a way which would or might prevent the Primary Beneficiary from becoming entitled to it, or to an interest in possession in it, on or before attaining the age of 25, nor in such a way that the income of it might meanwhile be dealt with except by being applied for the maintenance, education or otherwise for the benefit of one or more of the Primary Beneficiaries for the time being living and under the age of 25 or by being accumulated.

5.3 Subject as above, the income of the Share shall, during the Accumulation Period, be accumulated as an accretion to the capital of the Share. Any such accumulations may, at any time, be paid or applied in the manner set out in sub-clause 5.1 as if they were income of the Share arising in the then current year.

5.4 Subject as above, s 31 of the Trustee Act 1925 (as modified below) shall apply to the income of the Share.

5.5 Notwithstanding the above, the Trustees may, at any time during the Trust Period, by deed direct that the Primary Beneficiary shall become entitled to the income of all or any part of the Share from such a date as they shall specify. Such date shall not be earlier than the date of the deed, nor later than the date on which the Primary Beneficiary shall attain the age of 25. Such income shall be paid to the Primary Beneficiary from the date specified, or, if and so long as he is under the age of 18, applied or retained for his sole and absolute benefit and the trusts declared by sub-clauses 5.1 to 5.4 shall determine.

6. Trust to accumulate

Subject as above, during the Accumulation Period, so long as no Primary Beneficiary has attained the age of 25 and further Primary Beneficiaries may come into existence, the income of the Trust Fund shall be accumulated.

7. Ultimate default trusts

In the event of the failure or determination of the above trusts, the capital and income of the Trust Fund shall be held upon trust for [such of the Primary Beneficiaries as are living at the date of this Deed, and if more than one, in equal shares] absolutely.

8. Administrative powers

The Trustees shall, in addition and without prejudice to all statutory powers, have the powers and immunities set out in Part 2 of this Deed. No power conferred on the Trustees shall be exercised so as to conflict with the beneficial provisions of this Deed.

9. Extended power of maintenance

The statutory provisions for maintenance and education shall apply, but so that the power of maintenance shall be exercisable in the discretion of the Trustees and free from the obligation to apply part only of the income for maintenance where other income is available.

10. Extended power of advancement

The statutory provisions for advancement shall apply, but so that the power of advancement shall extend to the whole, rather than one half, of the share or interest of the person for whose benefit that advancement is made.

11. Restrictions on certain powers

11.1 In this clause, '**qualifying property**' means any part of the Trust Fund which is for the time being property to which s 71 of the Inheritance Tax Act 1984 (or any statutory modification or re-enactment of such section) applies.

11.2 Where the Trust Fund or any part of it would (in the absence of the restrictions imposed by this sub-clause) fail to be qualifying property by reason only of powers conferred on the Trustees by this Deed or by law, those powers shall be capable of being exercised only in a manner which does not prevent the Trust Fund or that part of it from being qualifying property.

12. Appointment of new trustees

12.1 During the lifetime of the Settlor, the power of appointing new trustees shall be vested in the Settlor.

12.2 A person may be appointed to be a trustee notwithstanding that such person is not resident in the United Kingdom. Remaining out of the United Kingdom for more than 12 months shall not be a ground for the removal of a trustee.

13. Proper law, forum and place of administration

13.1 The proper law of this Trust shall be that of England and Wales. All rights under this Deed and its construction and effect shall be subject to the jurisdiction of the courts, and construed according to the laws, of England and Wales.

13.2 The courts of England and Wales shall be the forum for the administration of these trusts.

13.3 Notwithstanding the provisions of sub-clause 13.1 and 13.2,

[(a)] The Trustees shall have power, subject to the application (if any) of the rule against perpetuities, to carry on the general administration of these truths in any jurisdiction in the world. This power shall be exercisable whether or not such jurisdiction is for the time being the proper law of this Trust or the courts or such jurisdiction are for the time being the forum for the administration of these trusts, and whether or not the Trustees or any of them are for the time being resident or domiciled in, or otherwise connected with, such jurisdiction.

[(b) The Trustees may at any time declare in writing that, from the date of such declaration, the proper law of this Trust shall be that of any specified jurisdiction. No exercise of this power shall be effective unless the law of the jurisdiction specified is one under which this Trust remains irrevocable and all, or substantially all, of the trusts, powers and provisions contained in this Deed remain enforceable and capable of being exercised and so taking effect.

(c) Following any exercise of the power contained in sub-clause 13.3(b), the Trustees shall by deed make such consequential alterations or additions to this Deed as they consider necessary or desirable to ensure that, so far as may be possible, the trusts, powers and provisions of this Deed shall be as valid and effective as they were immediately prior to such change.

(d) The Trustees may, at any time, declare in writing that, from the date of such declaration, the forum for the administration of these trusts shall be the courts of any specified jurisdiction.]

14. Exclusion of Settlor and spouse

14.1 No discretion or power conferred on the Trustees or any other person by this Deed or by law shall be exercised, and no provision of this Deed shall operate directly or indirectly, so as to cause or permit any part of the capital or income of the Trust Fund to become in any way payable to or applicable for the benefit of the Settlor or any person who shall previously have added property to the Trust Fund or the spouse for the time being of the Settlor or any such person.

14.2 The provisions of sub-clause 14.1 shall not preclude the Settlor or any such person from exercising any statutory right to claim reimbursement from the Trustees for any income tax or capital gains tax paid by him in respect of income arising to the Trustees or capital gains realised or deemed or treated as realised by them.

14.3 Subject to sub-clause 14.2, the prohibition in this clause shall apply notwithstanding anything else contained or implied in this Deed.

PART 2—ADMINISTRATIVE PROVISIONS

SCHEDULE

[*The initial Trust Fund*]

Signed as a deed and delivered   )
by [   ])
in the presence of:)

Appendix 6

TRUST DISTRIBUTION ACCOUNT

John Bale Trust

(1) Tom Bale set up an accumulation and maintenance trust for his nephew John under which John became entitled to the trust capital on his 18th birthday on 10 February 199–.

(2) The trustees being satisfied that no capital tax liability arises (no IHT since the trust is an accumulation and maintenance trust; no CGT because their annual exemption covers the gain on their deemed disposal caused by John's absolute entitlement) have transferred the investment in ABC plc to John.

(3) The dividend shown in the income account was received on 25 March 199– and it, together with the remaining cash has been transferred to John.

Capital account

		£
Assets held on 10 February 199–		
ABC plc ordinary shares		10,000.00
Cash		50.00
		10,050.00
Less:	Lowe, Snow & Co's costs, disbursements and VAT on distribution of the funds	30.00
Balance held for John Bale		10,020.00

Income account

	£
Income tax year 199–/9–	
Dividend	
ABC plc ordinary shares	10.00
Balance held for John Bale	10.00

Beneficiary's account

	£
Capital, per capital account	10,020.00
Income, per income account	10.00
Total due	10,030.00
Represented by	
ABC plc ordinary shares	10,000.00
Balance of cash, now due	30.00
	10,030.00

INDEX